Dear Mr. McKenna,

I finished reading your book *Spiritual Enlightenment: The Damnedest Thing* and I'm so mad, I could chew nails. While you tout your book by its very title as a spiritual book, it is nothing about spirituality and was very disturbing to boot. I wish I'd never read it but believe me, if you write another book, I'll not be buying it.

Do you realize that if people do as you suggest that their lives would be ruined? Maybe you never had anything to lose, but most people do. It's like some fairy tale world you live in, where you think everyone is independently wealthy and are able to come and go without commitments to an employer, to say nothing of family, friends, and community. Like you think a mother can leave her children to go off on this spiritual pursuit or wild goose chase, I'd call it. Who would do that? What for? Who would want to? Not realistic, not happening at all.

I have responsibilities to my family, friends and my community. I do volunteer work at a local shelter and organize food drives for the poor in my community. I am a member of the women's guild of our church. I help my children with their homework, provide good meals and a clean, happy home. They have extracurricular activities like dance, soccer, music lessons that enrich their spirit. You expect me to drop everything I value in my life, things that give meaning to my life. It would be flushing everything I value down the toilet. Real lives are at stake here and you talk as though it's nothing more than a stage. Get real. What you call enlightenment, I call a horrendous nightmare.

I can't imagine how or why you say such things. Just to sell books? Even if the things you say are true, who cares? What's so great about Truth? I'd rather have my family and my life where I believe real spirituality is available to each and every one of us through kindness, good will, an open heart and mind. What would you know of that with your nihilism and your void? I think it's rich that someone would write a book about spiritual enlightenment who admits they don't even know what the word spiritual means.

So, maybe you will sell a lot of books. I don't know why anyone would accept your version of spirituality. It's the opposite of everything that's good and beautiful about life. It is opposite of love and God and family and yet what's it all for? There's no point. Even you yourself say that there's no point. Yet you advocate to your readership that they put all else aside to become, in essence, total failures. The damage I would do to other's lives would be irrevocable, they would hate me and for what? Absolutely nothing.

Judging from all the rosy testimonials in the front of your book, there are people out there who believe you are a great spiritual master. I don't think you have a spiritual bone in your body. I've had the wonderful privilege of being in the presence of individuals who were truly enlightened but you are nothing like them. Put that in the front of your next book so people like me won't waste their time.

Reprinted by permission.
Name withheld by request.
Seattle, Washington

SPIRITUALLY INCORRECT ENLIGHTENMENT

Jed McKenna

www.WisefoolPress.com

Printed in the United States of America
ISBN 10: 0-9714352-5-1
ISBN 13: 978-0-9714352-5-4

10 9 8 7 6 5 4 3 2

Library of Congress Cataloging-in-Publication Data

McKenna, Jed
    Spiritually incorrect enlightenment / Jed McKenna.
        p. cm.
    ISBN 10: 0-9714352-5-1
    ISBN 13: 978-0-9714352-5-4
    1. Spiritual life. I. Title.
BL624 .M3974 2004
204'.2—dc22

                                                    2003020945

This book is dedicated to

HERMAN MELVILLE

Contents

Do not think the Buddhas

are other than you.

— Dogen —

1. Loomings

And that the great monster is indomitable,
you will yet have reason to know.

–*Herman Melville, Moby-Dick*

CALL ME AHAB.

Though, in truth, I am more Ahab than Ahab. I am the underlying reality of Ahab; the fact upon which the fiction is based. Captain Ahab is a rendering; the literary likeness of a true thing. I am that true thing.

One might reasonably expect the shelves of our libraries to be spilling over with tales of courageous men and women who've dedicated their lives to the selfless quest for truth, but, in fact, such tales are so exceedingly rare that we may fail to recognize them when they do appear. Herman Melville's *Moby-Dick* is not a book about whaling or madness or revenge, it's a book about one thing and one thing only: Man's pursuit of truth; truth at any price. Captain Ahab is not just a literary character, he is a human archetype; a fundamental yet unknown human archetype.

All the world's a stage, all the men and women merely players, and Captain Ahab is the final role; the role that sets us free. Whoever wishes to awaken from the dreamstate of duality into the reality of their being must step out of their current character and into the role of Ahab; must *become* Ahab. Ahab is monomaniacal—focused entirely on one thing to the exclusion of all else—and that's the way out of the dream.

The *only* way.

2. California Dreaming

The Spiritual Master is absurd, like everything else. He is a Function that serves to Enlighten or Awaken beings from this condition that is absurd and unnecessary to begin with. The occupation of the Spiritual Master is as absurd as anything anyone else does, you see. Therefore, it requires a Sense of Humor, or the Enlightened point of view.

–Da Avabhasa

I HATE LA.

There, I said it. I hate LA and LA hates me.

I don't know why Los Angeles and I hate each other, but I must admit I'm a little embarrassed about it. For me, LA is a no-flow zone where things don't work in the smooth, easy way to which I'm accustomed. Maybe it's only a no-flow zone because I hate it, but I think the no-flow came first.

I usually just try to stay out of LA, but that's hard to do when flying into LAX. Christine and I are picked up at the airport by Henry, a man who stayed with us at the house in Iowa for several months a few years ago. When he heard that I was coming out he was very eager to put us up. Now we're in LA and I have the uneasy Hotel California feeling I always get when coming here that once in, I'll never get out.

Christine is like my personal assistant, I suppose. A few years ago Sonaya started sending someone with me whenever I traveled to take care of things. I always argued against it but Sonaya wouldn't listen and now I'm hooked. The additional cost of a travel assistant is a small price to pay to avoid dealing with hotel clerks and rental car clerks and airline clerks and all the rest. She probably saves me more than she costs anyway. Usually, when I travel now, a few times a year, I call Sonaya and ask if she has anyone who'd like to go with me. Christine has done this several times. She's a bit on the small side and quiet, dresses in very conservative grays and blacks, but she eats clerks for breakfast and we never get jerked around. She runs interference for me, providing a protective layer between me and a world in which I no longer function very well. She's very religious, I think, and has no sense of humor; not a playful bone in her body. I think she sees me as a likable idiot, but I wouldn't bet on the likable part.

Henry is a very likable person. Very open and talkative. Unabashed. If penile dysfunction is what's on his mind, then that's what you're going to hear about. Penile dysfunction is not what's on his mind at the moment, but what *is* on his mind actually makes penile dysfunction sound pretty appealing. During the drive he speaks animatedly about the new spirituality they're inventing, he and his California friends, a fully integrated spiritual lifestyle that allows them to live their beliefs 24/7, as he says. A fully integrated spiritual lifestyle; that's what he keeps calling it.

Fizzle, I think. That's how the acronym would be pronounced.

Once again I am struck by the fortress-like impenetrability of the walls ego erects around itself. I remember Henry as an earnest, attentive, and thoughtful person. I don't recall ever thinking he might really buckle down and wake up in this life, but I do recall that he was trying to achieve some level of self-honesty and might manage to make a break from his ego. Now, listening to him talk about his newfound integrated spirituality as we drive through interminable LA, I am saddened to see that he has spun away from his honesty and is now cozily nestled in a self-gratifying, ego-preserving cloak of spiritual hedonism.

Oh well.

I'm trying to avoid saying that I hate California. I keep trying to think of something I like about California so I don't have to face this petty truth, but I can't do it. I hate California. Maybe California is really a lot of different places and there are probably parts I'd like, but I think that's just the denial talking. I should just say it and live with it: I hate California. I'm not sure why I hate California, but if pressed, I'd say that it has something to do with Californians.

"There's no area of our lives that isn't spiritually grounded," Henry informs me animatedly. "We've reconfigured our lives in every area. We've minimized the waste we create and maximized our utilization of replenishable resources. We're experimenting with a variety of alternative fuels and energy sources, and several of us are incorporating hydro—"

And on he goes. The drive takes forever and there's nothing to see the whole way. Henry goes on and on about the new paradigm he and his friends are creating and Christine is quietly absorbed in her knitting. The car is a high-end Mercedes so I can't complain about the ride, which also aggravates me. I'm curious as to where an eighty thousand dollar luxury sedan fits into this new spiritual lifestyle, but I'm afraid that if I ask, he'll answer.

When I use words like love and hate, what I really mean is more like attract and repel in the energetic sense. No-flow places and ego-bound people repel me, as do ego-saturated places where the greed and vanity of the people seem to permeate the place. Whatever doesn't repel me is either neutral or attracts me. This is true of everyone, but most people drown it out. It's much subtler than love and hate; it's at the level of energy, and when your energy is distorted, *you're* distorted. Los Angeles distorts me. California distorts me. These distinctions do not apply to me as a truth-realized being, but as a being detached from ego; a more common and accessible state. This book will attempt to cover the distinction between those two states in depth and gently encourage its readers away from the former and toward the latter.

I notice that Henry is still speaking.

"We all have green portfolios. That means—"

"Henry," I say.

"—that we only invest—"

"Henry."

"—in companies that have demonstrated—"

"Henry!"

"Yes?"

"You have to shut up. Don't talk anymore. Seriously, you're killing me."

"Oh, okay. Sure, that's not a problem. Yeah, heck, you've been flying and driving probably since all day. I should just shut up and let you refresh your spirit. There's a hot tub and a pool at the house and we don't use the dangerous chemicals—"

And on he goes. I feel my brain begin to swell inside my skull until finally the pressure is unbearable and it explodes, coating the interior of the car and my fellow occupants in a strawberry jam of blood and goo. Or is jelly the lumpier stuff? I can never remember.

❖

Since one of the things I'm trying to do with these books is hold the awakened state up for display, I should mention one of the more peculiar things about it, which is that I have nothing to do. I don't have any challenges left, and I can't just make one up. I can write this book and maybe stay involved with communicating on this subject in some minor way, but the fact remains; I have nothing to do. I like being alive, but I don't really have anything to do *while* alive. I like to sit and be, I like to appreciate the creative accomplishments of man, especially as they involve his attempts to get his situation figured out, but appreciation is a pretty flat pastime. I'm not complaining, just expressing something about this state that most people probably aren't aware of. I am content, and contentment is overrated. I have no framework within which anything is better than anything else, so what I do doesn't particularly matter. I have no ambition, nowhere to go, no one to be or become. I don't need to distract myself from anything or convince myself of anything. There's nothing that I think isn't as it should be, and I have no interest in how others see me. I have nothing to guide me except my own comfort and discomfort. I don't seem to be too bored or unhappy about it, so I guess it sounds weirder than it is.

❖

Stinkpig bastard Henry has sandbagged me by dragging us to a friend's house for a dinner party. There are five or six couples as well as Christine and me, who are not a couple. It's a spacious Spanish-style house surrounded by others like it, overlooking a valley of dirt and scrub and, if you turn the telescope on the balcony far enough to the left, I'm told, a glimmer of ocean.

The East Coast dinner parties of my youth were pretty formal affairs. Everyone arrives sevenish, drinks for an hourish, seated eightish, finished nine-ish, more drinks until two-ish. This doesn't look like that. Less formal, less uptight; this is more like an indoor picnic. Everyone comes and goes. Children with sitters or nannies stop in and leave, the occasional teenager zips in, consults with a parent about car keys or cash, and zips out. A neighbor pops in to discuss on-street parking and pops out. People are chatting in four or five different areas including the driveway, the balcony and the kitchen. There's no one making introductions, no proper young gents taking coats and drink orders, no enchanting hostess gliding through the scene, no one smoking, no dresses or ties, no cocktails— mostly wine and some beer—no soft chamber music, no candles because the house is flooded with sunlight.

Henry has pulled me aside and is continuing to batter me with

SPIRITUALLY INCORRECT ENLIGHTENMENT

details of Operation Fizzle. These people we're dining with are all a
part of it, he tells me. It's something they're creating and discovering
together. This dinner party is an example of it.

"Sometimes we get together just to discuss a single topic," he
informs me. "Have you ever done that? It usually has to do with
social responsibility. Sometimes we discuss a book. There are a lot of
us, not just what you see here. It's really gaining momentum. We're
creating a whole new paradigm."

Okay, too much.

"I have no idea what you're talking about with this new paradigm stuff, Henry," I tell him. "The paradigm I see here is denial and
petty self-interest, just like anywhere else. You might spin it differently, but it's the same life-structure that practically everyone is
living in. Is there something I'm not seeing? It looks like you're all
half a block off Main Street living perfectly ordinary, self-gratifying
lives and going to a lot of trouble to pretend you're not. How is this
different from what anyone else is doing?"

Henry is unflappable. "Do you think we should consider a less
self-centered approach?" he asks, rubbing his chin with a judicious
air. "That's something I've been wondering about. We participate in
quite a few charitable projects. I think we're all volunteers in various
organizations. We all recycle, of course, and we're very conscientious
about the environment. I guess we could be more giving, if you
think—"

"I don't think anything, Henry," I interrupt. "You're the one
talking about a new paradigm. I'm just saying I don't see it."

❖

On the one hand, these people, Henry and his friends, are clearly
very pleasant, very successful Americans living the American dream
of freedom and abundance. On the other hand, I can't help but see
them all as self-centered, self-important, self-righteous assholes; in

other words, youngsters. But they're not, not really, or, at least, not particularly. No more or less than anyone else at any other dinner party, certainly not those of my early years. It's just another sign that my good humor is wearing thin. How do mature, intelligent people manage to go through their lives in a state of such diminished capacity? And what do I care if they do?

In reality, there's only one thing going on. There's only one game being played in life, and these people have arrayed their mental and emotional forces expertly so as to convince themselves that they're on the field in the thick of it while actually standing in line at the snackbar. The American dream of freedom and abundance is just a child's rendering of true freedom and abundance, and serves only to convince people who haven't gone anywhere that they've already arrived.

To the awakened mind, the unawakened can be a source of frequent dismay. The distance between awake and asleep is so infinitesimal that it's hard to remember they're a universe apart. Zen parables about instant enlightenment seem suddenly probable, as if just the right event—the whack of a stick, a poignant *non sequitur*, an overturned bowl—could suddenly snap someone into full awareness. The unawakened mind sees an enormous barrier—the proverbial gate—between itself and the awakened mind. The awakened mind sees with perfect clarity that no such gate exists. Hence, frequent dismay. The really strange thing about being awake isn't being awake; it's the people that aren't. They're walking and talking in their dreamstates; some of them declaring their deep commitment to waking up while doing everything possible not to. Have you ever been around a sleepwalker who had their eyes open and was performing a task, even speaking? It's pretty eerie. Now imagine the whole world is like that. It's eerie and it's lonely, but more than that, it's dubious. It lacks credibility. It's not believable. Even at the level of consensual reality, it's hard to accept that these people are all really asleep. I'm able to interact to some degree with sleepwalkers, but they're speaking from within a dreamstate world that I can't see and only barely remember. They might *say* they want to wake up, but it quickly becomes apparent that they have some dreamworld notion of what awake means that might involve anything so long as it doesn't disturb their slumber. Ego's guard dog is ever-vigilant, and it bites. They say that sleepwalkers get violent if you try to wake them; a curiously apt parallel.

✧

I see Christine giving me a look. I understand what her look means, but not why she's giving it. She wants to know if I want her to do what she does, which is shield me from yucky stuff. She wants to know if I want her to get me out of here. That means I have to stop and think because I wasn't aware of anything here that I'd want to be shielded against besides spiritual banality, which wouldn't cause Christine to give me the look.

These are intelligent, successful people. I probably don't depict it well, but Henry alone has more intelligence in his nose than I have in my whole head. I was intelligent once, as I recall, in some previous life that I might have read about in a book for all the connection I feel to it. If I ever had much in the way of intelligence, I no longer do. I've gone soft in the head. I don't see beyond the surface of things anymore. I'm not naturally suspicious because the only thing in the universe that merits distrust is ego, and I tend to stay clear of it.

But now Christine is giving me the look and after a few seconds of thought I see why. I see that Henry has set me up. That's what's going on here; I am this evening's entertainment. Henry put me in this situation knowing that at some point I wouldn't be able to contain myself and I'd begin to talk, which for me, as Henry knows, means launching into a rant; a performance. Now that I see it, it's obvious. I laugh at my own gullibility. On the other hand, I don't get the chance to perform much anymore, so what the hell, we'll see what happens. I gesture to let Christine know it's okay.

✦

I sit at the dinner table and try to appear interested in the conversations around me. I'm drinking bottled water, Christine has sparkling cider. Everyone else is drinking wine and discussing wine.

Only Henry, his wife, and Christine know anything about me. Henry's wife's brother's wife, Barbara, is on my right. She brought the salad. I remark on how good it is and she provides some back-story.

"Indie—that's my boy, he's eight—"

"His name is Indie?" I ask, guessing that it's short for Indiana.

"Yes," she says. "It's short for Independence. He was born on the fourth of July."

I nod mutely.

"Well, Indie heard Mommy and Daddy talk about recycling and how it's a good thing, so he wanted to recycle the kitty litter. Isn't that sweet? He wanted to invent a way of reclaiming the used, you know, *soiled* gravel, from the clumps."

"Very environmentally aware for an eight year-old," I say, wondering how this ties in to the salad.

"Isn't he? Well, the little guy scooped practically the whole litter box into my salad spinner, you know, the cage in a bowl thing that spins and uses centrifugal force to dry the lettuce?"

I nod and force a smile, wondering if we'll all need our stomachs pumped at the end of this story.

"Indie filled it up with used kitty litter, straight out of the cat box, and was just pulling the string and spinning and spinning. Meanwhile, I'm in the kitchen looking everywhere for my salad spinner because I'm in the middle of preparing the salad and we're running late as it is."

I laugh in commiseration, really hoping that she'll skip forward to the part that explains the mysterious crunch in the salad.

"Finally, the housekeeper comes in carrying my beautiful salad spinner completely clogged with awful cat mess. I was furious!" she laughs.

"It seems dry," I say, coaxing her toward the bottom line.

"Yes! Well, I had no choice, did I?" she asks me, and I fear the worst. "I could hardly serve the salad wet, could I?"

"Uh, no?"

"Of course not. So I tossed it in a pillow case, tied off the opening, and threw it in the dryer for a few minutes."

"The salad?" I ask.

"Just the lettuce," she says.

"No shit?" I say.

"Nope," she says brightly, "not a drop!"

❖

I've decided to strangle the next one that swirls their wine and sniffs it. Not really, of course, but a larger part of me than I care to admit finds it hard to believe that I'd get in trouble for it.

I'm perfectly aware that these people's lives are theirs to do with as they wish. I'm perfectly aware that it's their party and that I'm the turd in the punchbowl. I'm perfectly aware that I'm the reality-freak and that they're just children playing in their own playground, minding their own business. It's not that I want to crack their shells just for the sake of shaking them up. I don't want to assume the role of spiritual mucky-muck with this crowd or any other, and I sure as hell don't want to save anybody. Save from what? Life? What always makes me buggy, though, is that life played by the rules is more wonderful and exciting by countless orders of magnitude than life played by make-believe. It's a great, amazing, perfect thing, and they're totally missing it. The game of their lives is passing them by as they sit around the dinner table swilling wine and inflicting their daintily coifed opinions on each other. They're busy playing dozens or hundreds of mind-numbing little games in order to avoid the only real game, and I can't help but think that if they'd just learn to deal with their fear a little bit, they could pull up a seat and get in on the game of their lives. It's about what really is, and what really is is actually very cool once you get to the place where you can look at it directly and begin to understand your relationship to it. It's not about truth-realization or spiritual enlightenment, it's just about facing facts, the facts of life, and most people go through their entire lives doing nothing other than avoiding the facts. What makes me buggy isn't that they're a bunch of fucking morons; we're *all* fucking morons. It's that I know something that I'm sure they'd really like to hear, and I'm sure that I could get through to them if I just express myself clearly.

I'm the real fucking moron, of course, the odd man out, and I'm sure my thinking closely resembles that of any wide-eyed fanatic who thinks they're the only one with the inside line. In my own defense, I'd like to say that I get caught up in situations like this one quite infrequently. For the last few years I've pretty much stayed clear of people altogether, and that's worked out to everyone's satisfaction.

❖

After dinner, everyone remains seated at the table. A few liqueurs are set out and everyone pours their own. Everybody's getting buzzed. The subject of terrorism and America's vulnerability comes up. The threat that has everyone spooked is some major combination-attack on the food and water supplies which, I take it, was narrowly averted in recent weeks. Had it been successful, they're saying, it would have left everyone to fend for themselves to stay alive. They seem to be almost morbidly fantasizing about possible scenarios in which a cascade failure of services occurs, followed by anarchy, rioting, and the eventual loss of the cities and infrastructure. The women are obviously very uncomfortable with the discussion, but the guys can't get enough.

"Oh, it's all just too terrible to think about," says one of the women.

"It's too terrible *not* to think about," says one of the men. "We live in a desert. It wouldn't be long before our situation was critical. A day or two."

"I'm sure there are food and water supplies somewhere—"

"The National Guard would be—"

"The president would—"

"I don't think so," says Henry. "Not for long and probably not out here. And say you get through the first few days with what you have. Then what? And what do you do when someone shows up with a gun to take what you have? You can't call the police. You don't even know who your friends are anymore."

They go on in this vein for a while; heaping on more horrors, remarking on how fragile our system really is, how terrible it would be if anything happened to it. They're simply oozing with the grim importance of it all. Finally, the dancing bear can stand it no more.

"Well, let's say the worst stuff you can think of really happens," I interrupt, "would that really be such a tragedy?"

The chatter stops as all eyes turn to me.

"Would it really be so bad if your world broke apart at the seams?" I ask. "Cascade failures and anarchy and all that. I could see where it might be a pretty *good* thing. Shake things up. Get the blood flowing."

They're exchanging glances with each other in smug bemusement; seeking an explanation for, or complicity against, the jackass making this unscheduled deviation from standard themes.

"I don't know any of you personally," I continue, "but it looks like your lives are fairly predictable. You know how this storyline plays out, right? So what would be so bad if this storyline shifted abruptly to something a little more exciting?"

For better or worse, I have their attention. Henry looks happy.

"I'm just playing the devil's advocate here, thinking out loud. Correct me if I'm wrong, but your lives are pretty much," I make a gesture indicating our current setting, "*this*, right? I mean, you make money, raise kids, socialize, fulfill your roles, just like everyone else; basically ambling in small circles toward your own graves while pretending you're not. Sure, you all meditate and do whatever spiritual practices, but you know that's not really going anywhere, right?"

A few pockets of resistance pop up, but I plow over them. Their indignation is as meaningless to me as the growls of little pink puppies. I'm indulging myself with a somewhat more forceful manner of communicating now, mainly for my own amusement, and their reaction at this stage is not a factor.

"This end-of-the-world thing of yours sounds so terrible," I say, "but maybe it would be your one real chance. You might not know it, but what you're fantasizing about is waking up; your own awakening. You've heard the Chinese saying that's both a blessing and a curse; May you live in interesting times. If you look at it, you'll see that we don't live in interesting times, but we could. That's what your terror scenario is really about, isn't it? The times becoming interesting? We'd have perfect seats for one of the greatest spectacles in the history of the world; the meltdown of an advanced technological civilization. As you've pointed out, it wouldn't take much. Food and water run out in a few days, and all pretense at decency and morality run out with them. Major cities panic and go berserk. Fire, riots, evacuation. It'd be the greatest unmasking the world has ever known. A mass awakening; millions of people getting very real, very fast. You don't think that'd be fun?"

They're looking at me like I'm crazy, stupid, or just unbelievably rude. I'm directing my words mainly to Henry so the others will feel that they're watching a conversation, and not being directly provoked. They see that Henry isn't offended, so they resist the urge to jump in.

"It's not too improbable, I guess. Terror, nuclear mishap, some planetary event, war, a microbe, an act of God. Things change, fall apart, end. No rule against it, right? Imagine America reduced to a land of warlords and city-states; marauding bands of peevish Merlot sniffers roaming the countryside."

Henry laughs and lifts his wine glass.

"Sultry bouquet! Sultry bouquet!" he shouts like a rallying cry.

I laugh too. This is fun.

"Any hope of a return to normalcy vanishes. The people we call primitive are unaffected and go on about their lives undisturbed while the entire wired world descends into savagery; not in years or months, but in weeks, days. We'd see how our deeply held values stand up to an empty stomach. How many meals do you miss before you stop loving thy neighbor and slit his throat? This civilized veneer is really quite thin. Make a study of the human *in extremis*—prison camps, lost at sea and all that—and you'll see it's not just the veneer of civilized behavior that's thin. Friendship, morality, honor, all disappear. Distinguishing physical characteristics disappear. And what about love? When the going gets tough, we'll steal food from our own starving children. We're wired to survive and love doesn't override wiring." This isn't going over at all well. "I don't really mean us, here, sitting at this table," I continue, "because this is all a veneer too. These cheerful, well-fed personas are just flimsy veils of consciousness laid over the animal within and don't survive even minor discomforts." Everyone's looking down and around, and my sense is that they'd like one among them to stand up and put me in my place. "Who we think we are can be stripped away forever," I make a poof gesture, "just like that. Right now, well fed, unthreatened, we have the luxury of pretending the Donners and the Nazis and the gang-bangers are someone else, but they're not. They're us; a veil's breadth away. There are no good guys and bad guys. People are people, all the same; only the circumstances change."

I take a breath and let all that sink in. I stand up and start to pace as I resume the diatribe, both for my own energy and so no one mistakes this for a conversation. They are silent now, watching the show. Maybe it's the words or the force behind them, or maybe it's just the spectacle, but they're all fixed on me. No swirling and sniffing. No smug, sideward glances. Henry is positively beaming with delight. He got his show.

I grab a carrot stick and take a bite.

"It could be the death-rebirth process, but on a planetary scale. Very interesting to think about. This whole ego-based society burns to the ground. Years of chaos and anarchy follow, but then something rises from the ashes. What? Probably another ego-based society born of might instead of right, of rancid fear, but maybe not. Maybe something else. Heaven on earth, right? Get ourselves back to the garden, don't you think? That's the process the individual has to go through, so why not a society? It's the kind of thing that seems like an unimaginable nightmare before and a Godsend after. The death and rebirth of Western civilization. A human evolution revolution. Pretty cool, huh?"

Henry seems to think so, the others aren't so sure. This hijacking of a conversation and blowing it out is something I can do as easily as popping a balloon. I just take the subject to a more interesting level and show everyone how it looks from there. You'd think people would get offended, but I don't slow down for that and their initial reaction quickly subsides as they see that something different from conversation is happening, and they get on board.

"Am I wrong about anything?" I ask and look at each of them. "This whole breakdown of services and infrastructure is *your* thing,

I'm just saying it might be a *good* thing. Amusing. Burn it all," I wave my carrot stick to indicate Western civilization, "I mean, why not? It's not really going anywhere, is it? Another tired storyline. Death and rebirth, right? Is there any other way?"

I look around. No one speaks.

"Now compare that to these bland little lives you're dozing through. What are you really doing? Crawling toward cancer and heart disease and prolonged agonizing deaths. Am I wrong? Oh, one or two of you might get lucky and die in a car accident or have a heart attack in your sleep or be murdered by your spouse, but that's really the best you can hope for. None of you seem self-determined enough for suicide. Compare that cheery outlook to this worst-case scenario of yours. Sure, you probably wouldn't last long, but what a way to go! A world in flames! But you people don't want that because—what? You got something more important going, I guess. Like what? Your plans? Your careers? Your future? Your children? Your children are just less developed versions of you and their hope of breaking out of the cycle of denial is no better than yours. And even if it were, that's no reason. The only reason is fear. Your fear gives birth to your denial and your cozy, insular delusions of permanence and continuity. Look at yourselves, getting together so you can reaffirm each other's self-image fantasies and tell scary stories about how the big bad wolf could huff and puff and blow your world down. 'Wow, we really dodged a bullet there,' you say about this terror thing, but what you dodged was your own lives. Sorry to be such a bore. Got any cake?"

I go into the kitchen and find coffee and Tiramisu. I serve myself and take it out onto the deck. The coffee is spiced, I discover, and toss it over the rail. Now there's no point to the Tiramisu. I scan the distant hills and wonder why everyone isn't more like me.

It was probably stupid of me to launch into a rant against these nice middle class people and their harmless middle class lives, but boredom makes me do stupid things. This is one of the pitfalls of venturing out into the world; I get sucked down in the quag of other people's bullshit. I don't have anything against people or their bullshit, I'm just not well-suited to getting sucked into it. I suppose I could have sat there all evening and suffered the minor indignity of nodding and feigning interest in wine, cars, politics, and worthy causes, perhaps even injecting the occasional inanity, but I think my tolerant days are behind me. And I mean, really, who gives a rat's ass what I say anyway? So I might as well speak my mind. At least tonight will be memorable.

I hear someone come out and turn to see Christine. She's probably pissed off at me too, though I don't think she looked up from her knitting during the entire performance.

"I suppose we've overstayed our welcome," I say. "Sorry if I embarrassed you. Please arrange a car and some rooms. We'll get the bags from Henry's. Don't let him take us."

She shakes her head. "You're a hit," she says. "They'd like you to come back in. They have questions."

"No kidding," I say. "Good for them." But I don't really feel like being a hit. "Find us a car anyway. Don't get us rooms, get us planes."

"Planes? Where?"

"Cedar Rapids for you, La Guardia or Newark for me."

"Really?"

"Really," I say. "Trip's over. I gotta get out of this place." But what I mean is, I gotta get away from people.

❖

"Well, what do you advise we do?" Henry asks when I return to the dining room. Everyone's still sitting around the table. I take my seat.

"I don't advise you do anything. Go on about your lives. Don't listen to anyone who tells you you're wrong. You're not wrong, that's a fact. Don't do anything different. I was just toying with ideas. Extrapolating. Exaggerating for comic effect."

"You don't think there'll be some sort of cataclysmic event?"

"Sadly, no. It doesn't appear to be indicated."

"Okay. Well, what would you do if you were in our position?"

"I'd chew my leg off to get *out* of your position," I say. "It would hurt like hell and probably kill me, but that's my automatic response to confinement. It's a decision I made long ago. I don't even have to think about it."

"But that's not what you'd advise any of us to do?"

"No."

"Why not?"

"Because you have lovely lives and even if you are asleep, so what? That's life. You're having a wonderful dream, so what's the point of waking up? Why mess with such a nice setup? Nothing hangs in the balance. Look at how you live; you're in the top one percent of the top one percent of the most fortunate people who've ever lived. You want to fuck with that?"

3. Dicking Around

Every man is tasked to make his life, even in its
details, worthy of the contemplation of his most
elevated and critical hour.

–H. D. Thoreau

I'M SITTING OUT ON THE balcony waiting for our car. It's
dark now and there's only one bench that has a proper view. A kid
of about twenty comes and sits there too. He has a beer and lights a
joint. We're far enough from the house that he could flick it over or
douse it in his bottle if anyone came out, assuming he'd care. He
offers it to me and I decline. He talks the way kids do about the way
his parents and the others inside are. He's got that tiresome teen
angst thing going and he's pretty buzzed. He asks why I'm here.

"I'm not," I say, recalling a conversation under similar circumstances from college.

"Huh?"

"I'm not really here," I repeat, wondering if he'll go for it, if he's
in the right state of mind.

"Okay, yeah, sure. So where the fuck are you really?"

"Same place you are. Another place and time."

He scoffs and takes another hit off the joint. He looks at me.

"How poetic. I'll say this, you're a lot more interesting than
those fucking cadavers inside."

"You're not."

He stiffens. "Yeah? Well, fuck you too."

"That's what I'm here to tell you. That's why I came here
tonight. In a few years you're exactly the same as those people in

there. That little heat you have now will be gone and you'll mock those in whom it appears. That's your future and you'll live for more than sixty years in a walking coma," I point inside, "just like them."

He laughs at me, pauses, considers, laughs again. "You're so full of shit you're almost interesting. What are you, some Philip K. Dick fanatic? Go around messing with people's heads?"

"Reality is that which, when you stop believing in it, doesn't go away," I say.

He scoffs. "What's that, more poetry?"

"Philip K. Dick," I say.

He doesn't speak for a few minutes. I enjoy the view and he enjoys his joint and his beer.

"Okay," he says after a while, "I'll bite. Where are we, you and I? Really."

"A private facility in the Canadian Rockies. Banff, British Columbia. It's called the Sheerer Institute."

"Uh huh. Okay. And what are we doing at the Sheerer Institute?"

"It's a hospice. You're dying of cancer. I'm working."

"Yeah," he says. "Sure fucking thing. So right now I'm lying in a bed dying of cancer someplace in Canada?"

"Yes, except it's not really right now."

"Oh yeah, how stupid of me. It's not now and we're not here. So what's this job you're doing?"

"I'm a patch."

"A patch, huh? Okay, so what the fuck is a patch?"

"Like a software patch. To fix a bug or correct a mistake. Heard of that?"

"Obviously, dude," he says. Now he's getting into it a bit. The dope is making him philosophical. Not believing or disbelieving, just getting into it a bit.

"So, I'm dying of cancer and you came back through time—?"

"No, I'm not a time traveler. I'm a patch."

"Oh yeah," he laughs. "You don't really think I believe any of this bullshit, do you?"

"I don't care."

"Okay. Then what the fuck do you want from me?"

"You don't have anything I want."

"Great. So what are you doing here?"

"I came to say something to you."

"So say it already and take your lame bullshit to someone who gives a fuck."

"I already said it. I'm done. Now I'm just enjoying the view."

"Yeah, and Monday morning you'll be enjoying the view from your desk where you sell insurance or write shitty TV or whatever you do, laughing about the clever bullshit you pulled on some kid, except you'll be lying because I just think you're just a fucking loser going through some bullshit about his lost youth or something."

"That should be easy enough to confirm."

"Yeah? How?"

"Do your parent's have mystery guests to dinner a lot? Find out my name. Find out how your parents know me. Come find me at my desk Monday morning and laugh at me."

He ponders thereon.

"You're a trip, dude, I'll say that."

"I'm just here to deliver the message."

"Huh. So you already said it, right? Said what, patch? What did you say? Go ahead, say it like I believe it."

"The year is 2066. We're at the Sheerer Institute. You're bedridden and dying. You're practically a cadaver yourself. All that's really left of you is your dreams, your memories. You're reliving parts of your life in your mind. It's why you went to Canada and the Sheerer Institute to die."

"Oh, so now I'm not here at all? I'm just dreaming all this? Dude, this just keeps getting better. Keep going."

"In looking back on your life, you see yourself as a failure. You believe that you wasted your whole life; slept it away. You remember that it wasn't always that way; that you were once awake, alive, but then you drifted off into a doze like those people in there and just stayed that way."

"Cool. So now I'm lying on my deathbed regretting the fact that I slept through my life, so I send in a patch to fix things so I'll live happily ever after. Maybe like you, huh? A real awake kind of guy?"

"Close, not quite. There is no happily ever after. This isn't your life, *that* is, the deathbed, and it's almost over. You're lying there in a semi-coma, dreaming your own life, and you want to dream it like it could have been, not like it was. So, at your request, a patch was inserted at the last point you remember having some balls. Not uncommon. I have pretty much this same conversation a dozen times a week."

I manage to look appropriately bored. It's awhile before he speaks again.

"You're full of shit, dude," he says.

"Yeah, maybe."

"Yeah, yeah, okay, so you played your little headtrip game. You delivered your little message. But it doesn't mean anything because I don't believe any of it. It's all just been a waste."

I look at him for the first time and turn back to the view. "Who's bullshitting who? Of course you believe it. You know it's true. Right now you have some juice, but you know it won't last. Those people in there, those cadavers? That's your future; that's you in there. They were just like you and you'll be just like them; a rat in a maze. It's true. You know it."

That shuts him up for a minute. Christine appears, Henry right behind her.

"Have a nice life, dude," I tell the kid as he departs.

"That was really something in there," Henry tells me excitedly.

"You have an awesome command presence. You should be on stage."

I look to Christine for some happy news.

"It'll be at least an hour for the car," she says.

"Oh, no way. Henry, keys please."

He hands them to me.

"I can take you," he says.

I stare at him. He grins sheepishly.

"You mad at me?" he asks.

"No," I say.

"Really?"

"Really."

"You sure?"

"Yes."

He looks glum.

"Henry, I'm sure."

He brightens up. "That was so great," he says. "That was so much fun. We'll be talking about tonight for years. You're absolutely right. There's so much more to life, so many possibilities. So what if it all came crashing down? What are we so afraid of? Are you sure you have to go? I thought you were—"

I stand and take the least peopled route to the driveway, Christine and Henry following. I open the passenger door of Henry's car for Christine and settle myself into the driver's seat. Henry says some more good-byes and makes me reassure him again that I'm not angry, which I'm not.

"You'll call me and let me know where to pick up the Benz?" he asks.

"The Benz? Jesus, Henry, you're killing me with this shit."

"You're right! You're absolutely right! When did I turn into such an asshole?" he asks, grinning crazily as if it's all so damn wonderful.

I laugh because it is and we drive away.

4. Fish Story

> "If man will strike, strike through the mask!
> How can the prisoner reach outside except
> by thrusting through the wall?"
>
> *—Herman Melville, Moby-Dick*

I WENT TO NEW YORK, but when I got there I didn't know why I was there. I visited the hole where the World Trade Center had been. I ate a pastrami sandwich and watched the cleanup. I went to the top of the Empire State Building. I walked the streets for several hours, gradually ambling toward Greenwich Village and NYU, finally ending up in Washington Square where I sat down on a bench. I sat there for an hour as the sun went down and told the Universe I was going to stay put until it came up with a better idea. After a while the phrase *Baptism of Solitude* appeared in my thoughts and quickly turned into a mellow yearning, so I figured what the hell, I asked for it. A deal's a deal. I took a cab to Kennedy and booked a flight for Rabat by way of Madrid. I stayed in Essaouira where I read Paul Bowles, Cormac McCarthy, some Faulkner, and a book of Civil War letters aloud to myself. When I'd had enough of that, I went to Marrakech where I read Pullman, Rowling and Tolkien silently to myself. I avoided people and news and did less than I thought possible while time reshaped itself around me. After a few months I didn't feel like being there anymore, I flew back to New York and got a reservation on the Friday afternoon Hamptons Reserve train, the Cannonball. Three hours later I was in Montauk and two months later it's now.

For these last few months I have been like Jonah, consumed by a whale. I have immersed myself in the book *Moby-Dick* and only now am I really coming to understand it, only now seeing it for what it really is. It's an exciting process because I don't think anyone has seen it for what it really is before. I only started reading it because I'm staying in the house of a woman for whom Melville and *Moby-Dick* have special meaning. She taught it years before when she was a college American Lit teacher, and then for many years she and her late husband shaped their private lives around nineteenth century American shipping and whaling, and at the center of it all was Herman Melville's *Moby-Dick*.

Eastern Long Island is a good place to live if you have an interest in nineteenth century American whaling. The industry's history is all within a few hours by car and ferry; Sag Harbor, Cold Spring Harbor, Mystic, New Bedford, Nantucket, Cape Cod, Martha's Vineyard. That's what Mary and Bill did for leisure; they traveled to these and similar places, visited the museums, read the books, bought the antiques and knick-knacks. They actually met at an ice cream parlor on Cape Cod—Four Seas, which is still in business—and they tried to get back there for every anniversary. Bill passed away nearly a decade ago. Since then, Mary has been working on a book about American whaling and *Moby-Dick* that she plans to dedicate to him.

Long Island is also a good place to live if you have an interest in nineteenth century American Transcendentalists. Whitman was born here in Suffolk County, and I'm probably within a two or three hour drive of Walden Pond, Concord, and Camden. I don't plan on taking the tour, but being here has a nice feel to it.

The den by the front door was used as Bill's office and except for the addition of a laptop computer it's probably pretty much the same as the last time he saw it. It's dark and warm and richly appointed in oak and leather. It holds a beautiful collection of law books and a separate collection of whaling and maritime books, including most everything ever written about Melville and the works of Melville, as well as hundreds of books relating to maritime life on the Eastern seaboard.

So, I could hardly stay in a house like this and not at least try to read *Moby-Dick*.

❖

Mary is in her middle sixties, tall, slender, Irish, Catholic. We've probably known each other since I was five years old because she and her husband were involved with my family's business and Mary especially was like a member of my family. We'd been out of touch for years, but then she helped out on some structural questions regarding my first book, *Spiritual Enlightenment: The Damnedest Thing*. She took a personal interest in the subject matter and we renewed our acquaintance. She repeatedly invited me to come stay with her for as long as I wanted, so that's what I'm doing.

Her house sits on Gardiners Bay on eastern Long Island, out among the Hamptons, Sag Harbor, Shelter Island and all that. There's a lot of money out here and a lot of tourism. I was raised on the other side of the Sound and I still have family there and in Manhattan. Normally I prefer to live well clear of money, tourists and family, but I find myself pretty comfortable at Mary's. It's off the beaten path, quiet, secluded, and surrounded with good places for walking and biking.

The front yard of Mary's house is mostly a peastone courtyard and driveway enclosed by a gated stone wall and thick, well-established trees. The house is small and quaint from the front, all white with a red front door, black shingles and shutters, well-developed shrubs and ivy, and a beachstone chimney. It's not attractive in front the way that many homes decorated for curb appeal are. It's not meant to impress guests and passers-by. Like many waterfront homes, the front of this house is more functional, and the back is where the emphasis has been put. It's a renovated 1920's fisherman cottage that

Mary and her late husband overhauled by gutting much of the interior to create large, high open spaces, and adding back-sweeping wings on both sides for bedrooms that enclose the outdoor living space of attached decks and shoreline behind. The house enfolds the backyard and is designed so that all the living spaces take full advantage of the view. The central part of the house contains a living room, dining room and gourmet kitchen which form one large, open space with cathedral ceilings and tall windows and French doors that allow the interior to integrate with the outdoor spaces.

The addition wings sweep out from the main part of the house, wrapping the yard in a gentle arc. There are two bedrooms in one of the wings; I'm staying in the outer and the inner is vacant. In the other wing is the master suite with a large bath and walk-in closets. All three bedrooms have large windows and French doors accessing the oversized deck. It's not really a big house, but it's light and open and feels simultaneously spacious and cozy. A house like this goes for something well into the seven figures from what I can tell by reading local real estate listings. Mary could rent it in-season for more a month than many people make a year, but she never has. This is the dream home she and her late husband bought and fixed up after raising their children, and she seems as attached to it as she is to her family.

It's a good house for indoor-outdoor living. The Gulf Stream has a favorable influence on the climate here, keeping it a bit cooler in summer and a bit warmer in winter. The back yard is half filled by an oversized white deck attached to the house and stepping down in two tiers before opening out onto a small lawn and a magnificent view of the bay. The upper tier of the deck connects to the rear of the house, corner to corner. It's partially covered by pergola-type slatting attached to the house like long white ribs. There's an umbrella-covered dining table and chairs, a barbecue, and a pair of lounge chairs. The back faces east, so there's plenty of morning sun and shadows begin extending from the house after noon.

The second level of the deck as you head down is more open and less used. There are some chairs, a built-in bench and railing to one side, and a hammock in its own frame tucked away in a spot of shade under an overhanging canopy of branches. Steps lead down through a low evergreen hedge to a sunny quarter-acre of well-groomed lawn and a path that leads down to the shore. The yard doesn't slope down to the water but stays level until it reaches a weathered wood deck that runs along Mary's entire bay frontage like a boardwalk. A floating dock extends twenty feet into the bay. There's no boat, but sometimes guests come that way. There are some faded Adirondack chairs down there and it's a great place to sit at dusk or dawn. Out in the bay, Orient Point, Gardiners Island and the infamous Plum Island are all visible in the distance.

❖

I'd always heard that *Moby-Dick* was the classic example of the classic book that everyone agreed was a masterpiece but that nobody actually read. Sitting at the table on the upper deck during one of my first days at Mary's house, I spent a few hours reading it and could easily see why on both counts. It certainly had its high points in the first quarter—Ishmael and Queequeg meeting and becoming friends, signing aboard the *Pequod*, Father Mapple's sermon, foreshadowings of "grand, ungodly, god-like" Ahab—but it was definitely heavy and oddly structured and I wasn't sure why I was reading it, or if I'd continue.

It would be chapter thirty-six, more than a hundred and fifty pages in, before I'd have the first of two delightful epiphanies about this book. It was Ahab himself who encouraged me to look a little deeper. It was in the scene where the ship has sailed and Ahab rallies the crew to his cause; the hunt of the white whale. His first mate, Starbuck, is hesitant to turn the ship and crew away from the business of whaling to the business of revenge. Ahab asks Starbuck if he is not game for Moby Dick:

> "I am game for his crooked jaw, and for the jaws of Death too, Captain Ahab, if it fairly comes in the way of the business we follow; but I came here to hunt whales, not my commander's vengeance."

Ahab takes Starbuck aside and says:

> "Hark ye yet again—the little lower layer. All visible objects, man, are but as pasteboard masks. But in each event—in the living act, the undoubted deed—there, some unknown but still reasoning thing puts forth the mouldings of its features from behind the unreasoning mask. If man will strike, strike through the mask! How can the prisoner reach outside except by thrusting through the wall? To me, the white whale is that wall, shoved near to me. Sometimes I think there's naught beyond. But 'tis enough."

It's a magnificent, exciting chapter and I was reading happily along when this paragraph locked me up. Did he just say what I think he said? I read and reread it a dozen times. Could it be? It didn't seem possible, and yet, there it was. *Moby-Dick* had just become a very interesting book indeed.

Just so we're all on the same page about this book, let me provide a quick summary. It starts with the most famous opening line in literature—Call me Ishmael—the significance of which has never been fully appreciated, and recounts the adventures of the narrator as he becomes gloomy and turns to the sea and a whaling voyage in order to escape his dark despair. He and his newfound cannibal friend Queequeg sign aboard the *Pequod* out of Nantucket, captained by a one-legged enigma named Ahab. As mentioned, we're in chapter thirty-six before we know what's really going on; that the captain is monomaniacally bent on a single purpose; to kill the white whale.

On a previous voyage it was Moby Dick who took off Ahab's leg. Now, to all appearances, Ahab wants his revenge. The hunt follows the *Pequod* through many oceans and many meetings with other ships. It's a delightful story delightfully told, abounding in unexpected humor and charm. The whole thing ends in a three day chase of Moby Dick wherein the *Pequod* and all hands, save Ishmael, are lost.

In his mad quest for vengeance, Ahab usurps the *Pequod* from its owners to serve his own monomaniacal lust for revenge, which results in the death of his crew of thirty men and leaves his wife widowed and son fatherless. He is basically a twisted psychopath, driven to starkest madness by the pain and humiliation of losing a leg to the white whale. He betrays everyone who trusts him and depends on him, and sends thirty men to their deaths to fulfill his mad obsession against a fish. In short, a pretty messed-up dude.

Or so he has been reckoned for these last hundred and fifty years, anyway. I read a few reviews and introductions before starting the book and found that the one thing everyone seemed to have in common regarding *Moby-Dick* was that they found it ambiguous; not open to definitive interpretation. After the first of my two epiphanies, I would investigate much more deeply. I would look through all the books in Mary's library, search the internet on the laptop in Bill's office, and even make a trip into the city for two days to do research in some libraries there including, through no conscious intent, the Epiphany Branch of the NYPL in Gramercy Park. What I finally concluded was that no one had ever formed a clear picture about this book. The general consensus seemed to be that no clear picture was even possible. Many reviewers would try to make sense of it by saying that the ocean represents this and the whale represents that and Ahab's quest represents the other thing, but never in ways that made much sense, as the authors of these theories would often admit.

Does *Moby-Dick* represent man's battle against nature? Against fate? Against God? Is Ahab a Prometheus? A Job? A Narcissus? Is he a tragic hero? Is *Moby-Dick* about good versus evil? Evil versus evil? Evil versus eviler? Whack-job versus fish? Is it an exploration of the human psyche? Is it political allegory? An antislavery manifesto? An indictment of capitalism and industrialization? A prodemocracy treatise? None of the above? What then? Let's keep it simple. What does it mean when a guy is so freakishly twisted that he would destroy everyone and everything just to take revenge on a stupid fish? What do we make of that? What *can* we make of it? Is it any wonder no one has come up with a clear explanation? Is any clear explanation even possible? Or was Melville, as critics have effectively concluded, vague and unclear in his own mind as to what he was writing about?

The answer, as we'll see, is no. Melville knew exactly what he was doing when he wrote *Moby-Dick*. There's nothing vague or unclear about it, and, as we'll also see, there's a very simple reason why no one has truly understood it before now.

All well and good, but the real question that concerns us here is this: Is *Moby-Dick*, understood correctly, of any possible interest to readers of a book called *Spiritually Incorrect Enlightenment*?

I'll answer that, for now, by saying this: Herman Melville was among the foremost spiritual pioneers of his race, and the book *Moby-Dick* is the captain's log of the journey he took.

So, yes, it's of some possible interest.

5. Spiritual Autolysis

> Nothing goes by luck in composition.
> It allows of no tricks. The best you can
> write will be the best you are.
>
> *—Henry David Thoreau*

I N *DAMNEDEST,* I INTRODUCED THE process of Spiritual Autolysis, which is really nothing more than a kind of journaling on steroids designed to help us burn through the seemingly endless layers of ego and delusion in the quickest and least painful manner. Try to write something true and keep at it until you do; that's the match that becomes the blaze.

Also in *Damnedest,* we met Julie, a bright and attractive young woman who had come to see me for the ostensible purpose of interviewing me for a holistic magazine. What she left with was a bit more than she came for, at least, more than she *thought* she came for. What actually transpired was that Julie took the one step she had been moving toward her entire life, and perhaps lifetimes before that; the First Step.

We ended *Damnedest* on that note, pointing out that, for Julie, nothing was over, but only just beginning. What it was the beginning *of* we are able to hold up for display here because Julie chose to use the process of Spiritual Autolysis as her primary method for waging the long battle she found herself facing. She also chose to use *me* as the target recipient for her writings, which makes very good sense. It allows her to write to someone she knows, to envision someone sitting across from her as she writes, or pacing with her as she paces, or accompanying her on long, thoughtful walks. I am someone she knows, and I am a graduate of the process she is undergoing. It is a very powerful tool for her to be able to address herself to an imagined me.

When I was in this same process, I didn't have someone like me to address myself to, so I addressed myself to *you,* my imagined reader. From my perspective, *Spiritual Enlightenment: The Damnedest Thing* had around fifteen predecessors written over the course of two years, more than a dozen years before I started *Damnedest,* each one of them written with the sincere intention that it should go to print, each one ending up burned or erased, and each one having served its real purpose.

❖

Early in my stay at Mary's house, I meet her housekeeper's son. Curtis is an eighteen year-old black kid who was picking his mother up one day and bitching about having to get a job flipping burgers until September when he starts at a community college where he has a partial soccer scholarship lined up. We talked for a few minutes, and I asked if he wanted to work for me instead of McDonald's. I always have a bunch of stuff to do that I don't want to do, especially with regard to writing and researching a second book. He said okay, so we asked his mom if it was okay. She figured I must be okay if I was Mary's guest, so she said okay.

Okay.

One of the things Curtis has to do is go through my huge backlog of email and make one of three decisions about each item; trash it if possible, file it if necessary, or show it to me if he can't possibly manage not to. This isn't easy for him because he starts out completely unfamiliar with spiritual stuff in general and my views in particular. Still, he gives it an honest effort. He reads *Damnedest* on the laptop, asks some good questions, and develops a feel for the way I work. He stays aloof, doesn't accept or reject anything, but he understands what I need and works efficiently and cheerfully. Over the course of the first week we get the hang of each other and start to develop a casual rapport.

As he is sorting through my email, Curtis comes upon the subdirectory where I route Julie's emails to me, often unread. I looked through the first dozen or so to see if I was needed for anything, but I wasn't. There is more than a year's worth of email and sometimes she sent as many as ten a day. One of the things I ask Curtis to do is go through it and see what's there. He comes to me with a thick stack of Julie's emails that he's printed out, wondering what should be done with them.

Julie was born for this process of awakening and she's shooting along as fast as anyone possibly could. I told her to put the word Beatrice in the subject header if she wanted my attention or response, but she hasn't done it yet. She sometimes goes from light and chatty to intense and scary in the space of a single paragraph. That's a good sign because it means she's not rereading and editing herself too much. That's the way to do it; just keep plowing ahead, don't waste a moment on appearances. What's behind you is behind you. She addresses her understanding of the importance of this ceaseless forward motion here:

> This process of Spiritual Autolysis is somewhat difficult on me for a silly reason. As a professional writer, and as a student aspiring to be a professional writer before that, I have always relied on the process of editing and rewriting to get my words the way I want them. I am absolutely loathe to simply write words and move on, leaving them in rough draft form. I see the value of it. I see how it works. I know no one is going to see them except maybe you Jed (probably not, but I have to proceed as if you're hanging on every word). I guess the thing that I am writing and rewriting and editing and reediting is the underlying thoughts more than merely the

words, so the process of constant refinement has simply moved to a different level. Still, I'm not accustomed to writing once and leave the words unpolished.

Discovering and creating the process is part of the process, meaning that you have to build your own process and be your own mechanic; fine-tune it to your needs and preferences, repair it on the fly, jettison whatever is unnecessary as it becomes unnecessary.

I've known forty or fifty supposedly enlightened men and women. I've interviewed them. I've read their books. I've listened to their words, attended more satsangs than I can remember. The magazines I wrote for opened doors and I always cast my subjects in the most flattering light, so I was always welcome.

I search my memories now and I can't think of one of those exalted personages that was anything more or less than a specialized, minimized, hybridized, accessorized or otherwise modified ego. Exalted egos. It seems so sad and pitiful now, looking back on it. Silly little men and women expounding their customized variations on safe, proven themes like unity, meditation, consciousness, living in the present, love, service, higher consciousness, and so forth, looking down on all the upturned faces of people so eagerly seeking not truth, but merely someone they could look up to. The blind leading the blind. Just children, really. That was me.

You called them the final level of containment, and that's really what they are. Not shepherds of freedom, but guardians of delusion. I am starting to see why that is and why it's not bad, but I'm not there yet – I'm still angry and resentful. I shouldn't be, but I am – or, I am, so I guess I should be. I know they're not evil or committing any crime, that they're just functionaries, performing in the service of Maya, and it's not that I'm angry at them but at myself for believing them, for being such a sheep, and for casting them in the most flattering light.

Julie is originally from Canada and her family has a cabin or a lodge or something that they use as a vacation getaway. That's where she is as she's writing this. She has the place to herself except for the occasional bear going through her garbage. She's working on a Macintosh Powerbook and I bet she types around a hundred and twenty words a minute when she gets going. That's how it feels to me sometimes when I'm reading them; like her fingers couldn't get the words out fast enough.

I look back on all that now as the height – or should I say depth? – of folly. If one of those much-vaunted spiritual teachers showed up on my front porch right now, offering to help me work through this thing I'm in, I wouldn't let them in, wouldn't even open the door. Why would I? They're of no possible use to me now. They have no familiarity whatsoever with this process, no acquaintance with the transformation from self to no-self. Better I should let in a hungry bear. The modern spiritual teacher could offer no more guidance to someone being consumed by the process of awakening than could the local fishing guide.

I'm already starting to appreciate the profound importance of the word Further. Part of me wants to stay and dwell on the fascinating workings of false teachings, gullibility, self-delusion, fear, ego, denial – the whole lot. The psychology of spiritual individuals and groups, especially in the teacher-student relationship, seems like a perfect topic for an article or a book, and I feel drawn to spend more time with it, but then I picture you, Jed, sitting here, across from me, and you don't even have to speak. I see my desire to find a distraction for what it is. I have to remember that I'm not here as a journalist or a sightseer, I'm on my own journey, just passing through, and there are always temptations and rationalizations that would take me from the journey. That's why the most important word is Further. I understand that. One must be ever vigilant because the enemy is. Everything about the world and about ourselves demands that we stop, and we have only that one thing to hold up against all those powerful temptations; the word Further. Here's where I find my own supposed goodness to be a most malicious adversary. It would be so easy to fall sway to my altruistic impulses, to justify stopping in the name of aiding others, of sharing what I've learned so far; some egoistic, Bodhisattva bullshit. It's there, now, the feeling that I have achieved an understanding that I must share, which, of course, would demand that I stop to develop my understanding and learn how best to share it, which, of course, amounts to nothing more than stopping. Yes, I want to share what I've learned. Yes, I want to help others, to show them the way. Yes, I want to oppose the darkness and ignorance that I myself have now begun to find my way out of, and yes, that's all an elaborate and painfully effective ploy by ego to get me to cease my journey – journey being just a metaphor for the process of ripping away the layers of ego, like peeling off my own skin. Am I ranting now? Again? Sorry, these understandings come in bursts and demand immediate expression – or attempts at expression, anyway. You should see all the stuff you're not seeing!

As we'll see, she's not always so sane and thoughtful.

It's very helpful to have a metaphor within which to conduct the process. This provides a familiar framework within which to navigate, identify features, monitor progress, and so forth. Reformatting the cluttered hard-drive of ego, or waging a battle on the armies of delusion are examples. The point is to create a mental space, a 3D construct like a virtual reality within which to conduct your journey, like generals supervising a war while standing over a map table. I gave her a few suggestions about how to provide a contextual framework for her process and she adopted the idea that exploring and cleaning her own interior space was not so very different from venturing into an attic that has been used indiscriminately for storage for many years.

> Where did all this shit come from? What a mess! I thought my mind was mine, but I come up here and find nothing but a dark, dank space stuffed to the rafters with every conceivable manner of garbage and junk! Some of it I recognize, some I don't. This is *my* mind, this is *me*, this is who I *am*, and I expected to find a clean, simple, organized, uncluttered, Zen-like space. Instead I find this horrible terrible disgusting mess. It's a miracle I've been able to function. I wish I had a flamethrower or a bomb. I wouldn't even care if it killed me. This is not an analogy, this is my *mind*, my *self*, and I am sickened and so fucking outraged I feel like my head is going to explode!

I laugh. Curtis seems a little perplexed. I look up at him over the teacherish half-moon glasses perched on the end of my nose.

"What?" I ask him.

"She seems pretty upset," he replies.

"It's okay," I tell him. "It's the best kind of upset. It's all good. Look through it and print what you think is interesting and we'll look at it for the book."

"Me?"

"Yeah."

"Why me?"

"Why not you?"

"How do *I* know what's interesting?"

"Because it interests you."

He stares at me blankly for a moment and turns to go back to the office where the laptop is. I return to the email I'm holding. Julie's only just started the process of venturing into her attic in this one, and her shock at what she's discovering there is quickly turning into outrage, an emotional intensity that will aid her greatly in what lies ahead.

> I feel like I'm burning in negative emotions, which I've always been taught not to do, but it feels good! Necessary! I feel contempt and scorn – even hatred. Everything that's a lie, everyone who perpetuates the lies, everything about me that is a lie, I'm burning with anger! I bury my face in my pillow and just SCREAM! I look around this attic – me! – and I feel like I was kidnapped as a baby and only now am I starting to understand the true nature of my captivity; that my entire identity is a fabrication, that my entire world is some sort of hallucination. Who am I? That's all it really is! Who the fuck am I? I look around at all this junk and I don't know how it got here. It's not me. I didn't put it here. I mean, some of it I did. Some of it I recognize. I see my ballet slippers, guitar, diaries. I see my books and journals. I see the pictures of me but I know that they're my exaggerated self-images, not what anyone else really sees and certainly not what's really me. But what *is* really me? The attic analogy is perfect, I get it, but my attic is dark. I have to find a window and let the sunlight in. LIGHT! MORE LIGHT! Somehow I think it's all about light. Light and lightness, not darkness and heaviness. Somehow I don't think there's much up here, good or bad, that would survive direct illumination. Illumination! That's the key to sorting out this mess. I know I'm babbling like a lunatic but I don't care. Whatever this is, I want to rip it open and find out what's real. None of this is real. I want to get to something real.

Most spiritually-oriented people would probably not even recognize what she's going through as being a part of the awakening process. Most people, spiritual or not, would chew off their own arm to avoid going where this woman is going. This woman is going to have to chew off her own *head*, but first she has to go through the process of becoming someone who would prefer chewing off her own head to the alternative.

She goes on in this vein for a few dozen paragraphs. Angry, embarrassed, apologetic, betrayed, angrier.

How many years have I spent lighting incense and candles? Meditating? Chasing after gurus and teachers, reading all that crap, following every stupid new fad, reading every stupid new book? But now I see clearly, perfectly clearly, that all I was ever doing, all it was all about, was avoiding *this*. Avoiding *me*. I see it now, there's only this. THIS! All I was doing was keeping myself distracted so I didn't have to do this one thing. Life, the world, reality, all depend on not doing *this*. *This* is the one true blasphemy. *This* is the one true heresy.

I'm pleased. My whole life seems to be about this one small motion, this inward-turning. I scan the pages I'm holding and read bits here and there.

There is no outside authority. I am my own authority. What a liberating realization! How could I not have known?

❖

There's a huge monstrous piece of furniture or a crate — I can't even see how large it is — it seems to be Christianity, or religion, but not. Nothing is labeled up here, nothing is clear or specific. It's something heavy and dark and vague, but it's more than that and different, and it's so big! I'll never be able to budge it. And that's just one thing. The place is full of things like that. Junk! Mountains of junk! There's a huge thing like black marble, like an insurance company or a bank, or all huge invasive greedy financial institutions as they exist in my mind, my heart, like an immovable mass of dread, sheer dread. I see a big box like a coffin with a flag on it. It's like, my patriotism, or maybe my politics or my national identity, or something. Everything is dark and vague and heavy. I can't make anything out for what it really is, or maybe none of it is really anything. Maybe that's the whole point. It seems obvious what it is but now that I look at it I have no real idea of what it is or why it's here or how it got here. That's what it's like with all this rubbish. Nothing is what it is.

✧

Am I really in here somewhere? Is something in here me? I must find a window. I have to let in some light. But the windows are blocked by debris and I can't even get to them. L I G H T ! ! ! This place is stifling. I am choking on thick dead air – on *me*. I'm choking on the dead air of me. The fact that this is how everyone is, that this is what it is to be a person, that no one's any better off than I am, means absolutely nothing. It's no consolation. I am nothing. I am clutter. I am debris.

✧

Garbage. Crammed to the rafters. Nothing seems better or worse than anything else, just bigger or smaller, heavier or lighter. There's Mom and Dad. There's my childhood. There's my God-awful teens. What's all this shit still doing here? Blocking the sun, that's what! Blocking. Obstructing. Causing putrefaction and dankness and decay. Causing me to be a closed, dark, fearful person behind a cheerful mask. This is oppressing. This is oppression. This is impossible. I can work at this for ten lifetimes and never get it clean. It's too much. But what else do I have to do? I have no other business than this. If it takes ten lifetimes, it takes ten lifetimes.

It doesn't take ten lifetimes, but it is a slow and profoundly intimidating process. You do what you can when you can, one piece at a time. That's within the context of the metaphor. What she's *really* doing is dismantling a massive ganglion of self that she actually had very little to do with creating, and what's she's really *really* doing is killing herself, one piece at a time.

6. No oasis situated yonder.

The words of U.G. Krishnamurti: Part I

The end of illusion is the end of you.

–U.G. Krishnamurti

There's a lot I really like about U.G. Krishnamurti, and there are times when I don't know what the hell he's talking about. The excerpts provided below, and in two later chapters, represent the overlap between his views and mine. I may have taken some of it a little out of context, but the point here is to try to convey tricky and often paradoxical ideas, as well as to hold up the state of the realized being for observation, and I think these selections do that.

For the sincere seeker, to be challenged is to be entertained—they are two sides of the same coin—and whatever else he may be, U. G. Krishnamurti is challenging and entertaining.

PEOPLE CALL ME AN 'ENLIGHTENED man' – I detest that term – they can't find any other word to describe the way I am functioning. At the same time, I point out that there is no such thing as enlightenment at all. I say that because all my life I've searched and wanted to be an enlightened man, and I discovered that there is no such thing as enlightenment at all, and so the question whether a particular person is enlightened or not doesn't arise. I don't give a hoot for a sixth-century-BC Buddha, let alone all the other claimants we have in our midst. They are a bunch of exploiters, thriving on the gullibility of the people. There is no power outside of man. Man has created God out of fear. So the problem is fear and not God.

I discovered for myself and by myself that there is no self to realize – that's the realization I am talking about. It comes as a shattering blow. It hits you like a thunderbolt. You have invested everything in one basket, self-realization, and, in the end, suddenly you discover that there is no self to discover, no self to realize – and you say to yourself "What the hell have I been doing all my life?!" That blasts you.

❖

We don't want to be free from fear. All that we want to do is to play games with it and talk about freeing ourselves from fear.

❖

Your constant utilization of thought to give continuity to your separate self is 'you'. There is nothing there inside you other than that.

❖

You see, the search takes you away from yourself – it is in the opposite direction – it has absolutely no relation.

❖

The search is always in the wrong direction, so all that you consider very profound, all that you consider sacred, is a contamination in that consciousness. You may not like the word 'contamination', but all that you consider sacred, holy and profound is a contamination.

❖

My life story goes up to a point, and then it stops – there is no more biography after that.

❖

Desirelessness, non-greed, non-anger – those things have no meaning to me; they are false, and they are not only false, they are falsifying me. I'm finished with the whole business.

❖

The holy men are all phonies – they are telling me only what is there in the books. That I can read – 'Do the same again and again' – that I don't want. Experiences I don't want. They are trying to share an experience with me. I'm not interested in experience. As far as experience goes, for me there is no difference between the religious experience and the sex experience or any other experience; the religious experience is like any other experience. I am not interested in experiencing Brahman; I am not interested in experiencing reality; I am not interested in experiencing truth. They might help others; but they cannot help me. I'm not interested in doing more of the same; what I have done is enough.

❖

Who am I to give it to you? You have what I have. We are all at 25 Sannidhi Street, and you are asking me "Where is 25 Sannidhi Street?" I say you are there. Not that I know I am there.

❖

The abstractions that you are throwing at me, I am not interested in. Is there anything behind the abstractions?

❖

I had arrived at a point where I said to myself "Buddha deluded himself and deluded others. All those teachers and saviors of mankind were damned fools – they fooled themselves – so I'm not interested in this kind of thing anymore," so it went out of my system completely.

✦

I am not trying to sell anything here. It is impossible for you to simulate this. This is a thing that has happened outside the field, the area, in which I expected, dreamed and wanted change, so I don't call this a 'change'. I really don't know what has happened to me. What I am telling you is the way I am functioning. There seems to be some difference between the way you are functioning and the way I am functioning, but basically there can't be any difference. How can there be any difference between you and me? There can't be; but from the way we are trying to express ourselves, there seems to be. I have the feeling that there is some difference, and what that difference is is all that I am trying to understand. So, this is the way I am functioning.

✦

You see, my difficulty with the people who come to see me is this: they don't seem to be able to understand the way I am functioning, and I don't seem to be able to understand the way they are functioning. How can we carry on a dialogue? Both of us have to stop. How can there be a dialogue between us both?

✦

Your natural state has no relationship whatsoever with the religious states of bliss, beatitude and ecstasy; they lie within the field of experience. Those who have led man on his search for religiousness throughout the centuries have perhaps experienced those religious states. So can you. They are thought-induced states of being, and as they come, so do they go. Krishna Consciousness, Buddha Consciousness, Christ Consciousness, or what have you, are all trips in the wrong direction: they are all within the field of time. The timeless can never be experienced, can never be grasped, contained, much less given expression to, by any man. That beaten track will lead you nowhere. There is no oasis situated yonder; you are stuck with the mirage.

❖

You see, people usually imagine that so-called enlightenment, self-realization, God-realization or what you will (I don't like to use these words) is something ecstatic, that you will be permanently happy, in a blissful state all the time – these are the images they have of those people... There's no relationship at all between the image you have of that, and what actually is the situation... That's why I very often tell people "If I could give you some glimpse of what this is all about, you wouldn't touch this with a barge pole, a ten foot pole." You would run away from this because this is not what you want. What you want does not exist, you see.

❖

If somebody asks me a question suddenly, I try to answer, emphasizing and pointing out that there is no answer to that question. So, I merely rephrase, restructure and throw the same question back at you. It's not game playing, because I'm not interested in winning you over to my point of view. It's not a question of offering opinions – of course I do have my opinions on everything from disease to divinity, but they're as worthless as anybody else's.

❖

Put it simply. I can't follow a very complex structure – I have that difficulty, you see. Probably I'm a low-grade moron or something, I don't know – I can't follow conceptual thinking. You can put it in very simple words. What exactly is the question? Because the answer is there; I don't have to give the answer. What I usually do is restructure the question, rephrase it in such a way that the question appears senseless to you.

✦

Understanding is a state of being where the question isn't there any more; there is nothing there that says "now I understand!" – that's the basic difficulty between us. By understanding what I am saying, you are not going to get anywhere.

✦

It is the questioner that creates the answer; and the questioner comes into being from the answer, otherwise there is no questioner. I am not trying to play with words. You know the answer, and you want a confirmation from me, or you want some kind of light to be thrown on your problem, or you're curious – if for any of these reasons you want to carry on a dialogue with me, you are just wasting your time; you'll have to go to a scholar, a pundit, a learned man – they can throw a lot of light on such questions. That's all that I am interested in in this kind of a dialogue: to help you to formulate your own question. Try and formulate a question which you can call your own.

7. Shadow Dwellers

Illusion recognized must disappear.

—A Course In Miracles

TWO IMPORTANT POINTS ARE TOUCHED upon by U.G. Krishnamurti in the preceding chapter, as shown in the following four excerpts:

> *If somebody asks me a question suddenly, I try to answer, emphasizing and pointing out that there is no answer to that question. So, I merely rephrase, restructure and throw the same question back at you.*
>
> *What exactly is the question? Because the answer is there; I don't have to give the answer. What I usually do is restructure the question, rephrase it in such a way that the question appears senseless to you.*
>
> *Understanding is a state of being where the question isn't there any more; there is nothing there that says "now I understand!"*
>
> *It is the questioner that creates the answer; and the questioner comes into being from the answer, otherwise there is no questioner.... That's all that I am interested in in this kind of a dialogue: to help you to formulate your own question. Try and formulate a question which you can call your own.*

First, the question itself is the obstacle to progress, not lack of an answer. The question is the key. Once we truly understand the question, we'll have the desired answer. The desired answer is always the removal of the obstruction a correct question represents. The question, understood correctly, is the obstruction. If it's not, see the second point.

Second, come up with the right question. There's always only one. Wherever you are right now is where you're stuck, and the only question that ever matters is the one that gets you unstuck, that takes you one step further. All other questions are fear-based ego-sparing time-killers. Forget concepts and ideas, forget past and future, forget mankind and society, forget God and love, forget truth and spirituality. Find that one question; the exact question that ego doesn't want you to ask. Put your full attention on it. That's how progress is made. Everything else is a stall tactic.

To move forward, you must figure out exactly what is obstructing you. Whatever it is, it isn't really there; it has no reality, no substance. It's your own creation, a phantom lurking in the shadows of your mind, a shadow demon. Your obstructions are your demons, and your demons are shadow dwellers. They live and thrive in the half-light of ignorance, so the way to slay a demon is by illuminating it with the full force and power of your focused attention; by looking at it, hard. Banish shadow with light and see for yourself that no obstruction exists, nor ever did. We create our demons and we feed them. To awaken we must slay them. That's really the whole process: Slay one demon, take one step.

Repeat.

8. The Damnedest Thing

Backward I see in my own days where I sweated
  through fog with linguists and contenders;
I have no mockings or arguments—
I witness and wait.

—Walt Whitman

I'M SITTING ON THE DECK watching boats in the bay through a pair of rubberized binoculars that are always left outside for this purpose. Thus occupied and thinking myself alone, I am startled to hear Curtis, three feet away, delivering a report on my standing in the polls.

"You got critics," he says.

"I wish," I reply.

"You don't gotta wish," he says. "Look."

"I don't gotta look," I say, "I got you."

"Well, *I* looked and I got this whole mess of stuff saying stuff that's critical about you." He has around twenty emails and amateur reviews printed out. Not bad considering how many I've asked him to look through.

"What kind of critical?"

"Some say you're kind of arrogant," he answers.

"Okay, that hurts. What else?"

"I don't know. You know, critical stuff."

"I know it looks critical, but it's not; not really. I wish there was some valid criticism. I don't mean against the core message of *Damnedest*, which is unassailable—if truth be with us, who can be against us, right?—but I was hoping for feedback that might expose any gaps in my expression of this subject in *Damnedest*. We put a lot of effort into making sure *Damnedest* was, uh, complete; that it didn't leave any questions unanswered, that it stood on it's own, that nothing else was required."

Curtis is giving me the blank look.

"You remember it says in *Damnedest* that there are many questions but only so many answers?"

"Yeah."

"Well, we—"

"We who? Like the queen we?"

"A bunch of people read through *Damnedest* before it went to print, looking for problems, gaps, omissions, logical flaws."

"Okay."

"We wanted to make sure those so many answers were in there. In fact, the original reason behind doing a second book was to reply to what you have in your hand."

"Critics."

"Right, kind of. Constructive criticism. We'd hoped that if we missed anything, forgot anything, left anything important out, that it would be brought to our attention by readers and that reader feedback would provide the basis for a second book."

"Which you're doing."

"A second book? Yes, but not the one we planned. This one's mostly for fun; provide some different perspectives, look at the developmental stages, describe the view from an uncommon vantage. Specifically, I think it'll focus on the distinction between the two most common goals of spirituality; Truth-Realization, which is enlightenment, and Human Adulthood, which is a whole different thing, but which is what I think most seekers really want. The second book's not a continuation of the first book, see what I mean? It's not like the next level or anything like that. *Damnedest*, as it turns out, was complete in itself. It stands alone. We done good."

He holds up the printouts. "Then what's all this?"

"Look for yourself and see. Look at it like a lawyer or a scientist. Look through the emotion and try to find the substance. See if anyone makes a valid argument and let me know. Really, that would be very useful to me."

"Some say you're not enlightened because you talk about me, me, me too much. Like you got too much ego."

I smile. "None of it has anything to do with me. This gets a little tricky. You sure you want to get into it?"

"Yeah."

I gesture to an empty chair and he sits.

"Well, any time you look at a group of people, any group, really, you can place the individuals on a spectrum of ego attachment. At one end of the spectrum are those who identify completely with their false self, and on the other are those who wear their ego impersonally, like a loose garment. Follow? In the world and *of* the world at one end, in the world but *not* of the world at the other. Since this degree of attachment is the only true measure of human age, the spectrum could just as well be represented in years; say, eight to sixteen, see?"

"Kinda," he says. "Not really."

"Good. Good to say you don't understand when you don't. We'll keep going and you'll start to see it. The audience for a spiritual book is the same; it can be viewed on a spectrum of ego attachment, which we're saying is like a more accurate way to look at people's age. A book like *Damnedest* is going to reach a much wider audience than it's really best suited for. It says harsh things; very grown-up things. It says no belief is true. It says gurus and meditation and spiritual teachings are all gentle deceptions meant to soothe the inner coward, not forge the inner hero. So *Damnedest* looks like a spiritual book, but it's actually an anti-spiritual book. It looks like it's for everyone, but it's really for very few."

"So when they say you can't be enlightened—"

"Me personally? It has nothing to do with me. Anyone who tries to drag me into it is just trying to distract themselves away from the real message, the grown up message, which is one of self-determination. Very scary stuff. If they say they don't believe I'm enlightened, they're right and they're wrong. They're *right* because no one is enlightened. I said so in *Damnedest*; there is no such thing as an enlightened person; it's an immutable contradiction. They're *wrong* because when you talk about enlightenment, what I am is what you're talking about, whether you know it or not, whether you like it or not. They're basing their statements on other things. They might feel that enlightenment is a subjective thing, an in-dreams thing, or perhaps they think that I, as an author, am seeking their approval or their verification; that my authenticity is for readers to decide. The spiritual marketplace seems to foster this buyer-seller dynamic rather than the most rigorous scientific-type inquiry, which would be much more appropriate for something so important."

"Sounds like a popularity contest."

"Exactly. There seems to be an attitude that opinion counts for something. Goethe said none are so hopelessly enslaved as those who falsely believe they're free. I think that applies here. People might say they're spiritual or that they want to know the truth or whatever, but they mostly just want what anyone wants regarding the big questions; just enough to get by, just enough so they can go on about their lives, maybe make things a little better, puff themselves up a bit. That's about all, really. When it comes to all this religion and spirituality stuff, the closer you look, the foggier it gets, and I think a lot of people are happy just to hang out in the fog."

"And so these people," he holds up the pages, "if they say you don't know what spiritual enlightenment means?"

"That's an interesting question: What does spiritual enlightenment mean? I take it to mean awake—truth-realization, abiding non-dual awareness—but I guess other people take it other ways.

There are really only three possible destinations; human adulthood, truth-realization, and altered states of consciousness. Truth is absolute, there's nothing more than that, so if someone says enlightenment doesn't mean truth-realization, then it's enlightenment they're diminishing, not truth. There's nothing more than truth, and anything less than true is false, so to say that enlightenment means something other than truth-realization necessarily means you're saying it's within delusion, which doesn't sound very enlightened. See what I mean?"

"A little," he shakes his head, puzzled. "It sounds like people are looking for something, but they don't really know what it is, and they don't really want to find it."

I laugh because that *is* what it sounds like.

"That's not crazy?" he asks.

"Crazy is a numbers game."

"Like if enough people do it—"

"—then it's not crazy anymore."

"So you write these books," he continues, "saying what it really is and and how to really find it for people who don't really want it."

"Well, yeah, maybe. I think some *are* meant for it, and I think anyone, anywhere on the spectrum, can always use a good map."

"Whole thing sounds kinda—"

"What?"

"—fucked up."

"Yeah," I agree, "kinda does."

I'm as confused regarding these issues as Curtis. Who wants what? How badly? Why? Who's sincere? Who's just accessorizing? Who's using waking up as a way to go more deeply asleep? Duality is a tangled forest in which many self-styled freedom-seekers wield the machete of discrimination with all the effect of a butter knife. Not knowing where, if anywhere, they want to go, they're happy enough where they are. Fearing the genuine, they embrace the counterfeit; opting for words and adornment over authentic change, fueling delusions of spiritual progress with empty practices and useless knowledge, turning in place to create a sense of motion. Most significantly, they inflict no damage on ego, using spirituality to reinforce rather than dismantle self-image. Anyone taking an objective view will conclude, like Goethe, that the less deceived we think ourselves, the more we probably are. Maya's hold over us is strongest when we think it weakest. They say nobody's perfect, and that's a literal fact. If you want to become perfect, become nobody. They only way to get free of Maya's grasp is if there's nothing for her to hold onto.

"You said in the book you hadn't achieved a better status, right?" asks Curtis. "Is that true? Like right now, you and me have the same status?"

"Sure. We're both sitting here, feeling the sun and the breeze. I'm not up on some mountaintop. You're not plumbing the depths of hell. Do I seem blissed out?"

"Blissed out?"

"Unnaturally happy."

"You seem like people."

"That's it. If there's a practical difference, it's that you have more range than I do. You have a lifetime of highs and lows ahead of you, and I have a lifetime of, uh, contentment."

"But contentment's a good thing."

"Not really. Contentment is an other-side-of-the-fence thing. Once you have it, you forget what seemed so appealing about it."

"So it's a bad thing?"

"You see the hammock down there?"

"Yeah."

"Nice, right? Swaying in a hammock. Gentle breeze. Not a care in the world. Sounds okay, right?"

"Sounds pretty good."

"It's good in contrast, not as a permanent state. Maybe for half an hour on the occasional Sunday afternoon, not as a living reality. See?"

"Yeah. And that's how you are?"

I smile. "Close. Swinging in a hammock with my hat pulled down and a stupid grin on my face is pretty much my life."

"Tough thing to complain about."

"Yes, it is. So anyway, the difference isn't something I have that you don't, it's something you believe that I don't. You think it's real and I don't even see it. At this point, I can't even remember it."

"And what's that?"

"Everything. Everything you believe. Everything you're absolutely certain about. Everything you'd bet your life is true."

Curtis knocks on the table. "I'd bet my life this table is true."

"Perfect example," I say. "It would never even occur to me that this table might have reality. I have no thought that even resembles that. I have no context in which such a thought could exist. Reality has no reality for me."

"You're saying there is no table?"

"I'm saying there is no question of a table."

He looks at me speculatively for a minute, trying to figure out if I'm really saying that I don't think the table we're both leaning on is real.

"You're living in the holodeck," he says, referring to the computer simulated reality environment in Star Trek. "Not just the table. Me? The ocean? Everything?"

I let him think about it. He puts it together quickly.

"Computer," he says, "end program."

He looks around expectantly, but nothing changes.

"Yeah, okay," he says, "I guess I got all that from the book, but it sounds like there's a deeper thing, like there's more to it than you said."

I'm impressed.

"Absolutely. Very good. There's the reality, the truth, but Jed McKenna can't express it and no reader can grasp it. And that's why I said in the book, come see for yourself. That's the only possible response. I know it doesn't make sense. No one who knew what they were talking about ever said it did. It's the paradigm gap. Jed McKenna might do a good job talking about the part that can be talked about, but Jed isn't any more real than this table and he can really only talk about what's not, not what is."

"But something is, right? I mean, like, not nothing?"

"I don't know. Maybe nothing is everything."

"Like nothing is something?"

"You got something against nothing?"

"It sounds, kind of, I don't know, unsatisfying."

I laugh again.

"Yeah, if you ordered it off the menu I think you'd have regrets."

"What does that mean?"

"It means that what we're talking about isn't something someone can desire or wish for. It's not achieved by wanting it, but by hating and destroying its opposite. That's why it's a process of negation. It can look like anger or hatred, but it's more than that. Does that make sense?"

"About as much as any of it."

"Yeah, well, that's the way of it. Two different paradigms. It doesn't add up in theory the way it does in practice, so the theorists can get a bit crabby."

"And this is the kind of stuff your audience, the spiritual community, is all about?"

"Not so much. The, uh, community, as it were, of spiritually oriented people is pretty diverse. There's no cohesion, no central tenet, no single guiding philosophy that unites them other than being outside the mainstream. There are currents of Buddhist and Hindu thought that run through it, but they don't really form any sort of basis to it all. There's a lot of metaphysical stuff, I don't know what all. A lot of lifestyle stuff, all sorts of healing modalities. So there's really no single defining quality you could ascribe to the spiritual audience beyond a certain independence of thought; a general rejection of common views on religion, health, lifestyle—well, pretty much everything, I suppose."

"So these people who write to you, I don't mean it's all bad, it's mostly good, *real* good, but the bad stuff—"

"Like stuff that says I can't be enlightened because I talk from the perspective of an egoic being?"

"Well, they don't say it like that—"

"That's the kind of thing that *Damnedest* addresses as well as it can be addressed. That's one of the answers that's not missing. You've read the book, could you address that objection based on what you read?"

He thinks about it.

"Yeah, I'm pretty sure. Yeah."

"Right. That's what I mean when I say it's a book for grown-ups. It's not a lazy man's guide to enlightenment, or enlightenment in thirty days, or whatever. Naturally, it gets into the hands of people who have a fairytale notion of spirituality, and those people are going to react adversely when someone tells them this is serious business with a nearly perfect failure rate."

"It's a book for grown-ups."

"Yeah, people able to face facts, even if it's just enough to see that they don't want to face facts."

"But not like an age thing?"

"No. True age is different from years since birth. You're older than I was at your age."

"Really? How old am I this way? The way you're saying."

"I don't know, a kid. Eleven? Twelve?"

"Twelve?" He stiffens, his eyes go wide. "I'm eighteen! I can fight in a war!"

I hold up my hands. "Relax," I say, "take a breath. No need for anger. Release that feeling." He quickly resettles. "Okay, now look at that feeling, that feeling of being insulted. Take a step back and observe yourself, your processes. Look at your reaction to my words. That's what you have in your hand. The people who wrote those notes were having the same reaction you just had. They believe things and beliefs have emotions in them. People take this stuff personally. It cuts close. It messes with who you are. It's all about discovering that you're not who you think you are. People can get a little feisty."

"So I'm not really eleven or twelve? You were just saying that?"

"I don't know. Let's cut you in half and count the rings."

He gives me the blank look again.

9. Radical Sanity

> So man's insanity is heaven's sense; and wandering from
> all mortal reason, man comes at last to that celestial
> thought, which, to reason, is absurd and frantic; and
> weal or woe, feels then uncompromised, indifferent as
> his God.
>
> *–Herman Melville, Moby-Dick*

MARY AND I HAVE DINNER together every Sunday night. Because of our odd schedules, it might be the only time of the week we see each other. She's always off in the city or New London or Groton, and I'm always out and about or sleeping odd hours, so we decided that we'd both make time on Sundays to get together. There are dozens of wonderful restaurants within a half-hour's drive, so we always go someplace new and alternate picking up the tab. I always plan on a steak and end up with seafood. Tonight we're at one of the area yacht clubs. We're sitting at a table outside on the deck overlooking the marina. I'm working on a lobster and she's got something like a braised sea bass Florentine. As usual, I have *Moby-Dick* on the brain, and I think Mary is happy to have someone to discuss it with again after so many years without Bill.

"So, you understand why Ahab is after the whale?" she asks me, well into our discussion. "It's not about revenge?"

"No, it's not revenge. Ahab isn't after the whale."

"Ahab isn't after the whale?"

"Nope."

"Captain Ahab isn't hunting Moby Dick?"

"Nope."

"Well, okay, that's quite a statement. What *is* he hunting?"

"I don't know. He doesn't know. It doesn't matter."

"But it's not Moby Dick?"

"No, Moby Dick is what's in the way. Moby Dick is what needs to be negated. He's just trying to go further. Moby Dick is blocking his way, so Moby Dick is the enemy."

"And that's one of your two epiphanies about the book?"

"No, that much is pretty clear. Ahab says that Moby Dick is the wall between him and freedom. That's why the whale is white; it's like a blank screen onto which we can project our own obstacle to freedom. The first of my two epiphanies is that *Moby-Dick* is one of the world's great spiritual books. Not a whaling tale or a sea adventure, but a spiritual inquiry, and a breathtaking one. Probably foolish to try to rate something like this, but from a practical point of view I'd say it's the most accurate map of the spiritual terrain ever produced and, therefore, the most useful spiritual book ever written and, therefore, the best book period. Or so my reasoning goes."

Mary tilts her head and smiles in mild bemusement. She finishes chewing and lifts her napkin to touch at her lips. She takes a sip of wine and sits quietly for a few moments before speaking.

"Jed, I don't know if you know this or not, maybe it hasn't occurred to you, but I think it very likely that *you* wrote the best spiritual book ever written." She holds up a hand to stop me from interrupting. "Please, I don't say this lightly. I know you don't care, and I doubt it will ever be recognized as such, but I don't think it's even a matter of opinion. I don't think any reasonable person who looked at it objectively could say otherwise. Your book is the clearest explanation of the highest subject. That's it right there; the clearest explanation of the highest subject. I'm not a New Age spiritual person or any of that, and I don't think I'll ever make the journey you made—not in this life anyway—but because of you I understand, really, for the first time in my life, for myself, not borrowed from someone else, what's really going on; what life really is, and what it's not." She pauses and I see that she's getting a little worked up. "I really don't see how there could be a better book than yours. Okay, I'm sorry, I'll stop. So now you say that *Moby-Dick* is a great spiritual book. I admit I'm a little skeptical, but I know you're not speaking lightly and I know you're not going to ask me to believe anything, so I'm very intrigued. But I doubt very sincerely that you will convince me that *Moby-Dick* is the greatest book, spiritual or otherwise, ever written. For me, that position is filled."

I turn my attention to my lobster. We eat quietly for a few minutes before she resumes the conversation. "So, *Moby-Dick*. You see something there that no one else has?"

"As far as I can tell, yes," I say. "There's a key that unlocks *Moby-Dick*. Once you have the key it becomes a completely different book. A truly great and important book."

"Many people think it's already a great and important book."

"Yes, I can't figure that out. The way it's currently interpreted, it's a failure of a book. It doesn't surprise me that the book failed and Melville died in obscurity. If anything, I'm surprised it ever got resurrected. It's wonderful in many respects, but fails at the highest level, so," I shrug, "what does that leave?"

"I guess I see what you mean. There's certainly no satisfactory interpretation of Ahab's monomania, which seems to be the central theme of the book."

"Yes, I've spent the last several weeks looking through commentaries on *Moby-Dick*. I looked through everything in your house, I went to some local libraries and into the city, I've looked at everything on the internet. I've read—well, skimmed—viewpoints concerning *Moby-Dick* from every imaginable perspective, and none of them seem to acknowledge the fact that they're admiring a false equation; that it doesn't add up. It seems bizarre, but the reality is that *Moby-Dick* only makes sense when interpreted correctly, and, as far as I've been able to discover, no one has done that. As it's commonly interpreted, it's a sad, pathetic story about a psychotic madman who destroys everyone and everything in his sphere of influence for no valid reason; for vengeance on a dumb brute, as Starbuck says, that smote him from blindest instinct. It's interesting to note that a hundred and fifty years of readers have not seen Melville any more clearly than Starbuck saw Ahab. Many reviewers try to squeeze some great importance from the book, as if they know it's a great classic so the equation must be right, but it's not. The equation is wrong. It's *obviously* wrong. The emperor is wearing no clothes. Some critics say it's the story of Man pitting himself against Fate or God because those are the biggest things they have names for. The modern-day equivalent of their tragic hero version of Ahab would be a guy who goes into a fast food restaurant and shoots thirty people because his car got scratched in the parking lot. That's Ahab. To say that *Moby-Dick* is a great book as it's commonly viewed is as ridiculous as defending the restaurant shooter by elevating him to some grand, mythic dimension. It's absurd."

This is obviously a lot for Mary to take in, and she's too astute to have failed to see her own name listed on my indictment.

"And yet, you're saying it *is* a great book."

"Oh yes, beyond mere literary greatness. That's what I'm saying. It's been one of the great pleasures of my life to discover this book and its author."

"Well, don't make me wait. What's this thing you see that everyone has missed? What's this key that unlocks *Moby-Dick* and turns it into a completely different book?"

"Captain Ahab was sane. Saner than sane. *Radically* sane."

She eyes me for a few moments to see if I'm serious. Finally, slowly, she speaks. "I've never heard a plausible argument in favor of Ahab's being sane. People have tried, but it always seems like a square peg in a round hole. I can't imagine *any* interpretation in which Captain Ahab could be perceived as sane."

"I know," I reply, "but *I* can. I see it perfectly. *Moby-Dick* is like a picture postcard sent to us by Melville. Up until now everyone thought it was a work of the imagination, a made up place, but it's not. It's a real picture of a real place and I recognize it because I've been there."

Mary regards me wordlessly. She's starting to look a bit uneasy. Melville's book, with which she has so long been so familiar, which is so much a part of her life and so near her own heart, is starting to look not so familiar, maybe even a little hostile.

"Herman Melville went off the map," I continue, "beyond the known, beyond where it's suspected there's anything beyond. It's not the book people think; it's not even the *kind* of book people think."

Mary's daughter and I were in dancing class together back when we were still leaving teeth under the pillow. We wore white gloves. She was the first girl to whom I ever bowed and I was the first boy to whom she curtsied. Mary called me her bonny lad back then. Now her bonny lad had grown into something strange and maybe not so bonny; something that could sit across from her on a beautiful evening overlooking the boats in the harbor and tell her she's never really seen the one thing she's looked most closely at. That even now, children grown, husband gone, life winding down, her journey might only be beginning. She's not uneasy because she senses a new beginning but, rather, because of the part that must come before beginnings. The cycles of life do not align with the cycles of the body. It can become a whole new world, a whole new life, at any age, but before we can embrace the new, we must release the old.

10. Whoever You Are, Holding Me Now in Hand

Walt Whitman

WHOEVER you are, holding me now in hand,
Without one thing, all will be useless,
I give you fair warning, before you attempt me further,
I am not what you supposed, but far different.

Who is he that would become my follower?
Who would sign himself a candidate for my affections?

The way is suspicious—the result uncertain, perhaps
    destructive;
You would have to give up all else—I alone would
    expect to be your God, sole and exclusive,
Your novitiate would even then be long and exhausting,
The whole past theory of your life, and all conformity to
    the lives around you, would have to be abandon'd;
Therefore release me now, before troubling yourself any
    further—Let go your hand from my shoulders,
Put me down, and depart on your way.

Or else, by stealth, in some wood, for trial,
Or back of a rock, in the open air,
(For in any roof'd room of a house I emerge not—
    nor in company,
And in libraries I lie as one dumb, a gawk, or unborn,
    or dead,)
But just possibly with you on a high hill—
    first watching lest any person, for miles
    around, approach unawares,
Or possibly with you sailing at sea, or on the beach of
    the sea, or some quiet island,

Here to put your lips upon mine I permit you,
With the comrade's long-dwelling kiss, or the new
    husband's kiss,
For I am the new husband, and I am the comrade.

Or, if you will, thrusting me beneath your clothing,
Where I may feel the throbs of your heart, or rest upon
    your hip,
Carry me when you go forth over land or sea;
For thus, merely touching you, is enough—is best,
And thus, touching you, would I silently sleep and
    be carried eternally.

But these leaves conning, you con at peril,
For these leaves, and me, you will not understand,
They will elude you at first, and still more afterward—
    I will certainly elude you,
Even while you should think you had unquestionably
    caught me, behold!
Already you see I have escaped from you.

For it is not for what I have put into it that I have
    written this book,
Nor is it by reading it you will acquire it,
Nor do those know me best who admire me, and
    vauntingly praise me,
Nor will the candidates for my love, (unless at most
    a very few,) prove victorious,
Nor will my poems do good only—they will do just
    as much evil, perhaps more;
For all is useless without that which you may guess
    at many times and not hit—that which I hinted at;
Therefore release me, and depart on your way.

11. Marquis de Sade

I realize that no contemplative path wants to advertise
the cross or the suffering entailed in the crossing over.
On the other hand we must not be naive about this or in
any way mislead others. The truth is that getting to the
other shore will stretch the human limits to the
breaking point, and not once, but again and again. Who
can take it? It is not for nothing that the cross is the
central Christian symbol.

—Bernadette Roberts

I DOUBT THAT THERE'S ANY other stage of development that
a person can undergo which progresses so rapidly and for so
prolonged a period as the one Julie's in now. For as long as it takes it
will never slow down, never pause. As long as there's fuel, the fire
rages on. Every day, sometimes every hour, it's a whole new game
because the player is a whole new person; simpler, less encumbered,
less false, more awake.

Oh darn, my crisis isn't going well! Boo hoo for me! My total meltdown isn't going as I'd hoped so I guess I'll whine and complain like
a little brat! What a coward! I'm so ashamed of myself even though
I know this is what it is. *No one* gets around this. *No one* has it any
easier. This is what it is. What I can't do today I'll do tomorrow.
Small steps. One step at a time. One step at a time. I can only do
what I can do. I never ever thought I could get this far, could get
to this point. Every day I go a little further, I get more done, I know
less and understand more. I know exactly what it means to be
amazed every day by how naive I was the day before. Of *course* it

looks impossible. I shouldn't even look! Why look ahead? Am I *trying* to break my spirit? Focus. FOCUS !!! The next thing is the *only* thing and the next thing might kill me anyway. I look at the thing after the next thing and I see a total impossibility, but the last thing was the thing after the next thing at one time and now I'm past that, so what the fuck do *I* know? Nothing! Just do the next thing. The *next* thing is the *only* thing.

She has the family Golden Retriever, Tilly, with her because it's a rule that anyone using the cabin bring her along for companionship and security. She doesn't see many other people. She goes for long walks and can go for miles in the woods without seeing another cabin. For groceries, she has to drive to a small general store twenty miles away. For anything else, she has a college town within a few hours. For an internet connection she has to pay for an expensive and unreliable wireless setup. She lives on energy bars, water and coffee. Her dog eats better than she does.

One thing I know from going through this is who hasn't gone through it. The Pope hasn't gone through this, so who the fuck is he? The Dalai Lama hasn't gone through this, but at least he admits it. I think about all the assholes I've looked up to like gods over the years and I want to throw up. Teachers, mentors, spiritual guides, all so full of themselves, but none of them came here, none of them went through this, so what are they? Nothing. Imposters. Sad little mouth-buckets. I've seen great saints performing miracles and I was so impressed it was as if I was in the presence of God. What could I have been thinking? What do I care about saints and miracles? Raise the dead, pull a pony out of your ass, who cares?!? Pull my finger, I'll give you a miracle. What do miracles have to do with anything? I think about the people I used to look up to as spiritual teachers with all their endless bullshit about higher states of consciousness and divine love and I'm just stunned. Children selling candy to children, that's all it is. I read your book every day, Jed. You're right, it's all in there. Sometimes I use bibliomancy! I set my question in my mind and open the book and there's exactly what I needed to find, though I might be slow to see it. You're right, the universe is magic – all magic – I am the universe and the universe is me and it's all magic. What's not a miracle? There's nothing that's not it, not a part of it, a part of me. I just opened your book this way before I started writing this and that part I opened to is this:

> I like happiness as much as the next guy, but it's not
> happiness that sends one in search of truth. It's rabid,
> feverish, clawing madness to stop being a lie, regardless
> of price, come heaven or hell. This isn't about higher
> consciousness or self-discovery or heaven on earth.
> This is about blood-caked swords and Buddha's
> rotting head and self-immolation, and anyone who
> says otherwise is selling something they don't have.

I know you, Jed. I know what you are. I know the part you haven't told. I know where you are and how you got there. Was this what it was like for you? Were you this scared? Were you this totally torn between fear and mania at every moment? Is this how it was for you? Am I doing this right? Will I ever get there? But there is no there, is there? I know what you say in the book about this – that you never really believe you'll emerge from this – but that doesn't mean I *will* emerge. It's too much. I don't know what's at the other end of this. I think of you and I read the book and I cling to the idea that there's something.

Jesus Christ, when did I start swearing like this? I sit at my keyboard and I am flooded with intensity and there are no words strong enough for the realizations I'm trying to formulate. You're right about looking back. I look at what I wrote to you Monday and I'm embarrassed to have been so stupid, so young, and I understand that I'll look back on what I write today the same way though I can't imagine it now; can't believe it. I look back to see all the enormous obstacles I have struggled so hard to overcome and I don't see them; there's nothing there. Did I imagine it all? Is there nothing to all this except thoughts? If so, what are thoughts, really? What is the thinker? Is the thinker just the sum of thoughts with no underlying reality? When the thoughts are gone, what remains? I don't know. I shouldn't be mucking around in questions like that, it's just my mind wandering during a lull.

Thank you for the book recommendation. It was perfect! I was so stuck I thought it was the end. It seems I always think that but this time was different It was a huge blockage and I was sure it wasn't something I could ever destroy, but I have – I just saw right through it – every step is its own mountain. If you had told me a year ago that the Marquis de Sade would be one of my spiritual teachers, I probably would have slapped you!

There have been a few times when I read her emails and made suggestions, usually just pointing her in the direction of a key to open the door she was currently stuck at. (I suggested the energy bars, fearing that she'd live on macaroni and cheese if a better alternative weren't presented.) The de Sade thing had to do with understanding the selfishness that motivates goodness, or something along those lines. She was stuck in that region and de Sade's *Justine* happens to hold an exact key to that lock. Since it's a public domain book that she could download off the internet and scan very quickly for the part she needed, it seemed like a worthwhile thing to suggest, despite the unlikely and spiritually incorrect source. I don't imagine the Marquis de Sade shows up as a solution-provider on spiritual bookshelves very often, but you don't get to choose where keys come from. Some you already have, some you have to make, and some you have to go out and find.

I'm starting to see that it's not this and not that. It doesn't matter what side of something you take – of an issue or a debate – if you take a side you've already lost; it has you, owns you. I don't get this yet but I'm starting to see. "Battles are lost in the same spirit in which they are won," said Whitman, and I'm starting to understand what he means, as if the outcome of a thing is secondary to the fact that you're engaged at the level of the thing. I take it to mean that you're not free of the battle if you're operating at the level of the battle. I don't know, but I know this is how it works. I try to understand the problem and I keep gnawing at it I finally get to the point where I understand the question, and somehow that always seems to provide the answer. This isn't like scientific inquiry or like solving an equation where there's a right answer you have to find. This isn't about answering questions or solving problems, it's about destroying them. It's about seeing a question or problem with perfect clarity, which makes it disappear as if it never was.

✦

In this attic is more than just some of my character traits. Everything that makes up my humanity is up here. Every role I've ever played is up here; every costume I've ever worn. None of it will survive, I see that now. Nothing will survive. What I know, Jed, I know from you; from your words, your book. As you said, it's like walking along a mountain path and suddenly you slip and find yourself hurtling down a muddy slope at breakneck speed and eventually hurtling down a muddy slope at breakneck speed becomes your reality. That's my reality; hurtling down a muddy slope at breakneck speed. I know it ends, even if I don't believe it, and I know what comes after, even if I can't imagine it. The First Step is the last step and I know I'll never experience firm footing again – the *illusion* of firm footing, that is. There is no such thing as *terra firma* because there's no *firma*, only *incognita*.

The passages of Julie's writing we're looking at, in not very particular order, were chosen because they exhibit the process itself; her awareness of it, her constant discovery of it, her relationship to it. The mass of her writings are very specific to her and not of general interest. She has two main sources of fuel. One is her mother, who has taken on exaggerated proportions in Julie's mind. The other fuel source for much of Julie's hottest burns is the long list of spiritual teachers she has come into contact with over the years, and by whom she feels particularly betrayed. She spends many hundreds of pages killing and dissecting various spiritual teachings; seeing what about them drew her and illuminating that thing in herself. However, we're not going to look at the actual contents of her process so much as the process itself. One person's particular set of locks and keys is of less value to observe than the process by which locks are identified and keys located.

I should have understood this from the beginning, should have understood a *lot* of things from the beginning. What I thought was going to be merely impossible I now see would be lightyears beyond impossible. I entered this conceptual attic assuming it would be something for me to investigate; explore myself, maybe do some cleaning and rearranging. Then I slowly came to realize that I'm not up here to investigate or discover or uncover, I'm not here to clean or rearrange, I'm here to *destroy*, to remove everything, whatever it takes, to completely empty this space and start from zero. My job is to empty this space, to scrub it down to the walls and floorboards, to let in clear light and clean air, and then, once I have reclaimed this space as mine, then I can, if I wish, if I exist, begin the process of bringing things back in, small things, one at a time, each one carefully selected by me. The irony is that this clutter *is* me, so who's left when all this garbage is gone? I don't pretend to understand it, but I'm not doing this as a self-improvement exercise, I'm doing this because I must, because "I" am not *me* so "I" must die and good riddance. What comes after is hardly a consideration. Only in this way can I ever call this space of me mine. I should have known this from reading your book, Jed, but you can't know something like this from reading. As you say, it's no good seeing the teacher do the math on the board, you have to do the calculations yourself, or else the answers are just words.

Now I'm beginning to see something I could never have understood if you had told me a thousand times; I'm not just up here to clear the space, I'm up here to burn. This attic is to become a furnace; is already *becoming* a furnace. This is where *I* burn, *me*. I can already feel the heat, the process has already begun. This is what's happening. As I write these words I am physically ill. I have been sick with this growing realization for days. I would rather be dead than continue. There is no torture I would not prefer to what I see ahead. I can't go on and I will not go on. I thought I could but I can't. I see things ahead that can't be. Nothing good comes of this. No one benefits, nothing is improved, nothing gets better. It's just nothing. What's the point of nothing? I must destroy everything, even the good, even the beautiful. That is the only way to proceed, so I can't proceed. Fine, I'll suffer as a slave, a prisoner of ignorance. I don't care. Who was I to think I could do this? No one could really do this. No *woman* could – certainly no mother. What a dreadful, revolting, sickening thing. It's over. I was such a fool! I am sick with myself and wish I could just die and be done with it all.

Every step is a mountain. That's the way of it.

12. The American Way

The United States themselves
are essentially the greatest poem.

—*Walt Whitman*

I HAVE BEEN COMING AROUND to an amusing realization for several years, but not until the white whale breached for me did it really click into a certainty. Melville's *Moby-Dick* is, to my mind, the capstone of this claim, and the claim is basically this:

America kicks spiritual ass.

I am confident in saying that the American seeker could do as well or better in his own language and in his own country than he could by searching all of the East and going back to the Buddha.

The modern seeker need not feel that the answers he seeks are buried in distant lands, in ancient texts, in foreign tongues. We've produced spirits every bit as courageous and clear-spoken as any found in the East. Although we don't have to, we can now comfortably dispense with India, Japan, China, Tibet and the rest. All anyone could possibly want is right here, in our own language and in our own general vicinity of time.

This isn't meant in the spirit of an East-West pissing contest. I'm just sharing what I feel is a pretty interesting observation: America is not the spiritual third-world. We don't have to become archeologists of spirit tramping desperately through the ages and around the world, as if what we seek was only to be found at the furthermost extremes of our reach, or just beyond. Our own time and place provides all we could need. Our own people have made their own journeys and have returned to tell us in our own language what they've found.

Wherever you go in time or place, the reality of the seeker's situation is always the same; that more is less, translations are untrustworthy, the spirituality that serves society is not the same that serves the individual, ego rules the roost, and 99.99% of all the world's so-called wisdom, East *and* West, is, for the purposes of awakening, about as useful as a glass of warm spit with a hair in it.

Ptui!

Having said that, and so eloquently, I'll limit my case for a superior and original American Spirituality to the following:

✧ If I could have only the *Bible,* the *Torah* and the *Koran,* or *A Course in Miracles,* I'd take the *Course.*

✧ If I could have only Lao Tzu or Thoreau, I'd take Thoreau.

✧ If I could have only Rumi or Whitman, I'd take Whitman.

✧ If I could have only the *Mahabharata* or *Moby-Dick,* I'd take *Moby-Dick.*

✧ If I could have only the *Upanishads* and the *Dhammapada* or Seth, Abraham and Michael, I'd stick with the channeled guys.

✧ If I could have the entire world's mystic literature or the writings of America's explorers of consciousness; Terence McKenna, Stanislav Grof, Michael Harner, Ken Kesey, John Lilly, Tim Leary, *et al*, I'd take the latter.

✧ And finally, at the risk of appearing spiritually correct, if I had to choose only one thing, or could only recommend only one thing, it would be the collected works of Deepak

Chopra. My advice to anyone who wants to know the truth is to come and get it, but few who venerate truth conceptually are game for the reality of it. The vast majority of spiritual seekers want sweet dreams, not the annihilation of the dreamstate. Dr. Chopra has, in his many books, extracted the best that the world's religions and systems of thought have to offer, and distilled it into a comprehensive, lucid expression of subjective reality and our place in it. For those who wish to create more health, wealth and happiness for self and family, more peace and prosperity for society, and a brighter future for planet and humanity, Dr. Chopra's writings will prove an invaluable and incomparable resource.

This list of resources could go on, of course, and certainly deserves to extend beyond America's shores, but the point is to create a shorter list, not a longer one. Less is definitely more when the crowning summit of all wisdom, East or West, is, "Think for yourself and figure out what's true."

To those who would argue, correctly, that the teachings of the East offer deeper, richer levels of subtlety and sophistication than the more youthful and boisterous Americans, I'd reply that waking up is a youthful, boisterous business and that those who seek ever deeper layers of understanding are merely fulfilling ego's agenda of stagnation and self-preservation.

I don't want to belabor the American thing here because I'm taking this nationalistic stance half in jest, (because, in turn, I don't see that spirituality and truth have much in common), but if anyone would contend that disincarnate entities can hardly be claimed as American, I'd respond that those particular entities—tellingly, perhaps—came through American channels. Similarly, a few of the incarnate entities listed weren't born in America, but they did their important work here, and so it all points to this: Youthful, boisterous

America is the spiritual center of the modern world.

❖

Herman Melville and Walt Whitman were born two months apart and died seventy-three years later, six months apart. That seems quite suggestive, though I don't know of what.

Moby-Dick isn't a novel and *Leaves of Grass* isn't a book of poetry. Whitman and Melville weren't mere authors or philosophers sitting at their desks wondering about the meaning of life; guessing, speculating, constructing elaborate theories. They were rough-hewn, self-determined men, deeply involved with life. Melville went to sea, went whaling, lived in foreign lands among exotic people. Whitman nursed the wounded and dying in Civil War hospitals, caring for men and boys in mortal anguish.

Whitman and Melville were pioneers, explorers of uncharted realms, cartographers of reality. They do not fall within the scope or competence of literary critics and reviewers. Whitman wasn't first and foremost a poet, he was a guy trying to make sense of his situation who devised an unconstrained writing style suited to expressing the journey he had taken, the person he had become, and the world as it appeared to that new man. Melville wasn't first and foremost a novelist, he was a guy who made a journey and told the tale. We can make interesting observations about the characters we meet in *Moby-Dick*—what they might represent, who they might really be—but ultimately, of course, they're all Herman Melville.

Here's something Nathaniel Hawthorne wrote after a meeting with Melville:

> Melville, as he always does, began to reason of
> Providence and futurity, and of everything that lies
> beyond human ken, and informed me that he had
> "pretty much made up his mind to be annihilated"; but
> still he does not seem to rest in that anticipation; and, I

think, will never rest until he gets hold of a definite belief. It is strange how he persists—and has persisted ever since I knew him, and probably long before—in wondering to-and-fro over these deserts, as dismal and monotonous as the sand hills amid which we were sitting. He can neither believe, nor be comfortable in his unbelief; and he is too honest and courageous not to try to do one or the other. If he were a religious man, he would be one of the most truly religious and reverential; he has a very high and noble nature, and better worth immortality than most of us.

In "The Poet of the Cosmos," a chapter on Whitman in his book *Accepting the Universe,* John Burroughs says:

> Let me say that whatever else *Leaves of Grass* may be, it is not poetry as the world uses that term. It is an inspired utterance, but it does not fall under any of the usual classifications of poetry. Lovers of Whitman no more go to him for poetry than they go to the ocean for the pretty shells and pebbles on the beach. They go to him for contact with his spirit; to be braced and refreshed by his attitude toward life and the universe; for his robust faith, his world-wide sympathies, for the breadth of his outlook, and the wisdom of his utterances.

13. Curtis on the Rocks

One who has seen his true nature no longer regards life
as being full of menace and misery as most people do.
His previously mistaken sense of personal volition and
responsibility has disappeared in such freedom and joy
that life is now just an amusing spectacle like a game or
a dream, in which he has no real part.

–Ramesh Balsekar

I'M DRIVING AN OLD JEEP while I'm here. It's faded red with
black padded rollbars and interior and a black softtop that I don't
use much. Mary has had the jeep sitting unused in her garage since
Bill died and told me I should use it. I had a mechanic clean the gas
tank and the carb, do some welding repairs on the frame, give it a
tune-up and put on some good used tires and it runs fine. When
Mary saw it all cleaned up and running smoothly she tried to give it
to me. I refused and we got into one of those dumb inverted negoti-
ations where everybody's going the wrong way. I finally talked her up
to nine-hundred and we shook on it. I had it put in my name and
insured, put in a CD player and some speakers, and now it's a pretty
cool ride.

Now that I had a jeep I felt like I had to do something jeepy,
which around here means something on the beach. I decide a nice
sunset viewing at the shoreline somewhere would be good. I ask
Curtis if he's up for it because he doesn't seem like someone who
stops to smell the roses very often. I want to spend some time with
Curtis so we can get to understand each other a bit better. I want him
to have a better sense of the things he's working on for me, and to do
that I need a better sense of him. He asks his mom and she agrees. I

ask her if it's okay for her son to have a beer or two if he wants and she says okay. She seems pleased to have an adult male taking an interest in her son since he doesn't have a father in his life. I don't have much in the way of the fatherly about me, but I reckon it's first do no harm like anything else.

We drive out to Montauk where there's a rock-lined alcove on the ocean I had already scouted out; obviously a popular site for clam-bakes and beach parties. We drive down onto the beach and set up the cooler, chairs, firewood and so forth. Then we have some fun with the jeep in the sand. Curtis doesn't know how to drive a stick, so we get started on that learning curve; no better way to learn than in an old jeep with rollbars and nothing to hit but drift fence and horseshoe crab shells. He's a fast learner and thinks driving in the surf is the funnest thing he's ever done. We do that until the sun starts drop-ping, then we park it by our freshly arranged firepit and settle in.

We have a good imported beer on ice and I brought some pricey Honduran cigars because it seems necessary when you're sitting around a fire on a beach on a starry night talking about big things drinking expensive beer that you have some good cigars. I don't drink or smoke much, but there are times for it and it's no fun not to do it right. Once we have everything arranged we settle into low-slung beach chairs near the fire pit, facing the ocean and the dark-ening sky like theater-goers attending the Time & Space show in the Amphitheater of Forever. We get the fire going and let it settle into a low blaze that doesn't interfere with our view. The sun setting behind us stretches our shadows down to the water. We chat about nothing for a while, sipping beer, watching boats and birds, waiting for the moon to show up. I lean my head back and fall into a light doze.

❖

I ask Curtis a few slow-pitch questions about himself and he's happy to talk. He coaches youth soccer and tells me about that. His other sport is tennis and he's gone to the Open for the last four years. He talks about his family a bit and after a while he tells me about his brother's violent death and the ordeal his mother went through to get him and his sister away from a place where such terrible things weren't uncommon. I mostly listen; my gaze settled somewhere on the distant blend of sea and sky. Curtis wants to know the same things everyone who has suffered tragedy wants to know: Why evil? Why ugliness and suffering? Why should pointless horror ransack our lives?

His questions are fine. They're the ones that slapped Prince Siddhartha out of lethargy, and probably many others. They're good questions to ask as you sit by a fire in the sand gazing out at the ocean and into space. I could answer his questions a hundred different ways for the next hundred hours, but it wouldn't do him any good. The answer is never the answer. It's not that I know the answers and Curtis doesn't. It's that I don't know the questions and he does. I see that the questions that haunt Curtis' mind have no reality outside of it. We want to ask questions and get answers, and when people ask us questions we want to give them answers, but there's only one true answer and it lies at the exact center of the question.

I could tell Curtis that there is no good and evil, only unity and the dream of non-unity, of separateness, and that the false sense of separateness is ego, and that ego is all there is of evil in the world, that dissonance is born of ignorance and appears as good and evil. Curtis insists that he has seen evil, he's sure of it. I could tell him that most of what he calls evil is fear, and that most of what he calls goodness is also fear. He tells me that his mother is good. I agree and tell him that his mother is something more than good, she's an adult, an adult human being, which is a surprisingly rare thing. He says his grandma is a strict, God-fearing woman and is also good, but I can tell her age from his words as he talks about her. I talk a little about true age and human development and how his grandma is still a child, just a very experienced one, although her daughter, Curtis' mother, is an adult.

I talk about these things in a deliberately impersonal tone so as to avoid giving offense. Curtis doesn't seem offended that I've called his grandma a child, which is a good sign. He has trouble with the distinction though, so we talk about other people, people we both know of, politicians and entertainers and athletes, and what it really means to be an adult and what it really means to operate at the level of fear and apartness. He has difficulty believing that presidents and movie stars and billionaires could be children while a single black mother who scrubs floors for a living is an adult. "Someday it will be the other way for you," I tell him. "Someday you'll see an adult in a position of power or influence and you'll wonder how it happened."

He asks me if that's what the Bible means when it says the meek shall inherit the earth and I say that I haven't thought about it before but it sounds right. Meek is a crappy word to describe someone who has surrendered to divine will, but it's no time to get tangled in clunky terminology. He sits quietly, trying to wrap his mind around the things we're discussing and see how they apply in his life. Most of what Curtis knows about spiritual stuff comes from his grandma and his church and his Christian upbringing. He seems to think of religion, philosophy and spirituality as one big thing, so that the pastor at his church and his grandma and me are all playing for the same team. He's never ventured beyond Christianity because he's never had a reason to. He doesn't have any questions that Christianity doesn't seem to satisfy, so he hasn't strayed from the fold in search of better answers. But now he's here with me, which is, on the face of it, so unlikely that I have to assume he's going to be coming hard about soon, or already is.

We talk through the night, most of the conversation revolving around ego-release stuff and how the things he's learned apply to what he's learning now. Like many people I've spoken to over the last few years, Curtis wants to translate everything into Christian terms. This is always awkward for me so I tend to be less responsive, only providing answers where clear answers exist.

Curtis has never taken time to do anything like this before; just sit back and relax and take a good look at where he was and what he was a part of. I would guess that the structure of his life has been pretty confining so far, but these surroundings are the most conducive imaginable to the process of expansion. We agree that we can talk about things just for understanding; that Curtis wants to know what I think and what all the emails and the book are about. He doesn't want to be sold or convinced, he just wants to understand.

I think I doze off for a few minutes. When Curtis speaks I open my eyes and now the moon is up, the birds are down, and the boats are in.

"Then what about sin and original sin and all that? You saying there ain't none of that?"

I rub my eyes and try to remember where the conversation was and how it got there. Then I wonder if I'm saying there ain't none of that, or if it translates into something worth talking about. As I often do, I answer out of my own curiosity, to see where this line of inquiry will take us.

"There's only one sin," I tell him. "The only sin is ignorance. Ignorance is sin, sin is ignorance. There's nothing else."

"Ignorance of what?"

"It's not that kind of ignorance. It's not the kind where you don't know something. It's the kind where you *do* know something that's not true."

"That sounds backward," he says.

"Yeah," I agree.

"Then what about heaven and hell?" he asks.

I make a *voila* gesture with both hands. "Here it is. More heaven at the moment, I'd say."

"And hell?"

"What was it like when your brother was killed?"

He spends a minute with that thought before continuing.

"And how about redemption? There's gotta be redemption, right? The only sin is ignorance, and all this, life, is heaven and hell, right? Like, here and now?"

"Pretty much."

"Then you're in heaven or hell right now? In life?"

"I suppose."

"Not later? Not in the future? Not when you're dead?"

"I don't know anything about later, future and dead."

"Huh," a long pause. "So then, how do you get out? How do you get redemption for your sin of ignorance and get out of hell into heaven?"

Curtis has obviously been in some serious conversations before. He seems to have an entire operations manual in his head. I've redefined a part and he wants to know how that redefines the whole. I decide to answer his question in a fairly complete way to see what he does with it. The fire has burned down to glowing embers, a salty breeze is blowing in, the moon is high, and I'm too comfortable to reach for another beer.

"Ignorance isn't a sin like something you pay for later, but like something you pay for now," I explain quietly, as if talking to the waves. "The price of ignorance is living in ignorance, just as the price of huddling in cold, damp shadows is living in cold, damp shadows. Step out of the shadows and into the warm sunlight and the sin, so to speak, is instantly forgiven. Your world instantly becomes one of radiant warmth and light, and the cold, damp shadows are forgotten. Karma is the same. Heard of karma?"

"I've heard of it," he says.

"It's like sin. It's reckoned a sort of debt."

"It builds up? Like you gotta pay?"

"Yeah, burn it off. The only way to burn karma is to burn ignorance, which is the same as burning self because ignorance and self are the same thing. Ignorance isn't an *aspect* of self; it's the *essence* of self. It's not nothing where there should be something, it's the delicate weaving of something *from* nothing. That nothingness woven into somethingness is what you call reality. The part you call *you* is ego."

"Please wait," he says.

"Okay."

"Ego is what?"

"The false self. The personality. Everything you think of as you. Everything that makes you different from everything that's not you."

"And the false self is bad?"

"No. It's false."

"False isn't bad?"

"Nothing is good or bad but thinking makes it so," I paraphrase Hamlet.

"And so things like heaven and hell and karma, which is like payback for sin, right? So all this isn't like something by itself, but something you get because you got a false personality."

"Kind of."

"Because the false self comes from ignorance?"

"Yes. The false self *is* ignorance. Everything that tells you that you are separate from everything else is false."

"I'm not separate from everything else?"

"No. There's only one thing. What it is is what you are. Everything that tells you otherwise is your own personal false interpretation. That's ego, that's you, and that's what ignorance and sin and evil really are."

After a few minutes of silence he asks for an example. I think about it.

"It's like you're a ghost wearing a mansuit, complaining about the rain. The rain is making you miserable, so you call the rain evil, but rain isn't evil, it's just rain. The rain isn't the problem, the problem is that you're wearing a mansuit. Take off the mansuit and the problem is gone."

Another silent minute passes.

"But then I don't get the good stuff about the mansuit either?"

"That's right."

"And it's not just that I'm wearing the mansuit, it's like that's what I think I am, like I forgot I was really a ghost."

"Yes."

"So the rain's not the problem."

"Right. It's not the rain that's the problem; it's the thing that gets rained on. The common understanding of sin is that it's okay to wear the mansuit, but not okay to get rained on."

"So the real sin isn't all the things about the mansuit, but the mansuit itself. Thinking you *are* the mansuit, forgetting you're a ghost."

"Yes."

"Okay, hold on a minute, please."

I wait. I appreciate the effort Curtis is bringing to this. Conversations about important stuff work differently from conversations about regular stuff. You have to stop to define terms a lot, and people want time to sit with new ideas to get the hang of them. A conversation with someone who is brave and receptive is slower because they're working harder. They ask more questions and need more time. This stuff is coming at Curtis from far afield, and he's being very respectful of views that are in conflict with his own by making such an effort.

"Okay, go ahead," he says about ten minutes later.

"I forget where we are."

"Karma. Hell. Ghosts in rain."

"Karma and hell and suffering aren't things in their own right but disturbances in this flimsy substance of false self. The problem isn't in the disturbing things but in the thing disturbed. The thing disturbed is the false thing and if it weren't there, there'd be nothing to be disturbed. Nothing to get pierced or burned or dried out. Nothing to be wounded or slain."

"Nothing to be wounded or slain," he repeats.

"In truth, there is no book wherein our records are kept. There are no karmic ribbons that need to be burned. There is no one sitting in judgment. There is only what we think is true and whatever happiness or suffering arises from that belief. The self is false and it is the self that carries the burden of its own ignorance; that suffers or is happy, that is subject to external, non-self forces. The belief in the reality of the false self is the origin of all suffering and all happiness."

"There is no one sitting in judgment?"

"What you really are is all there really is. Who's to judge?"

"I don't see how that can make any sense."

"I know. You don't have to make sense of it all. I was just hoping to give you some idea of what's going on in those emails and stuff."

"Okay. It's interesting. I like it. I'm not saying it's wrong, I just don't see how it can be. How self and sin is the same. And ignorance. How there's only one thing. It's confusing."

It's confusing because the lines are blurred. These lines always seem to be blurred. It's my fault for introducing truth into the conversation. Truth is irrelevant. We're covering too much ground because we're at cross-purposes. I want to touch on the truth stuff because that's what he's seeing a lot of when he's working for me. He wants to know about the stuff that's of practical value in his own life; the stuff that can help him grow into a person like his mother instead of his grandmother. That's what I want too, really, so I should leave the truth stuff out and let him get an unobscured view of fun important topics like selflessness, surrender, living with free access to the observer mode, releasing the tiller, and all that. On the other hand,

I don't choose my words and I'm as curious about this conversation as Curtis is. He's not a computer that needs to be fed with precise information, and no harm is done by dumping it all on him at once and letting him do the work of sorting it all out over time. Time is the ripening agent.

The night goes on. Conversations that can be read in two minutes take an hour. We both phase in and out. Clouds thread their way across the sky, but it stays mostly clear and starry. We spend a lot of time discussing the age thing, how humans who look like adults are usually just over-ripe children. Curtis likes this subject because he immediately recognizes the distinction in his own life, between his mother and his grandmother. It's personal to him, something he has a direct experience of, unlike the false self stuff which leaves one without anything to cling to or with.

"I want to be that," says Curtis when the difference between adult and child becomes more clear in his mind. I'm pleased that he sees the distinction, but not surprised by his choice. Anyone capable of seeing the distinction would make the same choice, intellectually, at least. No one wants to be small and petty and fearful. We're enslaved by our own fear and ignorance; two sides of the same coin. When we remove the blinders of ignorance, wrong-knowing, we'll see where we *can* be and that's where we'll *want* to be.

But saying "I want to be that" doesn't make you that or we'd all be chic, fabulous and live forever. Desire and the manifestation of desire isn't a crapshoot. It's an art and a science and it's something you can pay attention to and learn about and get better at, but it's not something you can dictate. You can't reduce it down to your size, you have to expand into it, and to do that you have to slice away the bindings that restrict such expansion. It's available to all, our natural birthright, and it works in us to the exact degree that we don't work against it; a degree that changes in everyone from minute to minute. If Curtis really wants this, it will really occur, but the kind of wanting required is the kind that starts in the mind and moves to the heart and then reaches out from the center. It takes time and it can be as much a pull toward one thing as a push from another.

"This is what my life has to be, I guess," says Curtis. "I can't see that anything else really comes before it. Thank you for showing me this."

❖

I operate my daily life at the level of patterns, not details, and I watch with bemused curiosity when the black son of a cleaning lady finds his way out of poverty and violence into an area of affluence, and further, into private dialogue with a being as rare as the being I am. There are no accidents, but there are gentle nudges and shoulder taps by an unseen hand. Why Curtis is here and what will become of him doesn't matter to me. However he got here, he's here. Whatever level he's at, he'll soon be at the next. He's going to step into adulthood. He sees what it is and what it means *not* to be an adult, so he'll make that transition. He'll make it by first seeing that there is such a transition to make, that what he presently considers normal and good is abnormal and bad, which he's beginning to do now. Then, through a death and rebirth process, the bindings of ego will start to itch and the itch will start to annoy him more and more until it's like he's allergic to his own skin, and at last he'll shed his false skin and be as if born anew into a world in which he knows he belongs; in which he is not a trespasser or debtor, which is his and which is not other *than* him. And that's where life begins, where learning begins, where adulthood begins. Thus are we cast out of the garden and thus do we regain it. Once regained, we can begin to explore our true relationship with our world and its relationship to us, and we learn that all there really is is consciousness and energy; that they're the same thing and what they really are is what *we* really are, which is just another way of saying life is but a dream. It's the distinction between self and Self; between Lower Self and Higher Self. Lower Self is petty and fearful and grating, Higher Self is open and easy and in tune with all rather than just itself. Higher Self is not the same as truth-realization, but just in case there's any question in your mind, it's the one you want. No one *wants* truth-realization. It can't be wanted. Higher Self, however, *can* be wanted and *can* be had, and is, in fact, what all seekers of all times and all places have, knowingly or not, truly sought.

Except for a brief description of Sonaya, who personifies the non-egoic state in its full expression, I swung wide of this topic in *Damnedest*. That was a book about spiritual enlightenment, which I interpret as meaning the supreme state. Higher Self is not truth or truth-related, it exists wholly within the dreamstate and contains, unlike the black and white truth, countless shades of gray. Truth-realization, abiding non-dual awareness, spiritual enlightenment; these terms apply to the supreme state. Supreme as in ultimate, beyondless. Higher Self is not the supreme state; it's the natural state. To have money and adoration and power is less than nothing compared to residing in the state of human adulthood, and so a lowly cleaning woman can be a regal being while a rich, beautiful, movie star can be a peasant. The first shall be last and the last shall be first, camels can't pass through the eyes of needles, the meek shall inherit the earth, and so on.

Once unshackled from the life-sucking demands of ego, we clearly see the unformed creatures we had hitherto been, like children. Not children in the happy, lyrical sense, but in the abrasive, self-absorbed, discordant sense. What we consider bright and beautiful in children is the inherent nature of the fully developed human. Our true state is one of playfulness, innocence, lack of guile, unboundedness of spirit, robust health and inner light, a natural confidence and unerring sense of right, imperturbability, grace, a calm eye and easy good humor, balance, freedom from malice and pettiness, the absence of fear, the presence of largesse and a permeating sense of gratitude. Creativity. Connectedness. Correctness. This is the clear and rightful state of the human being. One must die of the flesh to be born of the spirit. One's life energy, formerly squandered by ego, can then be turned to the higher purposes and potentials of life in the magnificent amusement park of duality.

❖

We both fall asleep in our chairs. When I awake, the fire is down to ash-covered coals and the first light of the new day is just starting to warm the air. I go to the water to stretch and write my name in the sand and when I return to my chair Curtis is awake and watching the first rays of the sun coming up over the Atlantic Ocean. I remove some apples, grapes, pears, gorp and bottled water from the cooler and set them between us. We eat and watch the sunrise.

14. There is no other.

Chapter 11 from *The Mysterious Stranger* by Mark Twain.

"The dream-marks are all present; you
should have recognized them earlier."

—Mark Twain

FOR AS MUCH AS A year Satan continued these visits, but at
last he came less often, and then for a long time he did not come
at all. This always made me lonely and melancholy. I felt that he was
losing interest in our tiny world and might at any time abandon his
visits entirely. When one day he finally came to me I was overjoyed,
but only for a little while. He had come to say good-by, he told me,
and for the last time. He had investigations and undertakings in
other corners of the universe, he said, that would keep him busy for
a longer period than I could wait for his return.

"And you are going away, and will not come back any more?"

"Yes," he said. "We have comraded long together, and it has been
pleasant—pleasant for both; but I must go now, and we shall not see
each other any more."

"In this life, Satan, but in another? We shall meet in another,
surely?"

Then, all tranquilly and soberly, he made the strange answer,
"There is no other."

A subtle influence blew upon my spirit from his, bringing with
it a vague, dim, but blessed and hopeful feeling that the incredible
words might be true—even must be true.

"Have you never suspected this, Theodor?"

"No. How could I? But if it can only be true —"

"It is true."

A gust of thankfulness rose in my breast, but a doubt checked it before it could issue in words, and I said, "But—but—we have seen that future life—seen it in its actuality, and so —"

"It was a vision—it had no existence."

I could hardly breathe for the great hope that was struggling in me. "A vision?—a vi —"

"Life itself is only a vision, a dream."

It was electrical. By God! I had had that very thought a thousand times in my musings!

"Nothing exists; all is a dream. God—man—the world—the sun, the moon, the wilderness of stars—a dream, all a dream; they have no existence. Nothing exists save empty space—and you!"

"I!"

"And you are not you—you have no body, no blood, no bones, you are but a thought. I myself have no existence; I am but a dream—your dream, creature of your imagination. In a moment you will have realized this, then you will banish me from your visions and I shall dissolve into the nothingness out of which you made me...

"I am perishing already—I am failing—I am passing away. In a little while you will be alone in shoreless space, to wander its limitless solitudes without friend or comrade forever—for you will remain a thought, the only existent thought, and by your nature inextinguishable, indestructible. But I, your poor servant, have revealed you to yourself and set you free. Dream other dreams, and better!

"Strange! that you should not have suspected years ago—centuries, ages, eons, ago!—for you have existed, companionless, through all the eternities. Strange, indeed, that you should not have suspected that your universe and its contents were only dreams, visions, fiction! Strange, because they are so frankly and hysterically insane—like all dreams: a God who could make good children as easily as bad, yet preferred to make bad ones; who could have made every one of them happy, yet never made a single happy one; who made them prize their bitter life, yet stingily cut it short; who gave his angels eternal happiness unearned, yet required his other children to earn it; who gave his angels painless lives, yet cursed his other children with biting miseries and maladies of mind and body; who mouths justice and invented hell—mouths mercy and invented hell—mouths Golden Rules, and forgiveness multiplied by seventy times seven, and invented hell; who mouths morals to other people and has none himself; who frowns upon crimes, yet commits them all; who created man without invitation, then tries to shuffle the responsibility for man's acts upon man, instead of honorably placing it where it belongs, upon himself; and finally, with altogether divine obtuseness, invites this poor, abused slave to worship him!...

"You perceive, now, that these things are all impossible except in a dream. You perceive that they are pure and puerile insanities, the silly creations of an imagination that is not conscious of its freaks—in a word, that they are a dream, and you the maker of it. The dream-marks are all present; you should have recognized them earlier.

"It is true, that which I have revealed to you; there is no God, no universe, no human race, no earthly life, no heaven, no hell. It is all a dream—a grotesque and foolish dream. Nothing exists but you. And you are but a thought—a vagrant thought, a useless thought, a homeless thought, wandering forlorn among the empty eternities!"

He vanished, and left me appalled; for I knew, and realized, that all he had said was true.

15. The Break-Out Archetype

"He's a grand, ungodly, god-like man, Captain Ahab;
doesn't speak much; but, when he does speak, then you
may well listen. Mark ye, be forewarned; Ahab's above
the common; Ahab's been in colleges, as well as 'mong
the cannibals; been used to deeper wonders than the
waves; fixed his fiery lance in mightier, stranger foes
than whales."

—Herman Melville, Moby-Dick

AHAB IS AN EXQUISITE CREATION, and a unique one.
No other character in literature, philosophy or religion
fulfills, even approximately, the description of the unknown archetype. Ahab not only fulfills it, he defines it.

It is an archetype because it is a universal role in the human
drama, transcending place, time and culture; common to all, accessible to all. It is the *unknown* archetype because the awakened state is
an undiscovered and unsuspected country. It is the *ultimate* archetype
because it is the *final* archetype, and it is final because it breaks out
of the confines within which the dramatic play of *all* archetypes
occurs.

Hence, the Break-Out Archetype.

The Break-Out Archetype is unknown, and will remain
unknown. Very few people are likely to understand it conceptually,
and far fewer will understand it directly, by playing or having played
the role. And of those who understand it directly, nearly none will
care to think or speak of it.

Captain Ahab is definitive, as we'll see, because Melville knew
exactly what he was doing when he created Ahab. Mary suggested

that I list the reasons why I believe Captain Ahab was designed from the ground up to be the unknown archetype. She also suggested I list any features of this archetype that might be *missing* from Ahab. I brought her my list and my notes and we worked on it together for a few evenings. Her deeper knowledge of *Moby-Dick*, combined with her familiarity with *Damnedest*, allowed her to understand the archetype conceptually, so she was able to identify features common to both Ahab and the Break-Out Archetype and cite supportive examples and contradictions. But even at that, my one all-crowning realization about Ahab and the Break-Out Archetype was still at this point unsettled in my mind. I didn't discuss it with Mary then, or include it in this list.

Among the most significant features of Ahab when considering the Break-Out Archetype is his profound and mysterious relationship to fire. Fire is *of the essence* of the Break-Out Archetype and it is *of the essence* of Ahab. Melville makes this point many times in many ways, starting with Ahab's appearance:

> He looked like a man cut away from the stake, when
> the fire has overrunningly wasted all the limbs without
> consuming them, or taking away one particle from their
> compacted aged robustness.

Ahab is marked from head and face to neck (to feet, it's hinted) with a brand-like scar that resembles the perpendicular seam of a lightning strike on a great tree. We are given reason to suspect that Ahab's present state didn't begin when the whale took his leg, but sometime before that when he got involved with worshippers and sacraments of fire. In one of the most sensational scenes in the book, the ship's masts are lit up like nine candles as lightning blazes and Ahab wields a flaming harpoon like a torch as he delivers the speech of his full defiance, after which, burning harpoon in hand, he addresses his panic-stricken crew:

Petrified by his aspect, and still more shrinking from
the fiery dart that he held, the men fell back in dismay,
and Ahab again spoke:—

"And that ye may know to what tune this heart beats;
look ye here; thus I blow out the last fear!" And with
one blast of his breath he extinguished the flame.

❖

Moby-Dick, viewed aright, is a very simple story: Man, Ocean and
Whale are Ego, Universe and Delusion. Fire is negation. Everything
else is everything else. Ahab is in sole command of his ship on the
sea of the infinite, launched on a kill-or-die quest to win his freedom.
Armed with pure intent and a weapon "tempered in blood, and
tempered by lightning," Ahab brings his entire being to bear on this
one single purpose. The white whale is Ahab's dragon; his current
layer of ignorance. It doesn't matter what the dragon represents, only
that it exists. As long as there is a dragon, there's an Ahab, and as
long as there's an Ahab, the hunt goes on.

The following items are true of both Ahab and the individual
who has taken the First Step and is in the process of awakening; the
Break-Out Archetype:

❖   Ahab possesses purity of intent: Monomania.

❖   Ahab acts, but does not reflect on the fruit of the act.

❖   Ahab is imperious; sovereign and self-sovereign.

❖   Ahab is amoral.

❖   Ahab has lost a significant, irreplaceable part of himself.

❖   Ahab knows he is alone. He says:

> "Ahab stands alone among the millions of the peopled
> earth, nor gods nor men his neighbors!"

❖   Ahab has undergone a radical transformation.

> Ahab and anguish lay stretched together in one
> hammock, rounding in mid winter that dreary, howling
> Patagonian Cape; then it was, that his torn body and
> gashed soul bled into one another; and so interfusing,
> made him mad.

❖   Ahab's objective is not, as it appears, the whale. The whale
is just in the way:

> "If man will strike, strike through the mask! How can
> the prisoner reach outside except by thrusting through
> the wall? To me, the white whale is that wall, shoved
> near to me. Sometimes I think there's naught beyond.
> But 'tis enough."

Further, come what may. That's what Ahab is saying.
Those are the orders he sails under. It really has nothing to
do with the whale. That's why no consensus has ever been
arrived at as to what the whale, and the whiteness of the
whale, represent. Beyond our furthest charted regions,
where it is written, "Here be dragons!" is where this hunt
takes us. Each person's white whale is whatever keeps
them from advancing in that direction.

❖   Ahab is *hyper*-Promethean in his defiance. Stealing fire
from the gods is petty larceny compared to stealing illusion from Maya.

> "Thou canst blind; but I can then grope. Thou canst
> consume; but I can then be ashes. Take the homage of
> these poor eyes, and shutter-hands. I would not take it.
> The lightning flashes through my skull; mine eye-balls
> ache and ache; my whole beaten brain seems as
> beheaded, and rolling on some stunning ground... There
> is some unsuffusing thing beyond thee, thou clear spirit,

to whom all thy eternity is but time, all thy creativeness
mechanical. Through thee, thy flaming self, my
scorched eyes do dimly see it."

❖ Ahab is driven, not drawn. He does not act from desire.
He is not pulled by the lure of some imagined betterment
of self or world. He is not motivated by altruism or self-
interest.

❖ Ahab cannot be swerved from his purpose:

"Swerve me? The path to my fixed purpose is laid
with iron rails, whereon my soul is grooved to run. Over
unsounded gorges, through the rifled hearts of mountains, under torrents' beds, unerringly I rush! Naught's
an obstacle, naught's an angle to the iron way!"

❖ Nor can he swerve himself:

"This whole act's immutably decreed. 'Twas rehearsed
by thee and me a billion years before this ocean rolled.
Fool! I am the Fates' lieutenant; I act under orders."

Ahab is lashed to the front of a speeding locomotive
hurtling toward imminent collision. He is a force of
nature, a tidal wave that started as a minor oceanic event
and which has swelled to a magnitude that can erase cities
from the earth. "Nothing personal," says the wave, "it's
immutably decreed." And so it is.

"All your oaths to hunt the White Whale are as
binding as mine; and heart, soul, and body, lungs and
life, old Ahab is bound."

❖ Here, five important expressions of the Break-Out
Archetype are voiced by Ahab in the space of five
sentences:

"I'd strike the sun if it insulted me. For could the sun
do that, then could I do the other; since there is ever a
sort of fair play herein, jealousy presiding over all
creations. But not my master, man, is even that fair play.
Who's over me? Truth hath no confines."

That first sentence deserves a chapter of its own.

"I'd strike the sun if it insulted me."

"I will fight whatever enemy is before me," Ahab is
effectively saying. "I am moving forward and whatever
stands in my way is therefore my enemy and I will throw
myself unreservedly against it." The battle is absolute, and
because the goal is always forward progress, whatever is in
the way is always what the battle is against. The goal is
not survival or happiness or continued well-being. There
is only one goal and it is always the same: Further.

The second idea conveyed, that there is ever a sort of fair
play herein, is a critical observation that is at the very
heart of one's ability to stand up and fight the fight. The
jealousy presiding over all creations can be understood as
the balance of opposites as in the yin-yang symbol, but the
fact that Ahab understands that no task before us can be
beyond us demonstrates a profound grasp of a rule that
applies to all but is known by few: The universe always
plays fair. If we must, we can.

Third:

"But not my master, man, is even that fair play."

That fair play is the balance of opposites; causality,
action and reaction, the dualistic universe. Ahab is, in
effect, declaring that he grasps non-dualism.

The fourth important point to be drawn from this excerpt comes from these words:

"Who's over me?"

Those may sound like the words of a megalomaniac, but in Ahab it's not ego talking. It's a man declaring his self-sovereignty, which is well-established in the heart and mind of the Break-Out Archetype. Anyone found over us would merely represent another obstacle to our progress.

The fifth insight worth noting in this passage is this:

"Truth hath no confines."

This perfect statement is the diamond heart of both Captain Ahab and *Moby-Dick*. It's one of those Golden Keys, like not-two or *tat tvam asi*, that unlocks the entire mystery. If truth hath no confines, then all confines are false. One who dedicates himself to striking through *all* confines must eventually arrive at truth. Hence, further.

✧ Ahab embraces his madness. He knows that it is indispensable to his endeavor:

> "For this hunt, my malady becomes my most desired health."

✧ Ahab views his madness as a form of sanity. He finds it strange that others seem to be in similar circumstances, but not reacting similarly. When the life-battered blacksmith tells Ahab, "I am past scorching; not easily can'st thou scorch a scar," Ahab replies:

> "Thy shrunk voice sounds too calmly, sanely woeful to me. In no Paradise myself, I am impatient of all misery

in others that is not mad. Thou should'st go mad, blacksmith; say, why dost thou not go mad? How can'st thou
endure without being mad? Do the heavens yet hate
thee, that thou can'st not go mad?"

✧   Ahab knows the truth of his being:

"Nor white whale, nor man, nor fiend, can so much
as graze old Ahab in his own proper and inaccessible
being."

Compare that to the *Bhagavad-Gita*:

I say to thee weapons reach not the Life,
Flame burns it not, waters cannot o'erwhelm,
Nor dry winds wither it. Impenetrable,
Unentered, unassailed, unharmed, untouched,
Immortal, all-arriving, stable, sure,
Invisible, ineffable, by word
And thought uncompassed, ever all itself,
Thus is the Soul declared!

And the *Tao Te Ching*:

He who knows how to live can walk abroad
Without fear of rhinoceros or tiger.
He will not be wounded in battle.
For in him rhinoceroses can find no place
   to thrust their horn,
Tigers no place to use their claws,
And weapons no place to pierce.
Why is this so?
Because he has no place for death to enter.

✧   Captain Ahab utilizes non-ordinary ways of knowing. He
breaks away from the conventional methods of navigation
in favor of higher, more intuitive ways:

"Curse thee, thou quadrant!" dashing it to the deck,
"no longer will I guide my earthly way by thee."

Ahab states that he never thinks, only feels. His "evil shadow" Fedallah is, among other things, an oracle, and serves Ahab as an unconventional source of knowledge.

✧ Ahab never counts cost. Nothing true can be destroyed, nothing false exists. Ahab's quest will sink his ship, bring ruin upon its owners, kill his crew and two boys, leave his wife widowed and child fatherless, and destroy Ahab. It's not that he's unaware of the cost, but that he knows it to be irrelevant; a non-issue.

✧ Ahab is both player and spectator. He is undergoing the process as well as monitoring it. He often soliloquizes and shows himself to be in the observer mode:

"What I've dared, I've willed; and what I've willed, I'll do! They think me mad—Starbuck does; but I'm demoniac, I am madness maddened! That wild madness that's only calm to comprehend itself!"

✧ Captain Ahab operates from a place of perfect certainty. He may be the source of tremendous conflict, but he himself is unconflicted. Although composed, like everyone, of two aspects, the "living principle" and the "characterizing mind," and although at times one seems haunted by the other, and although at times Ahab grieves for his lost humanity, the fact remains that he is clear and unwavering in his purpose.

✧ It cannot be clearly determined whether Ahab chose his destiny or was chosen by it, even by Ahab:

> "Is Ahab, Ahab? Is it I, or God, that lifts this arm? If the great sun moves not of himself, but is as an errand-boy in heaven; nor one single star can revolve, but by some invisible power; how can this one small heart beat; this one small brain think thoughts; unless God does that beating, does that thinking, does that living, and not I."

✧ Ahab lacks the "low, enjoying power." All the normal pleasures of life are lost to him. He's in an amusement park he can't enjoy, or, as he calls it, Paradise:

> "Oh! time was, when as the sunrise nobly spurred me, so the sunset soothed. No more. This lovely light, it lights not me; all loveliness is anguish to me, since I can ne'er enjoy. Gifted with the high perception, I lack the low, enjoying power; damned, most subtly and most malignantly! damned in the midst of Paradise!"

✧ Captain Ahab appears insane. Onlookers, both Ahab's crew and Melville's readers, assume that Ahab has chosen his course and could alter it, and since he doesn't, he must therefore be insane. Perfectly correct. There is no way to interpret Ahab as sane *except* within the context of the Break-Out Archetype.

✧ Ahab is absolute. He is holding nothing back. He has no Plan B; no secondary considerations or objectives. All the power and force of his being is being brought to bear on a single endeavor. He never acknowledges any future beyond Moby Dick.

✧ Ahab is still human; still in *this* paradigm. He displays genuine, heart-felt nostalgia for what he has lost, for the price he has paid. He's going, not yet gone.

✧ Ahab is overwhelmed. He is driven, as if possessed, to an incomprehensible fate, far beyond human bounds:

> "What is it, what nameless, inscrutable, unearthly thing is it; what cozening, hidden lord and master, and cruel, remorseless emperor commands me; that against all natural lovings and longings, I so keep pushing, and crowding, and jamming myself on all the time; recklessly making me ready to do what in my own proper, natural heart, I durst not so much as dare?"

✧ Ahab has no regrets or misgivings. He may feel overwhelmed, and he may have nostalgic longings, but he does not express the wish that his situation was otherwise.

✧ Ahab doesn't pass the cup. To all outward appearances, he could turn back from the fate into which he's leading himself and his crew as easily as nodding his head, but the inward reality is very different.

✧ Ahab is discovering his role as he plays it. We see this when he throws down his quadrant, a tool of lower, scientific knowing, in favor of a higher way of knowing. We also see it when he realizes that smoking no longer gives him pleasure. First comes realization:

> "Oh, my pipe! hard must it go with me if thy charm be gone!"

Then resolution:

> "What business have I with this pipe? This thing that is meant for sereneness, to send up mild white vapours among mild white hairs, not among torn iron-grey locks like mine. I'll smoke no more—"
> He tossed the still lighted pipe into the sea.

❖ Ahab is a deceiver. He is inwardly honest, not outwardly. He presents a false face to the world in order to carry out his task:

> Now, in his heart, Ahab had some glimpse of this, namely: all my means are sane, my motive and my object mad. Yet without power to kill, or change, or shun the fact; he likewise knew that to mankind he did long dissemble; in some sort, did still.

❖ But his deceit is outward only. He is not deceiving himself:

> But that thing of his dissembling was only subject to his perceptibility, not to his will determinate.

❖ Ahab has already jettisoned most of himself. He is streamlined for the hunt; his ego is stripped to the bone. He is no longer wasting his lifeforce on projecting an outward self. In his more normal days he must have been very conscious of presenting himself as pious, honest, honorable, dependable; worthy of a ship, worthy of marrying, worthy of sailing under. Now, all such considerations, except as necessary to his plans, are forgotten. He no longer maintains a religious, national, community, professional, or family identity. He is no longer burdened with the need to fulfill his role.

❖ "Let what will befall," says Ahab. He is resigned to his fate. He knows it's out of his hands, as shown when he parts from recently befriended Pip, knowing that death may be near for them both:

> "True art thou, lad, as the circumference to its centre. So: God for ever bless thee; and if it come to that,—God for ever save thee, let what will befall."

❖ Ahab is a pure, unapologetic nihilist. He creates a weapon, a harpoon, which will "weld together like glue from the melted bones of murderers." He tempers his weapon not in water, but in blood.

> *"Ego non baptizo te in nomine patris, sed in nomine diaboli!"* deliriously howled Ahab, as the malignant iron scorchingly devoured the baptismal blood.

"I baptize you not in the name of the father, but in the name of the devil." What does that mean? Does Ahab worship the devil? That might be how nihilism appears to many, but to Ahab such a distinction would be meaningless. Ahab is not forging a tool to create or a container to preserve, he's forging a weapon to destroy. He is a nihilist; he seeks to arrive at the real by destroying the unreal.

Correctly understood, this is also what Melville created in *Moby-Dick*; a weapon to destroy. He told his friend Nathaniel Hawthorne, to whom *Moby-Dick* is dedicated, that this line—*Ego non baptizo te in nomine patris, sed in nomine diaboli!*—is the book's motto.

❖

A final quality shared by Ahab and the Break-Out Archetype is the one that keeps them undiscovered and unsuspected. By dwelling in the outskirts of the paradigm, they are effectively shrouded in the blurred edges of the observer's perceptual range. This shroud allows Ahab to stand before his crew unseen for what he really is, and *Moby-Dick* to lay open before readers unseen for what *it* really is. The observer, not knowing the finiteness of his own reality, must say that Ahab is a great character, but ultimately insane. He must say that *Moby-Dick* is a great book, but ultimately incomprehensible. He must say that the Break-Out Archetype is interesting in theory, but of no practical value because you can't break out of reality. Where would you go?

Critics often point out the flaws in Ahab that lead to his downfall in order to support their theory that he is, in the Aristotelean sense, a tragic hero, but that's just the kind of error that must occur when we unknowingly translate from another paradigm into our own. That's why *Moby-Dick* has defied all interpretations. It's about going somewhere that we don't even *suspect* the existence of.

Captain Ahab is not a tragic hero. He exhibits no flaw and experiences no downfall. He is set on a single path from the time we first see him until his final encounter with the white whale. He is a harpoon that speeds unerringly toward its target. He never veers in the least and in no sense does he fail to achieve his objective.

The *dis*similarities between Captain Ahab and the individual who has taken the First Step and is launched on the trajectory of awakening are few. I have only noted one omission worth mentioning: Elation.

Lunatic joy.

Stark, raving happiness.

Transcendental exultation.

Ahab appears at different times to be enraged, insane, reasonable, tormented, heartbroken, and introspective, but never radiantly triumphant, which he would most certainly be. He has every reason to be leaning off the prow of the *Pequod*, arms flung wide like Jack Dawson in the 1997 film *Titanic*, shouting "I'm the king of the world!" But what Jack Dawson was playing at would, for Ahab, be true. For Ahab, all the uncertainty, fear, doubt, mediocrity, pettiness, striving, ambiguity and myriad other chains that bind us and weigh us down have been sliced away. His fate is known, his success certain. He is hurtling at thrilling velocity into perfect freedom. He knows it, and he would be unspeakably happy about it.

16. Irreconcilable Differences

Are you the new person drawn toward me?
To begin with, take warning—I am surely far
  different from what you suppose;
Do you suppose you will find in me your ideal?
Do you think it so easy to have me become
  your lover?
Do you think the friendship of me would be
  unalloy'd satisfaction?
Do you think I am trusty and faithful?
Do you see no further than this façade—
  this smooth and tolerant manner of me?
Do you suppose yourself advancing on real
  ground toward a real heroic man?
Have you no thought, O dreamer, that it
  may be all maya, illusion?

—Walt Whitman

I ENTER THE OFFICES OF the public relations firm I've been asked to meet with. I'm a few minutes early for our appointment so I sit in the waiting area and wait. After a while Mark comes out and waves me in. It's his firm. He's a PR guy specializing in New Age books and music. I was made to promise that I'd at least talk to him while I was in Manhattan, so here I am.

Unfortunately, I didn't sleep last night because I got caught up in a reading and note-taking jag and didn't look up from my work until sunrise. The result has been two meetings on personal business where the best I could do was collect information and postpone decisions, and now this meeting, which is really no more than a courtesy because I'm already pretty sure that it will bear no fruit. Not the intended fruit, anyway.

I was reading *Moby-Dick* last night and I was just about to turn off the light and go to sleep, very mindful of the fact that today would require more than usual alertness, when something caught my eye that I had missed in previous readings:

> Glimpses do ye seem to see of that mortally intoler-able truth; that all deep, earnest thinking is but the intrepid effort of the soul to keep the open independence of her sea; while the wildest winds of heaven and earth conspire to cast her on the treacherous, slavish shore?
>
> But as in landlessness alone resides highest truth, shoreless, indefinite as God—so, better is it to perish in that howling infinite, than be ingloriously dashed upon the lee, even if that were safety! For worm-like, then, oh! who would craven crawl to land! Terrors of the terrible! is all this agony so vain?

In landlessness alone resides highest truth. That woke me up instantly, and it wasn't until five hours later that I realized I had effectively sabotaged what was already sure to be an arduous day.

Dragging Curtis along was a last minute decision. I don't function well when tired and I thought it would be a good idea to have an alert person around to keep me from getting hit by a non-metaphorical bus.

On the ride in we saw a sign advertising a *Star Wars* movie and Curtis brought up the subject of a paper he had done for a college English class on the Hero's Journey as described by Joseph Campbell. He based his paper on the first *Star Wars* movie, using Luke Skywalker to illustrate the key points of the hero's progress. It was an interesting topic for Curtis, so it was interesting to hear him talk about it. He seemed to be finished before I thought he was finished, though.

"Is that it?" I asked.

"What do you mean? What else?"

"What about relevance? Why is it important? What does it matter?"

He doesn't seem to understand what I'm asking.

"How does it translate to real life? What is the value of understanding the Hero's Journey to you and me?"

"Oh, yeah," he says, nodding. "No."

"No?"

"We didn't cover that."

I nod too, pretending that makes sense to me, wondering if the reason it doesn't is because my brain is fogged in, but suspecting not.

❖

Mark is my third and last meeting of the day. Curtis is where I wish I was, across the street in a Greek restaurant, probably eating something involving slow-cooked lamb. Not only am I unrested, I'm unfed. I haven't eaten anything all day but half a cellophane-wrapped lemon pastry.

I take the seat Mark indicates and allow my eyes to wander over the pictures and certificates on the wall behind his desk. There's a calligraphic rendering of a line from Rumi, very artfully done and expensively framed, prominently placed on his desk facing whoever sits in the chair I now occupy:

> Beyond our ideas of right-doing and wrong-doing,
> there is a field. I'll meet you there.
>
> — *Rumi* —

I read it several times, trying to see it through different eyes each time, trying to understand why he has it on his desk facing his visitors as if it's something he's personally saying to them; that he'll meet them in this improbable field. I'm too tired to think about this, but the stupid thing is staring right at me. I read it through my own eyes and can't make any sense of it. What does Mark think it means, I wonder. Does he view it as some sort of ideal or truism? A declaration of love or compassion? I've talked to the guy. I've seen the books he displays, the ones he wants people to know he likes. I have a pretty good idea of where he's located in the spiritual terrain and I know exactly what kind of progress he's making. What I don't know is what he thinks that Rumi quotation means. It's like putting pretty Chinese calligraphy on your wall without knowing it says "Roundeye Sucks." Mark speaks English, though. Maybe it was a gift from Coleman Barks. I can't think of another explanation.

❖

After all the pleasantries about how wonderful my book is and how everybody in the office has been stealing it from each other, we settle in around a conference table, everyone armed with notepads, pens, bottled water and various other accoutrements of comfort and productivity. Mark sits at the head with Megan on his right. Janet and I sit across from each other near the middle. Rosalyn, Mark's executive assistant, sits at the foot with calendar, notepad, appointment book and a copy of Radio-TV Interview Report spread out in front of her.

Everyone knows why they're here except me. These people are in the business of getting publicity for authors; reviews, talkshows, radio interviews, articles, and so forth. We're here to see about prepping me for a blitz of radio interviews that are really super, I'm told, because I can do them while sitting at my kitchen table in my underwear. Mark and his people know why they're here, but they don't yet know that their efforts shall not be rewarded, even though I've been pretty upfront about it. As delightful as the prospect of doing radio interviews while sitting at my kitchen table in my underwear may be, the visible purpose of this meeting—me promoting a book—is not going to happen. So why am I here wasting people's time?

To find out what the true purpose is, the one behind the visible purpose. I don't do or not do things based on what's visible, but based on tendencies and currents. I've been asked to do this, it fell together with other plans, it's obviously worth doing for some reason, though not the stated one. Why then? Who knows. We'll see. Or not.

❖

"Some of these questions are from people here in the office," Janet tells me. "I actually went on the web for most of them. I just went to some spiritual newsgroups and asked for examples of the sort of questions people might ask of a purportedly enlightened spiritual teacher. I'm going to record this so that, once we're all comfortable with giving it a go-ahead, we can bring some focus and control to the process. We're not going to script you, but it's much better if you're able to develop a small repertoire of smooth responses and a few control techniques. We provide the radio stations with fact sheets and suggested questions which hosts like to stick to, but the topics can go pretty far afield, especially if they allow call-ins. Your ability to steer questions back into your own familiar territory will determine whether you sound crisp and knowledgeable or unfocused and garbled. Does that all make sense?"

"Sounds good."

"Okay. We'll worry about intro, tone and general banter later. For now we just want to throw a variety of questions at you and see how the whole thing plays out. Ready?"

"Ready."

"Okay. Question number one. Is it possible to have an experience without knowing who is having the experience?"

She looks up from her notes to await my answer. I just stare back at her. Behind my moronic facade lies the brain of a moron, scrambling to make sense of her words. After several moments of strenuous contemplation I am able to articulate the following response:

"Huh?"

"Excuse me?"

"Uh, I don't think I understood the question."

"Is it possible to have an experience—?"

"Say it differently, please."

"You can't really ask a host or a caller to—"

"I understand. I'm sorry. I don't know what to do with the question."

"Should I repeat it?"

"I heard all the words, I just didn't catch the meaning or intent of the question. Can you rephrase it?"

"This is the kind of thing we're looking for," she says, "this sort of stumbling. Hopefully, we can get you to the point where you take a question that seems irrelevant or off-topic and just bring it smoothly back into your own area of expertise. It doesn't just happen. It's something you have to practice. That's why we're here."

"Okay, I guess this question would be the same as saying 'Can one ask a question without knowing who's doing the asking?' Does that sound right?"

Janet nods tentatively.

"The question reduces to 'Can one *be* without knowing who one *is*?' Or 'Can the doer do without knowing the doer?' It's either gibberish or ridiculous, don't you think?"

"Um, I don't know," she says. "You can't say that to a caller though."

I look at Mark, who just shrugs.

"Okay," I say, "well, to me it sounds like that. It sounds like someone is asking if it's possible to exist without knowing one's true nature. The way they asked it made it sound like a real question, and the way I rephrased it made it sound a little goofy, but that's basically what the question is really asking. 'Can I not know my true nature?' It might be a little tough to answer without seeming to make fun of the person asking. Would you like to just go to the next question?"

"Yes."

"Okay."

"Uh, let's see, is enlightenment a natural evolutionary step?"

"Oh, that's a good one. The answer is no. If anything, enlightenment is evolution derailed. I mean, I take the question to mean evolution of a reincarnating individual or an evolving species, but the answer is the same either way. Evolution is about change and enlightenment is about truth, which is unchanging. Evolution takes place in a larger context than day-to-day existence, but it's still encased within a dualistic context. In other words, evolution, growth, development, change, whatever, are all parts of the dramatic event of dualistic being. Enlightenment isn't."

"But wait," injects Mark, "is enlightenment the end of the evolutionary line?"

"You might get questions for clarification or follow-up," Janet points out.

"That's fine," I say. "It's an amusing question. Will I myself experience growth beyond truth-realization in this life? No. Will I reincarnate back into an ignorant state, which is to say, will unseen forces put me back to sleep? No. The question assumes the existence of a differentiated true self, like a separate entity, and uh, that wouldn't be an accurate assumption. Differentiated and true are mutually exclusive."

"Then who are we talking to?"

"You mean Jed McKenna? I have no idea. A character in a dream."

"You're enlightened and you don't know who you are?"

"Can't know, doesn't matter, don't care. You're talking about reconciling the dreamstate with reality, like it all has to add up.

Everyone seems to get hooked on that, but you can't do it. Truth and non-truth are irreconcilable. Truth is, non-truth isn't. The false is purely an apparition; it exists only in the eye of the beholder. True and false aren't opposites; they're not like the black and white of the yin-yang symbol. There is no true self and the false self is irrelevant. We can't insist on a truth that makes sense in light of what we know because we don't know anything. Again, differentiated and true are mutually exclusive, not two halves of the whole."

"Wow, this is good," says Janet. "Nice sharp soundbites. A little long on some of the answers, but we can trim them down. That's what this process is all about; making you succinct. There's good material here. Very interesting. Okay, next question. If love is all there is—?"

"No way. Next question, please."

"Excuse me?"

"Let's just move on."

"You don't want to answer—?"

"It's not a real question, it's a veiled assertion. Anyway, there's no question that starts, 'If love is all there is,' that I could possibly answer. Even if the question was, 'If love is all there is, what's your favorite color?' I couldn't answer."

"Is there something about love—?"

"Listen, I don't want to bore you guys to tears with all this. Do you really need to hear an explanation for every question I don't want to respond to?"

"I think so," said Janet. "For one, it's not boring. Two, it helps us come up with ways to maintain control in an open question format. I'll let you know if we're getting bored," she smiles.

"Okay."

"So, is there something about love?"

"It has nothing to do with love. You can make it, 'If intense gamma radiation is all there is,' or, 'If walnut veneer is all there is,'

The question is really, 'If my beliefs are correct, then how do your beliefs fit in?' I don't have any beliefs and I can't answer a question that's based on someone else's. It's like asking, "Where does freedom fit within my confinement?" It doesn't. If the question is, 'Is love all there is?' then we can proceed, but we can't simply grant the premise that love is all there is."

"Okay, is love all there is?"

"Sure. If someone wishes to refer to all-there-is as love, they're free to do so. I don't see where that would be a particularly useful thing to call all-that-is for the purposes of waking up, but you can call it whatever you want; God, Universe, Consciousness, Tao and Mind are all common examples. Why not love?"

She smiles, but chastises me. "You're coming off a bit arrogant."

"I know it appears as arrogance, but it's really something else, and I'm doing my best to spin it in a fairly docile manner."

She looks at me sternly. "This isn't going well, is it?"

"Depends on your preferred outcome."

"Don't you want to do interviews to promote the book?"

I smile. "Next question please."

"Hmm," she looks at me quizzically. "Alright. Non-dual philosophy asserts that—"

"There's no such thing as a non-dual philosophy. Let's try the next one."

"Hold on," says Mark. "There's actually a large community of non-dualists around the world and on the web. And Advaita, of which you've said good things, actually means not-two, as in non-dual."

"Alright," I say, "but it really doesn't make for a philosophy. Non-duality isn't a philosophy, or if someone has turned it into one then they've created a Faux-Advaita for personal or financial gain. Non-duality isn't a philosophy, it's a concept. You can't live a concept. You can liken it to two-dimensionality. You can have a conceptual grasp of two-dimensionality, but it's of no practical value in three-dimensional reality, and if you want to enter *into* two-dimensionality, you're going to have to leave three-dimensionality and your three-dimensional self to do it."

"That sort of statement is like a blanket indictment," says Mark. "That might piss a lot of people off."

"Which bring us to the core problem at this table," I reply around a jaw-cracking double yawn. "If I'm not pissing people off, I'm not doing my job. That's not bravado, that's the reality of it. I slap people. I slap them to wake them up because they have somehow, in some way, asked me to do so. But that dynamic isn't at work here. Here, I'm supposed to be asking people to trust me, to believe me, to buy my book. I don't want to ask people to trust me or believe me. I wouldn't know how or why."

"You don't want people to trust you?" asks Megan, with some doubt in her voice.

"No. It's not a trust business, it's a self-verification business. We're all sitting here now with the seemingly common goal of promoting a book, but my priority isn't selling books. My priority is to try to communicate well, and this is taking me in the opposite direction from that. You guys have the job of turning me into a polished frontman for the book. I'm here to see if there's a way to participate in the promotion of this book as a favor to someone, but I'm pretty sure there's not."

This earns me four sets of unamused stares. These guys are here because they want to receive a hefty check from the publishers, and I'm getting in the way of that. Mark spends the next few minutes explaining the book promotion process again in case there was some-thing I was not understanding about the whole thing. They feel that *Damnedest* can be a bestseller, but bestsellers don't just happen; they require careful planning and orchestration.

I'm not keeping secrets from them. I explained to Mark the

lengths we'd gone to in order to keep the book projects from turning back on me. I'm a private person, I told him. I've done my bit. I'm writing a book or two because it seems I have to, but that's it. I guess he thinks I'm kidding him or myself though, because we proceed as if I hadn't said a word. I know it's not proper business meeting etiquette to rock back and forth while humming and drooling, so I try to look attentive and nod at the right times, but it's hard. I'm very tired, I'm very hungry, and nobody speaks my language.

"Okay," Mark says, "let's just keep going and see if we have something we can work with, okay?"

"Okay," I say.

Megan speaks up. "Okay, here's a question. How can I live more deeply in the moment?"

I search the question for meaning and come up empty.

"What for?"

"What?"

"What do you want to live more deeply in the moment for? What does that mean?"

"I'm working on being more fully present—"

"Where?"

"What?"

"More present where? Deeper in the moment when?"

"In the present," she says, like it's obvious. "In the now."

"When?"

"What?"

"What's the now? The present, uh, time?"

"Yes," she says in a clipped way as if speaking to a dolt, which she may well be. Again, tiredness is throwing a shroud over everything, so I can't tell if I'm being thick or if I've descended into a place of thickness.

"You want to be more present in the present?"

"Yes," she says. "I'm trying to deepen my awareness, to live more fully in each moment."

I feel like I'm trapped in a Monty Python skit.

"Can I ask why?" I ask tentatively, trying not to offend, but a little curious as to what the appeal might be of this deeper awareness.

"To live more fully in each moment," she answers, speaking slowly to help me get it. "To be in deeper touch with my life."

"Okay, to be deeper in touch with your life. And how would you go about that?"

"By deepening my awareness," she replies in exasperation, and it's finally clear to me that we're talking in circles and that I'm pissing her off for no good reason. Someone sold this woman something and now she's all excited and coming to me to ask how it works, but I don't even know what the hell it is.

"I don't know why anyone would think to ask me about living in the moment," is my polite attempt at getting away from this discussion. I often wonder how much of the New Age community is made up of people who had some nice experiences with dope, acid, mushrooms and whatnot in their younger days and would like to have those experiences again; maybe even make them permanent. It seems to me that a lot of teachers and techniques catch on with the spiritual crowd by promising them some hope of reliving their psychedelic glory days. If this woman, Megan, were a student of mine, someone with whom I could speak openly, I'd tell her to stop bullshitting herself and go take acid if that's what she wants to do. I know that's what I'd say because I've said it to dozens of people before. Figure out what you really want. If you don't, you'll continue having this Pavlovian response every time you hear the bells of a new spiritual snake-oil salesman rolling into town. If what you want is to revisit the interior spaces to which drugs granted access, then stop dicking around with placebos and go find your drugs. If you can't find the drugs, or you've been scared or shamed away from them, then hook up with Stan Grof or Michael Harner or someone who's come up with a viable alternate route.

"But you're a spiritual teacher, aren't you?" Megan asks.

"No, not really. More like the opposite," I sigh and rub my eyes. "I don't want to get pulled into that kind of discussion. If someone calls and asks what I think of the flavor-of-the-month teacher, technique, or book, nothing good can come of it. It puts me into a no-comment position, or I'm going to come off as insulting, and I know that's not good."

"Well," offers Janet, "we can just set you up with a stock response to use whenever something like this comes up. Something like, 'I recognize the merit of so-and-so's teachings,' or 'I have a lot of respect for that book.' You know, just have a stock response ready that's favorable but non-committal. I'll get a few ideas down on paper tonight and we'll put together something you like."

I don't bother telling her not to bother.

"Oh, here's a good one," she says. "Free will or predetermination?"

"Uh, really, I'm not doing this to be difficult, but that's not a valid question either."

"How can it not be valid?"

"It's not freestanding. It sits atop various assumptions that haven't first been verified. It presupposes other things to be accepted as true that can't be accepted as true. See, that's the thing; for every person, at any time, there is only one right question. My job is to help them find it, not to answer it."

"Thus spake Jed McKenna," laughs Janet. "You're not one of those *fun* teachers, are you?"

"I'm sure not coming off that way. That's why this needed testing. In my ideal teaching environment there's a structure and an accepted process that doesn't include asking questions just for the sake of asking questions. To me, that's just aimless small talk and it's not fun. Of all these questions we've looked at, not one was from someone who was stuck at a certain point and trying to move forward. None were from someone looking for the key to unlock the next door. They were all spiritual jerk-off questions that you'd expect from people with fearful, ego-reinforcing agendas. That's why I agreed to dry-run this process and that's why I won't be exposing myself to this sort of unstructured dialogue. No one benefits. I'm used to dealing with hungry, desperate, serious people. I'm not going to develop some spiritual bad-boy gimmick or crazy-wisdom shtick just to shake down the tourists. This is the most wondrous and exhilarating stuff in the world when you take it seriously, and the most dreadful, toxic sludge when you don't."

I stand up.

"I'm sorry to have wasted your time."

❖

Mark catches up with me as I'm trying to figure out which elevator button means down. He feels that the meeting actually went pretty well for a first run-through and that we should get together again. I smile and nod. Then he tells me about a group of people in Queens he gets together with to study the *Bhagavad-Gita*. There's a meeting tonight, he says, and asks me to attend. I beg out, explaining how tired I am; bad day, poor sleep, long way home and all that, but he's insistent and I'm muddled in the headbone, so I agree to stop by.

17. Gita Life

How hath this weakness taken thee? Whence springs
The inglorious trouble, shameful to the brave,
Barring the path of virtue? Nay, Arjun!
Forbid thyself to feebleness! it mars
Thy warrior-name! cast off the coward-fit!
Wake! Be thyself! Arise, Scourge of thy foes!

–Krishna, Bhagavad-Gita

C URTIS AND I GET OFF the train at the Jamaica station and catch a cab for the ten minute ride to the address Mark provided. The meeting is in the basement of a church that is Catholic, but not; some new and improved version that still doesn't have female priests, so not really much of an improvement. There is juice and a platter of butter-free cookies on a table in the back of the room. The stained drop-ceiling, enameled cinder-block walls, buzzing fluorescent lights and cracking linoleum floor tiles are all tinged milky brown from years of cigarette smoke, creating the ambience of a city morgue that has hosted decades of AA meetings. The long Formica tables are sticky, the molded plastic chairs are slippery, the air is stale, I'm tired and hungry, and as if all that's not enough, Curtis is cheerful.

The tables are arranged in a large square and eventually the thirty some-odd people take their seats, two and three deep in some places. There's a foil-wrapped cardboard cutout of the *Om* symbol hanging by a thread from the ceiling grid. Curtis asks me what it is but I'm in no mood to explain sacred syllables to anyone right now, not that I really could anyway. A tall, thin, mid-thirties guy in a pony tail and glasses stands up diagonally to my right and addresses the group.

"Good evening, everyone," he begins, and damn me if he's not cheerful too. What's everyone so happy about? Curtis grins at me. I give him the badeye in return, but I guess I'm not very good at it because his smile widens. "It's nice to see so many new faces," the speaker continues as my eyes and heart fasten on the exit sign. "Maybe before we get started we can go around the room quickly and introduce ourselves."

The horror. The horror.

Somehow, this is all my fault. How did I let this happen? I don't mind offending people, certainly not that Mark guy who, I note with no small degree of resentment, isn't here. So why am *I* here? Because I was tired. That's how errors happen. That's how toes get stubbed and cars get wrecked. Being tired is the surest way to make a mess. Be Well Rested is the first rule of life's happy motorist, or maybe second or third, but it's high on the list, right up there with Waiting Is, Think Less, and Dance More. This whole day has been littered with minor errors that would normally not even be possible, but because I didn't come into it properly rested, it's like I'm sinking into a murky dreamstate where events conspire against, not for, and where caricaturish, funny-talking creatures abound.

"My name is Govinda," says our guide. "I don't really see myself as a teacher so much as a facilitator." He smiles benevolently. My brain has gone numb and I can't even muster the energy to close my mouth. Govinda has a lilt, I notice, a little sing-song inflection as if his last gig was in daycare. He continues. "I've been studying Hindu scripture in general and the *Bhagavad-Gita* in particular for fifteen years, but I like to think that there's still more for me to learn so, in a way, I'm just a student of the *Song of the Lord*, just like any of you."

I do a quick personal inventory and find I have nothing with which to fashion a noose or open a vein. I wiggle my tongue around in my mouth, but it seems unswallowable. If I have anything approaching a guiding philosophy in life—and I suppose I must, what with being all enlightened and everything—it revolves in very large part around not being in this basement with these people and their tin foil *Om* and their butter-free cookies. I'm simply not a person who does things he doesn't want to.

And I like butter.

The introductions begin at Govinda's right so there are a bunch of people ahead of me, including Curtis. The person on my immediate right is a portly, wheelchair-bound gentleman in his early fifties, and from the few words we exchange I get the impression that he attends church basement functions pretty indiscriminately, especially during summer reruns. He, Barry, has a battered Penguin *Gita* in front of him. In fact, everyone but me and Curtis has a *Gita* in front of them; mostly Penguins, a few Stephen Mitchells, one I recognize as being from the Theosophical Society, and a variety of others.

The introductions continue. Melanie is a customer service rep who is very curious and always interested in new things. Rohan enjoys exploring the beauty of other cultures, though he looks pretty Hindu and I suspect he's a *Gita* ringer. Kurt is trying to practice the lessons of the *Gita* in his own life. Max is one of those disorienting people without clear gender markings and says something about service and duty. There's a gay couple and a straight couple, a Hispanic guy with prison tats, a few Hindus and New Agers. About half the people around the table seem like sincere students who want to get more from the *Gita*. The other half, who knows.

As the introductions continue, sap dullard misanthrope Curtis is just grinning away, his bright beaming smile welcoming each and all into his ever-expanding embrace. A Folger's coffee can with a rectangular slot cut in the plastic lid is being passed around to help pay for the use of the basement. By the time it's Curtis' turn to introduce himself, my eyes have come loose in my head, my head loose on my shoulders, and my ass loose on my chair. "I'm here with my new friend Je-, uh, Mack," says Curtis, "and I don't really know what a *Bhagdad-Gita* is, but I feel you're all a very special, sincere group of people and I'm very happy to be here with you." They applaud Curtis' comments. My hands reflexively start to clap but I command them to stillness. Where did I go wrong? The universe has turned on me. It's my turn to say hello. I start oozing out of my chair.

"Hi," I mumble. One of my hands gives a little wave, the traitor. "Just want to go where the knowledge is," says I with a small laugh shared by none. "We, uh, me and my friend—" I can't remember if we came up with a code name for Curtis so that I was about to blow his cover, but by stumbling on his name it sounds to my ears like a gay white guy going to *Gita* study with his young black stud, and I start giggling. I only manage to say, "Thanks for having us. Hope to learn a lot."

When the coffee can comes to me, I conspicuously stuff a wad of bills into it as if to redeem myself, though probably only making myself seem somehow more unhinged. This brain-dead stunt will haunt me later when it comes time to pay the cabbie.

Once the introductions are done, Govinda asks us all to turn to the fourth discourse. Noticing that Curtis and I don't have books, he asks our neighbors to share with us. My wheelchair guy turns his Penguin grudgingly toward me; the good student made to suffer for the bad. I pretend to carefully read the open page with an air of scholarly appreciation to satisfy him.

In the movie *The Matrix*, there's a scene where the adept Morpheus effortlessly glides through throngs of people on a bustling city sidewalk while inept Neo bumbles and collides and apologizes. Flow and non-flow. Having no preferences, having no ego that requires constant monitoring and reinforcing, having a calm, untroubled mind, most of my life resembles Morpheus' smooth navigation rather than Neo's manic, pinball mode. When that flow is disrupted, even in a small way, I am acutely aware of it. I stop what I'm doing until I find the obstruction that caused the error. I make sure my breathing is deep and stable, my mind clear, and get myself back to the place of smooth, effortless functioning. The error itself doesn't matter so much as eradicating or circumnavigating the source of the error. When something impedes flow, returning to smooth flow is the objective, not making a study of obstructions.

Everyone navigates in this higher mode to one degree or another, and anyone can learn to do it better and more often. Actually, most people would function a lot more smoothly and easily a lot more of the time if they'd just learn to breathe correctly. Practically everyone restricts their breathing to the upper part of the lungs, so that the chest expands and not the belly. The result of this shallow breathing is that we operate in a perpetual panic mode, as if all of life was a fight-or-flight situation. This causes the mental state of dis-ease that we accept as normal and from which we seek escape through addictions and distractions. It disrupts our activity during the day and our rest at night. When we breathe into our entire lungs by expanding the diaphragm, we automatically create a mental state of composure and ease, which is then reflected in our environment.

How telling is it that we are a society of people who don't even know how to breathe? Hello? At what more basic level could we possibly fail? And what's more than that, how telling is it that when we are made aware of this crippling flaw, most of us will do absolutely nothing to correct it because our vanity won't allow us to expand our tummies?

✦

My brain is sludge. I never suffer from the other maladies that might cause one to be in discord with the energetic flow of things, so not being tired is really all I have to worry about, and today I botched it and my world has spun off its axis as a result. Wrong is right, I know, and there's a reason for everything, even this, but adopting a philosophical outlook doesn't make it any more pleasant.

Govinda begins reading from his *Gita* and I can barely distinguish one word from another. Curtis is practically snuggling with the pretty co-ed on his left with whom he's sharing a book. Govinda gets about a minute into his reading when he stops and looks at me, as do most of the others. Am I drooling?

"You okay?" asks Curtis in a whisper.

"Yes," I say slowly, wondering why all eyes are on me. I revisit the last few moments in my mind and come to suspect that a groan I thought was internal might have found voice.

"Is there something you'd like to add?" asks Govinda. "Excuse me, I've forgotten your name."

So have I. I look at Curtis.

"Mack," he whispers.

"Mack," I tell Govinda.

"You don't sound like you agree with the words of Lord Krishna, Mack. I'm sure we'd all be very interested in your comments, if you'd care to share them with us."

"Well, uh, not really, no. Thank you. Sorry. Please go on."

"Okay," Govinda says, and returns to the part where Krishna tells Arjuna that he's showing him his universal form because Arjuna is such a devoted pal. I make a bathroom sound on the mental plane and am startled to hear it manifest on the physical plane as well. Govinda stops and turns to me.

"Please, Mack. If you have anything to say—"

❖

The Great Master attended a class disguised as a
Lowly Student. The Inept Teacher held up the
Great Book and spoke words that were loathsome
to the Great Master's ears. Unable to endure the

Inept Teacher's false interpretation of the Great
Book any longer, the Great Master picked up his
chair and beat the Inept Teacher to death. Instantly,
the Lowly Students burst into Full Enlightenment.

*—The Zen Teachings of
Master Addlebrain*

❖

"He's lying," I blurt. Blurting is one of the negative effects of
being tired for me. I speak when I otherwise wouldn't and say things
I probably shouldn't.

"Who's lying, Mack? Lord Krishna?"

"Yes. Lord Krishna. Lying. I'm sorry, really. Please just go ahead.
I'll be good—"

"It's okay, Mack. I think the Lord can handle a little constructive
criticism." That gets a laugh from the group.

I look at Curtis. He shrugs slightly as if to say, why not?

Yeah, why not.

"He's not the Lord," I say. "That just confuses things. You can't
make any sense of the *Gita* if you don't understand who's who."

Govinda laughs a little nervously. "Lord," he says, holding up the
cover of his book for me to see. "*The Song of the Lord*. The *Bhagavad-
Gita* is the story of how the Lord reveals his full glory to his
devotee—"

"Yuck," I blurt. "No it's not. You're making it a Christian thing.
It's not a Christian thing, or a Hindu thing, or anyone else's thing.
It's, like, the coolest thing in the world and you're just breezing right
past it. You're not getting what a fun and important thing this really
is."

There's a reason for me to be in this sorry place in this sorry state.
I feel like I'm stuck in the role of a proselytizer, which is the last
thing I want to be. If I had to guess, I'd say that one person in this

room was on the verge of something, and so my unlikely and reluctant presence has been orchestrated for that one person's benefit; to help them take the next step. Just a guess, of course, but the setup is so clumsy that it has to be something along those lines. Time, perhaps, will tell.

"Look for yourself," I say. "Look at what Krishna just told Arjuna; 'I'm showing you all this because you're my friend and devotee.' Even accounting for sloppy translations, that's not true. Krishna is obviously lying. The question is, why? Why is Krishna lying?"

I'm getting a lot of dirty looks. I made a heresy. Oops. I guess you can't come to Friday night *Gita* study in Queens and call the blessed Lord a big fat liar. I stand up and touch Curtis' shoulder.

"Look, I'm sorry. You're right, I don't know what I'm saying. We have to go. We were just supposed to meet someone—"

"Please stay, Mack," says Govinda, gesturing to my seat. "If you have a theory about Lord Krishna that we haven't considered, I think that's the purpose of this group; to consider different viewpoints and decide for ourselves." He looks around the group for support and doesn't get much. "Please, stay. Continue."

I'm so fatigued I'm about to start blubbering. I've somehow wandered out of the sunlight and into this dreary underworld. I'm trapped in this absurd role on this shabby stage and it looks like the only way out is straight through. There's nothing to do but play it out. I take a breath and try to establish some degree of clarity.

"Okay," I sit back down so as not to appear to be competing for the leadership role with Govinda. "Krishna is lying. Krishna is not revealing himself to Arjuna for the reasons he states."

Govinda appears bemused by my presumptuousness. "So why is Lord Krishna lying, Mack?" He still has that condescending lilt in his voice, but I don't mind.

"You've been studying the *Gita* for fifteen years, Govinda, so you already know why he's lying. He wants something. What does Krishna want? Why is he really talking to Arjuna?"

Govinda doesn't look happy to have the tables turned on him and I didn't really mean to do it, but here we are.

"He wants Arjuna to get back up," replies Govinda. "He wants him to blow the conch and launch the war."

"Of course, so it's not really true that Krishna has chosen this time and place, seated between two massive armies poised to attack, to reward friendship and devotion, is it?"

"Well, you can look at it from the persp—"

"Don't make excuses for the *Gita*, Govinda. Like you say, it can stand a little constructive criticism, but maybe some interpretations can't. In any event, the point is that Krishna doesn't matter. It's not about Krishna. That doesn't concern us here."

"Okay Mack," says Govinda with a look of gentle encouragement. "What *does* matter? What *does* concern us here?"

"Why did Arjuna fall down?" I ask.

Govinda doesn't miss a beat.

"Arjuna fell down because he saw his own beloved teachers and relatives among the opposing army and he realized that no amount of wealth or glory could make the slaughter of his beloved—"

"No, no," I interrupt, "don't waste your time on that, that's just the story, the metaphor." How did I get drawn into this? Where's the damned exit? "That's the little story of Arjuna and Krishna on the battlefield. We don't care about that. This isn't a story about foreign people in an ancient culture clashing for a throne. It's all about the *reader*. Nothing else. That's why this book matters. It's not about the people *in* the story, it's all about the person *reading* the story."

I say this to Govinda, but then turn to everyone seated around the tables. "It's not theory, it's practice. It's about *you*, your life, right now, this very minute. You should be taking this book very personally. You, the reader, are Arjuna. This is *your* war. The *Bhagavad-Gita* is about why Arjuna gets back up and launches the war, but you can't understand why he got back up until you understand why he fell which, no offense, none of you do."

Tired or not, once I get going I can't stop until the idea I'm trying to express is fully expressed.

"When you see for yourself what Arjuna saw, the sight that made the world's mightiest warrior collapse in fear and confusion, you'll do exactly what he did, collapse in fear and confusion, and you'll be unable to give the signal to launch the war. Until that happens to *you*, it's all theoretical, irrelevant. Until you see what Arjuna saw, firsthand, in your own life, the *Gita* is of no more value to you than a book of scribble. The *Bhagavad-Gita* begins when Arjuna falls and then it's all about one thing and one thing only: Why did Arjuna get back up?"

I pause. The idea seems fully expressed. The end is in sight.

"Sorry, really, I'm almost finished. The *Gita* isn't some sterile, intellectual pursuit. It's the great, rollicking, swashbuckling adventure of life—truth, reality, freedom, the real treasures—and it doesn't matter whether you're in a wheelchair or you're young or old, rich, poor, guy, girl, Jewish, Shinto, whatever. It's beyond all that. But it's not a book you read, it's a journey you take, and it's not Arjuna's journey, it's *yours*."

I stand up and grab Curtis by the arm.

"Okay, that's it. Sorry to spout off like such a dreadful idiot. Hope I didn't ruin everyone's evening. Gotta go. Bye."

We flee.

❖

This seems to be a recurring theme lately so I guess it's something I'm supposed to pay attention to and talk about. Curtis brings me letters people have written about *Damnedest* and one thing many of the letters have in common is that the writers are making the book about something besides themselves, as if *Damnedest* was about the characters in the book rather than the character reading it. Then, Curtis expresses his interest in the Hero's Journey, Campbell, *Star Wars* and all that, but stays in the role of the audience member, not seeing or being shown that life is not a spectator sport; that the hero of his life is him and the journey is his to make. Now again, this *Gita* group, and I see that one reason I was guided into that quaggy weirdness was to show me this thing again, this quality that affords us the cuddly illusion that life is somehow elsewhere or elsewhen, somehow other than right here and right now. We are, many of us, not merely living in a dream, but asleep within it.

And here I'll say that the usual disclaimers apply. There is no right and wrong, no better or worse. Truth isn't good and delusion isn't evil. No one is ahead or behind. The worms won't care how your epitaph reads and the truth of you will outlive time itself. All is vanity.

All.

18. Why Arjuna Fell

My members fail, my tongue dries in my mouth,
A shudder thrills my body, and my hair
Bristles with horror; from my weak hand slips
Gandîv, the goodly bow; a fever burns
My skin to parching; hardly may I stand;
The life within me seems to swim and faint;
Nothing do I foresee save woe and wail!

It is not good, O Keshav! nought of good
Can spring from mutual slaughter! Lo, I hate
Triumph and domination, wealth and ease,
Thus sadly won! Aho! what victory
Can bring delight, Govinda! what rich spoils
Could profit; what rule recompense; what span
Of life itself seem sweet, bought with such blood?

–Arjuna, Bhagavad-Gita

JULIE IS ABOUT TO SEE for herself what no book or teacher could possibly show her. She's about to know, directly, in her own life, what *the price of truth is everything* really means.

For some people this particular stage of the process is easier, for some it's harder. Some people have had years to soften to it and slip more or less comfortably into it. Some, like Julie, hit it hard, without warning or preparation, and have a worse time of it than can be expressed by words on the page. This is where people can end up straightjacketed—as does Ahab—or worse.

I'm so scared at times I'm practically frozen, frozen with fear, literally *sick* with fear. What else is up here? Even the air seems too heavy to move. There are parts of this attic I can't even see into. I can make out large forms, menacing shapes, huge immovable dark objects. There are no demons but these, I now know, but some of these demons I *love*. That's the scariest thing. They are me, but they're not, but they are! My mother is up here. My father is here. My music. Pets, dreams, family, friends. It's not all bleak and horrible. There are moments; magic, love, beauty. Poems, flowers, songs. Boys and men I've loved. My teachers. You, Jed. The places and smells and friends from my childhood. There seems to be no end, there's so much. I've lived a beautiful, lovely, blessed life. What do I do? It's not just junk, it's not all bad. This is the scariest part of all. What about the good? Friends! Love! Dance! My heart! Isn't all that real? Aren't these memories real? Isn't my heart real? What of that? What?

This isn't where the battle is fought, this is where the battlefield is first fully apprehended. The person who arrives at this point is not the person who goes beyond. In this process, resistance is conquered and non-resistance takes its place; acceptance, recognition, surrender. The segregated self is slain and the integrated self is born. Death and resurrection, caterpillar and butterfly, human and vampire. To the onlooker it looks like one becomes the other, but to the participant it is quite unmistakably the end of one thing and the beginning of another.

I try to summon the courage to focus on one thing; my mother. I can hardly do it. I don't even understand what her presence here is really composed of, but it seems like *mother* is a ridiculously inadequate term for countless thousands – millions! – of bits and pieces of emotions of varying intensities, memories, images. Not my mother, of course, but all somehow related to her, coming from her, feeling like her; fears, images, scraps of sound, memories, hopes, some pleasant, some oppressive.

Money is another one. Money and security. I thought I was level-headed when it came to money, spiritually attuned and well-balanced, but what I really am is infested by it like a cancer that has silently metastasized into every organ and tissue. Amazing! Just amazing! It's everywhere! And it's so foul and putrid and fear-infected that I'm sickened to think of it. And the thing is, I *was* level-headed when it came to money. What does this infection look like in those I always scorned for their love of money? Or in those I pitied for their enslavement to it? It makes me ill to even think about it. You talk about icebergs Jed, the larger mass that hides beneath the surface, but this reminds me more of the mushrooms I once wrote a piece about. Most people think the blue whale is the largest living thing on earth, but it's actually the honey mushroom which, as I recall, can spread its underground root system over more than two-thousand acres. You would hardly suspect by seeing the visible portion that grows above ground that it stretches for miles in all directions and can actually wipe out forests! This is what the sickness of money has made me think about as I've discovered its vast and pernicious root system; the way it's fairly small and benign in its visible aspect and so vast and devastating below.

One thing I am beginning to see is that nothing is really a thing apart. Everything is intertwined and forms part of something larger and something larger than that, some energetically interconnected labyrinth of self. This is the complexity of the fabric of self, and the threads don't run in neat lines, but in chaotic, multidimensional, swirling patterns, some visible, some deep and unseen. This is my attic. This is my tapestry, my fabric. The fabric is me but I am not its weaver. Looked at as a whole it seems to represent me, but as soon as I get close and see what it's really made up of and distinguish the component patterns, the millions of threads, then "I" disappear and all that remains is a haphazard patchwork of memories and emotions. That's what I am. That's *all* I am.

Resist this process with a rigid ego and it will break you. I don't personally know of anyone committing suicide at this juncture, but I suppose it's not uncommon. Julie certainly considered it. You can't not. In this situation—can't go forward, can't go back—death is the *tertium quid*; the third thing. It might well have been that very thought, the thought of death, that opened her to the necessary letting-go; itself a kind of death. In fact, many or even most suicides might take place right here, which will seem more plausible as we get a better idea of where "right here" really is.

That exact point, the point where the person who fell becomes the person who gets back up, is the exact line of division between two beings. Ego may desire enlightenment, but ego can't cross that line. The person who stands up is not the person who fell. It's the primary death/birth process, and nothing proceeds until it happens.

Julie is learning the one thing about the *Bhagavad-Gita* that no amount of studying and dedication could ever reveal. She's about to see what you can only see by approaching your own battlefield. She's about to see what Arjuna saw. She's about to see why Arjuna fell.

I don't know what I've gotten myself into. This is too much – it can't be done. What a fool I am to have started this! What a pathetic fool. How could I let this happen? Where does this go? There is no doubt, I am the stupidest stupidest person. This is bad, this will kill me, this is the end of me. No way back, no way through. There's no way I can ever do this. I don't know how anyone can. No one can. No one could ever choose this. Not me. Not me. This is something for a whole different kind of person, I don't even know what kind. It can't be done. I can't do it. I wish I had never started this. I just want to be back the way I was. I can't breathe. My insides are twisted. This is horror. This is so far beyond me. My soul is sick to death and my heart is crushed.

At this point, Julie is catching her first glimpse of what's really going on. She hasn't started the battle yet, but she's coming to see what the battle truly entails. She is beginning to see where the battlefield really is, *what* the battlefield really is. She is beginning to see what anyone who comes to this will see; that it's not the dark, evil, noxious stuff that's the problem. It's not the ignorance or the sin. It's not the stuff we can't identify or the stuff we didn't know was there. What Julie is beginning to see is the same thing that drove Arjuna, the world's greatest warrior, to drop his weapon and crumple to the ground in fear and confusion when *he* saw it.

> And that the great monster is indomitable,
> you will yet have reason to know.
>
> — *Herman Melville* —

All attachments to the dreamstate are made of energy. That energy is called emotion. All emotions, positive and negative, are attachments. Humans are emotion-based creatures and all emotions derive their energy from one core emotion; fear. Fear cannot be confronted or slain because it is fear of nothing, of no-self. The desire to slay fear is itself a fear-based emotion. Fear can only be surrendered to; the thing feared, entered. You can spend your life hacking away at the million-headed hydra of attachment and never make any progress, or you can follow emotional energy back to its source, its lair, and see Leviathan, enemy of light, for what it really is:

Your heart.

That's what Arjuna saw. That's why Arjuna fell.

19. Come, Ahab's compliments to ye.

Ahab's soliloquy after rallying the crew, from chapter 37: Sunset.

The prophecy was that I should be dismembered;
and—Aye! I lost this leg. I now prophesy that I
will dismember my dismemberer.

–*Herman Melville, Moby-Dick*

*(The cabin; by the stern windows;
Ahab sitting alone, and gazing out.)*

I LEAVE A WHITE AND turbid wake; pale waters, paler cheeks,
where'er I sail. The envious billows sidelong swell to whelm my
track; let them; but first I pass.

Yonder, by ever-brimming goblet's rim, the warm waves blush
like wine. The gold brow plumbs the blue. The diver sun—slow
dived from noon—goes down; my soul mounts up! she wearies with
her endless hill. Is, then, the crown too heavy that I wear? this Iron
Crown of Lombardy. Yet is it bright with many a gem; I the wearer,
see not its far flashings; but darkly feel that I wear that, that
dazzlingly confounds. 'Tis iron—that I know—not gold. 'Tis split,
too—that I feel; the jagged edge galls me so, my brain seems to beat
against the solid metal; aye, steel skull, mine; the sort that needs no
helmet in the most brain-battering fight!

Dry heat upon my brow? Oh! time was, when as the sunrise
nobly spurred me, so the sunset soothed. No more. This lovely light,
it lights not me; all loveliness is anguish to me, since I can ne'er
enjoy. Gifted with the high perception, I lack the low, enjoying
power; damned, most subtly and most malignantly! damned in the

midst of Paradise! Good night—good night! *(waving his hand, he moves from the window.)*

'Twas not so hard a task. I thought to find one stubborn, at the least; but my one cogged circle fits into all their various wheels, and they revolve. Or, if you will, like so many ant-hills of powder, they all stand before me; and I their match. Oh, hard! that to fire others, the match itself must needs be wasting! What I've dared, I've willed; and what I've willed, I'll do! They think me mad—Starbuck does; but I'm demoniac, I am madness maddened! That wild madness that's only calm to comprehend itself! The prophecy was that I should be dismembered; and—Aye! I lost this leg. I now prophesy that I will dismember my dismemberer. Now, then, be the prophet and the fulfiller one. That's more than ye, ye great gods, ever were. I laugh and hoot at ye, ye cricket-players, ye pugilists, ye deaf Burkes and blinded Bendigoes!* I will not say as schoolboys do to bullies— Take some one of your own size; don't pommel me! No, ye've knocked me down, and I am up again; but ye have run and hidden. Come forth from behind your cotton bags! I have no long gun to reach ye. Come, Ahab's compliments to ye; come and see if ye can swerve me. Swerve me? ye cannot swerve me, else ye swerve yourselves! man has ye there. Swerve me? The path to my fixed purpose is laid with iron rails, whereon my soul is grooved to run. Over unsounded gorges, through the rifled hearts of mountains, under torrents' beds, unerringly I rush! Naught's an obstacle, naught's an angle to the iron way!

Burke and Bendigo were English boxing champions.

20. Why Arjuna Got Back Up

The soul that with a strong and constant calm
Takes sorrow and takes joy indifferently,
Lives in the life undying! That which is
Can never cease to be; that which is not
Will not exist. To see this truth of both
Is theirs who part essence from accident,
Substance from shadow. Indestructible,
Learn thou! the Life is, spreading life through all;
It cannot anywhere, by any means,
Be anywise diminished, stayed, or changed.

But for these fleeting frames which it informs
With spirit deathless, endless, infinite,
They perish. Let them perish, Prince! and fight!

He who shall say, "Lo! I have slain a man!"
He who shall think, "Lo! I am slain!" those both
Know naught! Life cannot slay. Life is not slain!
Never the spirit was born;
    the spirit shall cease to be never;
Never was time it was not;
End and Beginning are dreams!

–Krishna, Bhagavad-Gita

I'M SITTING AT THE OUTDOOR dining table on the upper deck, shaded by its tilted umbrella, with several books and a collection of handwritten notes spread out in front of me. Curtis is inside working on the laptop in the office, so when the doorbell rings, both indoors and through an outdoor speaker, I assume he'll take care of it, which is wrong because it rings again a minute later.

"I guess I'll get that," he shouts.

A minute later Curtis leads Govinda through the French doors. Govinda starts to speak, but I cut him off.

"Have a seat," I say. "Here," I indicate a drink tray, "pour yourself an iced tea." He sits down and pours his drink, without adding sugar, I notice. He has that frail body and blanched pallor one sees in healthfood stores and wherever cheeseburgers and sunlight are shunned.

"Listen to this," I say.

> "*Ego non baptizo te in nomine patris, sed in nomine diaboli!*" deliriously howled Ahab, as the malignant iron scorchingly devoured the baptismal blood.

"'*I baptize you not in the name of the father, but in the name of the devil!*' Have you read *Moby-Dick*?"

Govinda looks a bit disoriented, which is fine. I'm sure he's given plenty of thought to what he'd say to me when he got here, and we'll get to that, but I want to introduce him to my way of conducting a dialogue right from the beginning.

"Uh, yeah, in high school," he answers. "Cliff Notes, anyway, or maybe I saw the movie. Who's baptizing who?"

"Ahab is baptizing his newly forged harpoon. In blood. Welded together like 'glue from the melted bones of murderers.' Rock 'n roll, eh?"

My grin is probably a bit fiendish and Govinda is probably wondering if he's made a big mistake by coming here. Maybe he has. My grin isn't for his benefit, I just really enjoy the chapter where Ahab creates his weapon and I've been bursting to share it with someone all morning.

"Sounds kinda Satanic," he replies.

"Yeah," I agree, "sure does. Melville told Nathaniel Hawthorne that that was the book's motto."

"Um, I don't know if you remem—"

"How could I forget. Govinda. Nice to see you. Did you cover this in high school?"

"Cover what?"

"Why the book's motto seems Satanic."

"I doubt it. You're probably surprised to see me again—"

"Not really. I was pretty much expecting someone from that night. Makes sense that it's you."

"Oh," he says.

"So what happened after we left? Was everyone dazzled by my supreme wisdom?"

"Mostly they thought you were drunk."

"Understandable. Let's go for a walk. You up for it? Come on."

"Oh," he says again. "Okay, yeah. Sure."

We head into the house where I grab a Mets cap and my wallet and slip on some good walking sandals. I'm a bit energetically buzzed from the excitement of diving down through the layers of *Moby-Dick*, so a walk will be a good way to expend the build-up.

We hop in the jeep and drive a couple of miles to a boat landing which is a good starting point for walking because it will give us several options for scenery and distance. We park and set off down a pleasantly shabby wooded lane. Govinda produces a small bundle of folded cash from his shirt pocket and hands it to me.

"You put a hundred and seventy-one dollars in the can," he explains. "I kept ten, which still makes you our largest contributor."

"I was a little tired," I explain. "I was pretty eager to get out of there."

"Yeah, I think we noticed."

We walk in silence for a while.

"I didn't track you down just to return the money," he says.

I wait.

"I read your book," he says. "I got a preview copy from Mark. I read it, I don't know, like five times. It's all dog-eared and highlighted. It's really great. Really. I read a lot—"

"That louse," I exclaim. "He was supposed to be there that night. And now he's revealing my secret identity and my hidden lair."

"I guess his grandmother died that night. She'd been sick—"

"Oh," I reply, "a death in the family. The king of excuses; shame to waste it on me."

"And I think I'm the only one he told about you."

"So I shouldn't expect any more surprise visits?"

"No, not that I know of. I don't think so."

"Good. It's not my house. I can't let it turn into a whole weird thing out here."

"Look, I hope you don't mind—"

"Don't worry about it," I say, but I'm a little worried about it, and already my thoughts are turning back to the charming, ego-free zone I maintained in Morocco.

We veer off the lane onto a sandy shoreline path.

"I want to know why Arjuna fell," he says.

"What you mean is, you want to know why Arjuna got back up and you realize that you must first know why he fell."

He thinks about that for a minute. "Yes, I guess so."

What to do... what to do...

Kill Krishna. Kill Arjuna. That's the first thing Govinda needs. He's stuck on the *Gita* and we have to get him unstuck.

"You know," I tell him, "Arjuna wasn't like you. He wasn't a seeker, a spiritual guy. He wasn't a student of philosophy or truth. His experience with Krishna in the *Gita* was not the result of his own effort or intent. He didn't become truth-realized through his own processes. He got a free pass—*revealed by mystic spell*. Krishna cheated, as Krishna will do. He picked Arjuna up in a helicopter, gave him the grand tour, and set him back down, all in order to get Arjuna to do what he, Krishna, wanted done."

"I haven't really thought about it that way before," he says.

"The *Bhagavad-Gita* really isn't worth much. I like it, but it's not of much practical value to anyone who wants to wake up. It has a few good points, but it's much more effective at conveying duality than non-duality. For Arjuna, truth-realization is a temporary phenomenon. He wakes up enough to do as Krishna wishes, and then he returns to his ordinary dream-state. His non-dual awareness was non-abiding."

Govinda is silent, contemplative.

"If you want to see a guy getting back up, read *Moby-Dick*."

I bring up *Moby-Dick* because it applies and it's on my mind, and because I like talking things through to see them better for myself.

"Here's Captain Ahab, right? Before his first meeting with Moby Dick. He's still got both legs, still a normal, respectable guy, right? He's a ship's captain, a trusted career man from Nantucket, a husband and father. He's made his life whaling, which is the business of Nantucket. He's a Quaker, which is the religion of Nantucket. We don't really know much about why he fell, but we see him when he gets back up. He's out in the middle of the ocean, maybe a few years since he set foot on solid ground. He's in the middle of a fierce fight with a huge, white-headed whale. Picture it. He and his men are in small, fragile whaleboats engaged in a raging battle. The boats are smashed and splintered, the water is churned white with froth and red with blood from the thrashing leviathan. Leviathan! Enemy of light! Tangled lines and floating debris everywhere, men thrashing in the water, yelling over the din, boats crushed, and at the center of it all a frenzied beast the size of a house fighting for its life. Pretty hairy, huh?"

Govinda grunts.

"So, the whale is winning. The boats that were launched to kill him are smashed, the bloody churning water is strewn with ropes and splintered wood and crewmen. And what does Ahab do?"

Govinda shakes his head.

"He grabs a six-inch knife and attacks the whale. Like a child attacking a Sumo wrestler with a thumbtack. He hurls himself at the whale and tries to kill it with a knife."

"Christ."

"What a thing to do, right? What is it that built up in him, for how long, to make him do something like that? Who knows, but he did."

"What happens?"

"The whale bites off his leg."

"Ouch."

"That's where the line is crossed. That's the division between two things. That kind of battle wasn't unusual in whaling; boats get busted up, men end up in the water, whales get away with harpoons and lances in them. A captain of Ahab's experience would have seen a similar scene dozens of times, maybe hundreds."

"Really?"

"But this time it's different. This time there's something in Ahab that won't be turned back. Who knows what or why? Ahab has no prior relationship to this whale. It should be just another whale to him, but this time Ahab grabs a knife and hurls himself at the whale, and from the exact instant when that impulse went forth from his brain on its way to his legs and arms, one thing was over and another thing had begun."

We walk for a while in silence.

"The *Gita* is still a valuable tool," I eventually continue, "but if you look at it as some sort of sacred text, or as some divine, unimpeachable authority, you'll be making the only real mistake you can."

"Stopping," he says.

"Yes. It's all about moving forward. Nothing is sacred or holy or divine; only true or not. So, you want to know why Arjuna fell. Well, you don't, really, but I know what you mean. You want to climb out of this hole you've spent fifteen years digging yourself into and take the journey you've been avoiding. Sound about right?"

He winces and nods. "Yes."

"Cool. Well, there's reason to be optimistic. I don't always know what tune the universe is playing, but it's definitely playing one now. We've been brought together through some pretty unlikely circumstances and I don't know why, but there are reasons. Maybe it's for you, maybe it's for the book I'm working on, maybe something else. All of the above probably. Who knows? Doesn't matter. The reasons are always there, whether we see them or not."

We continue walking for another hour or so during which time I begin to understand something that's not easy for me to understand. I let Govinda do most of the talking while I just walk, my mind in neutral, and the thing that starts to become clear to me is that the whole releasing-the-tiller thing I talked about in *Damnedest* has not gotten through to him. Maybe he thought it was optional; a step that could be skipped. Listening to him talk, it seems that he's simply ignoring it, and this, right here, is the really weird thing about working with spiritual seekers; they will do anything and everything necessary to make the journey, except move. They're totally committed to going, as long as they can stay right where they are. They would give anything to be there, as long as they can do it from here. Ego wants the goodies, so if the price of the goodies is ego, what's the point? It doesn't make much sense to trade your horse for a saddle. So what's the solution?

You can have your cake and eat it too! This is the bestselling formula that had Govinda marching in place for fifteen years; the promise that one can soar majestically as an eagle without actually leaving the nest. Virtual reality, I guess. Virtual spirituality. Virtual life. I finally had to stop reading spiritual books and magazines several years ago when it became embarrassingly apparent that this same formula, endlessly rehashed, formed the basis upon which the entire spiritual marketplace thrives. The last thing of a spiritual nature I recall reading was a magazine interview with an old Indian guy who said that if I recited a certain mantra for six months I'd get rich, if I stood on hot rocks for six months I'd conquer my sexual desires, and if I lived on air alone for six months I'd get enlightened. I wondered if all three could be done simultaneously so I could be a rich enlightened eunuch in time for the holidays, but the article didn't address that. Rather than risk a really shitty six months with nothing, or just the eunuch part, to show for it, I bid farewell to my days as an interested observer of human spirituality and haven't looked back.

❖

What I'm noticing about Govinda is something that's been bubbling up in my awareness all week, and now it's coming to the surface. Julie talked about it in some of her emails that I've recently read. That got me watching Mary and Curtis and some other people to see how they operated. Now Govinda is here and I'm really starting to see that the most basic yet most important thing is the least recognized. And not the most important thing just in the waking-up sense, but in the sweet-dreams sense as well. And the reason I may be slow in realizing this is because the quality to which I refer has been so fully integrated in me for so long that I assume it's shared by all, or I've forgotten that it's not. That, or, due to my ego-shunning lifestyle of late, I've simply managed to block it out.

This may be the point of this whole curious chain of events, starting with my poor sleep the night before heading into the city, Megan's Be Here Now remix, the *Gita* meeting in Queens, the talk on the beach with Curtis, Govinda tracking me down and showing up in person, and who knows what's next. Foolish to pretend to know where anything begins or ends, of course, but handy to isolate smaller trends in order to guess at larger patterns. The point of this chain of events certainly doesn't have to be just one thing, like me realizing that I have a blind spot regarding other people's mastery of higher navigation, or that many people are living their own lives as impartial observers. It can also be, and certainly is, about Govinda and his progress, and I'm sure there are many other threads woven into this small section of the tapestry as well. Infinite intelligence means just that; as vast and incomprehensibly complex as the workings of things may appear to us, there is no such thing as big or small, simple or hard, many or few, to the perfect intelligence that governs all and is all, and I think the thing I might have failed to notice is the fact that not everyone knows this and lives their life in accordance with it. I think the thing I might have forgotten along the way is that most people, including many of those around me, operate from the level of the finite brain rather than infinite mind.

So there's the next piece in this ever-unfolding puzzle. It has somehow escaped my notice that most people function at an immeasurably inferior manner than that which is rightly theirs; beggars with a winning lottery ticket in an unchecked pocket. This isn't really an enlightenment thing so much as a human development thing. This was discussed in *Damnedest*, but it can't be overemphasized—not mine, but Thy will be done; the will of Allah; Brahma is the charioteer—if you don't get this, you don't get anything. If this isn't your living reality, then you are, like most people, stuck in the ego-clad, nestling state. If so, my advice is this: Observe this state. Make a study of it as it appears in yourself and others. Turn the light of your mind upon it. See it everywhere. Learn to recognize the workings and reasonings of ego. Dissect thoughts, words and actions to find the kernel of fear within. To know the lie is to hate it; to see it is to slay it. There is no nobility in spiritual poverty. If you desire release from this state, you should pray for it. If you don't desire release from this state, you should pray for the desire. The nest isn't life, as anyone who has taken wing will attest.

Enlightenment, a fancy word for awake, is for every single person to arrive at eventually, whereas this higher, unbounded mode of being is here now for whoever truly wants it. If you made a wishlist of anything and everything you could ever want from spiritual pursuits and practices, Human Adulthood would fulfill it, or provide the means. Of course, most people are hopelessly locked into their lives and that's why something so natural and universally desirable is so rare, but there it is: Most people stop growing at around the age of ten or twelve and die in the nest they were born in. It would be easy to believe that many, if not most, of the woes of mankind, on both the individual and societal levels, stem from this state of arrested development. Yes, it's as true of society as of the individuals that make up society. Look for yourself. Look *at* yourself. Look at the news, at politics, at religion. Look at education, healthcare, business, entertainment. Look at the why, and the why of the why. All you'll see is greed and vanity, the offspring of fear, all fear being, ultimately, the fear of no-self. Thumb through any magazine, flip through the channels of the TV, go wherever there are people, and you'll see nothing but a morbidly juvenile, fear-infected, stunted, runtish race over which Maya reigns supreme and unchallenged.

It's not that a better way is available and that most people fail to take advantage of it, but that a better way is at all times in full force and effect, and to function from the level of the puny separate self is to work in opposition to it. In other words, it works in our lives *not* to the degree that we harness it or master it, but to the degree that we get out of its way. It's really nothing more than coming of age; of fully developing into our own potential. You'd think it would be the primary subject in every home and school, but most adults are just children who don't know they're children, unwittingly perpetuating an endless cycle of complacent mediocrity. Believing themselves fully and normally developed, they raise their children to become adults who don't know they're children, passing the torch of spiritual dwarfism onto the next generation, who will pass it onto the next.

We hope that our children might grow up to be president, or a rich doctor or a powerful lawyer, as if that were any sort of success. Rather, we should hope that they grow up to be grown-up human beings, and redefine our notions of success accordingly.

The prison door of self is never closed, but very few wish to walk through it. The chains that confine us in Plato's cave are not locked, but very few are aware of their captive status. Those who have slipped their chains may be more effectively confined yet, thinking themselves free merely because their cell is larger and others are less free. Thinking themselves free, they don't seek freedom. They are content in their captivity.

I think of people I know and have known, and I'm forced to concede that this fuller development I'm talking about isn't so much good or bad as something that's right when it's right. It's something for people to worry about when they get to it and not before. Juvenile rambunctiousness provides the dramatic element of life; after all, what fun is a playground full of well-behaved adults? Pride. Envy. Gluttony. Lust. Anger. Greed. Sloth. The seven deadly sins, like it or not, are the spice of life. Maybe there's a choice about things and maybe there's not, but we're acting like there is, so why not choose not to choose? The confines of self can be heaven or hell, and there's no sense in clawing your way out of heaven. When heaven becomes hell, as all heavens must, that open door will start looking pretty good. Until that time, we lack the motivation necessary to pass through it anyway. The point of the advice I gave above—pray—is to make that time come sooner.

Is that good advice? I don't know. I think of Henry and his friends with their Special Blend spirituality, and how events conspired to make me visit them in their cells and mouth off like I knew what they needed, but what they needed was what they already had. The point of a dream is to dream, not to wake up. Their lives would suffocate me in a minute, but they live them comfortably, happily, so why mess with that? That's why I make a point of not visiting people in their cells. If they want to step out, they can. When they want to, they will. If they have questions and know how to ask, the answers will come.

Now you, on the other hand, reading this book, might take a moment to consider how *your* thread weaves through this section of the tapestry. It's our little conceit that we possess free will, so you might want to exert some now. You have either left your cell already or you're sniffing around at the open door, so this might be a good time to stop and ask yourself what you want, and what you're willing to give for it. Not all fires are started by conscious intent according to convenient schedules. Sometimes they just flare up where you didn't even know it was getting warm, and then you learn two things fast; fire doesn't negotiate and nothing doesn't burn. What do you really want? If you've got the kids and the house and the cars and the career, or any sort of life you're fond of, and you're looking at the subjects discussed here as a way to spiritually enhance your existing lifestyle, then I should remind you that dreams are highly flammable things and suggest that you ask yourself, *really* ask yourself, why you're reading books about setting your world on fire.

> Whoever battles monsters should take care
> not to become a monster too,
> For if you stare long enough into the Abyss,
> the Abyss stares also into you.
>
> — *Friedrich Nietzsche* —

21. The First Step

His three boats stove around him, and oars and men
both whirling in the eddies; one captain, seizing the
line-knife from his broken prow, had dashed at the
whale, as an Arkansas duellist at his foe, blindly seeking
with a six inch blade to reach the fathom-deep life of the
whale. That captain was Ahab.

—Herman Melville, Moby-Dick

THE FIRST STEP, HOWEVER ONE comes to it, marks the
end of one thing and the start of another. Until the First Step
is taken, awakening from the dreamstate isn't possible. After the
First Step is taken, staying in the dreamstate isn't possible. When we
are first introduced to Ahab, he is already beyond the First Step, but
Ishmael recounts the early effects of it for us:

It is not probable that this monomania in him took its
instant rise at the precise time of his bodily dismember-
ment. Then, in darting at the monster, knife in hand, he
had but given loose to a sudden, passionate, corporal
animosity; and when he received the stroke that tore
him, he probably but felt the agonizing bodily lacera-
tion, but nothing more. Yet, when by this collision
forced to turn towards home, and for long months of
days and weeks, Ahab and anguish lay stretched together
in one hammock, rounding in mid winter that dreary,
howling Patagonian Cape; then it was, that his torn
body and gashed soul bled into one another; and so
interfusing, made him mad. That it was only then, on
the homeward voyage, after the encounter, that the final
monomania seized him, seems all but certain from the
fact that, at intervals during the passage, he was a raving

> lunatic; and, though unlimbed of a leg, yet such vital
> strength yet lurked in his Egyptian chest, and was more-
> over intensified by his delirium, that his mates were
> forced to lace him fast, even there, as he sailed, raving in
> his hammock. In a strait-jacket, he swung to the mad
> rockings of the gales.

Whatever it was in Ahab that made him grab a knife and make that leap in a hopelessly futile bid to kill the whale didn't just appear in him at that moment. There are hinted presaging events, but in that act Ahab expressed his intent. He told the universe, in the only language the universe understands, what he wanted. He made a wish and now he gets what he wished for. So it begins.

An interesting question is whether Ahab chose his destiny or it chose him. From the knife passage it might seem that he was just a whaling captain who was going about his normal business when the First Step struck him like a bolt from the blue; hit him like a bus. However, we see that there was something in Ahab before that turning point that makes it unclear where the line between volition and fate is really drawn when it comes to the First Step, or anything else for that matter. It didn't come upon him during his raving madness while lashed in a swaying hammock for "long months of days and weeks" after the loss of his leg. It may look black and white, as if a sane, responsible man suddenly snapped in the heat of battle, but Melville hints at a series of grays leading up to it, things involving fire and sacraments and the mysterious Parsees and Fedallah. In terms of Plato's cave allegory, by the time Ahab made his lunge at the whale, he had long since rejected one layer of reality, and was now declaring war on another. He had already slipped his chains and quietly explored the cave. Now, with the First Step, he was rejecting the cave itself and bolting for the exit.

The First Step has now been taken and the shearing away of the self begins with an initial impact of such enormity that Ahab is profoundly and forever changed. After taking that First Step, Ahab, as is certain to occur, has a piece of himself torn away; a piece that can never heal, never grow back.

> And then it was, that suddenly sweeping his sickle-shaped lower jaw beneath him, Moby Dick had reaped away Ahab's leg, as a mower a blade of grass in the field.

First, Ahab experiences a massive and permanent alteration. Next, he will endure a prolonged state of glaring lucidity from which he'll find no respite. He will not be able to sink back down into the slumber he'd formerly called his life. It may look like howling madness and shrieking pain, but it's practically an entomological description of the chrysalis stage of development; a man in a dark cabin, lashed cocoon-like in a swinging hammock, dying and being reborn. Captain Ahab of Nantucket is dying and Crazy Ahab is being born:

> Small reason was there to doubt, then, that ever since that almost fatal encounter, Ahab had cherished a wild vindictiveness against the whale, all the more fell for that in his frantic morbidness he at last came to identify with him, not only all his bodily woes, but all his intellectual and spiritual exasperations. The White Whale swam before him as the monomaniac incarnation of all those malicious agencies which some deep men feel eating in them, till they are left living on with half a heart and half a lung. That intangible malignity which has been from the beginning; to whose dominion even the modern Christians ascribe one-half of the worlds; which the ancient Ophites of the east reverenced in their statue devil;—Ahab did not fall down and worship it like them; but deliriously transferring its idea to the abhorred white whale, he pitted himself, all mutilated, against it. All that most maddens and torments; all that stirs up the lees of things; all truth with malice in it; all that cracks the sinews and cakes the brain; all the subtle

> demonisms of life and thought; all evil, to crazy Ahab,
> were visibly personified, and made practically assailable
> in Moby Dick. He piled upon the whale's white hump
> the sum of all the general rage and hate felt by his whole
> race from Adam down; and then, as if his chest had been
> a mortar, he burst his hot heart's shell upon it.

And after the initial impact is survived? Then Crazy Ahab emerges. But he's not just a different being, he's a different *order* of being. He functions differently. He sees differently. He thinks differently. Because the perceiver is changed, the perceived is changed, and Ahab emerges into a different world than the one he left.

One thing he knows about his new state is to keep quiet about it, so he emerges from the chrysalis looking and acting *not* like Crazy Ahab, but like respectable Captain Ahab of Nantucket. He dissembles. He creates a false front, not because he cares what others think, but because he has a purpose, and nothing but his purpose matters.

> And, when running into more sufferable latitudes, the
> ship, with mild stun'sails spread, floated across the tran-
> quil tropics, and, to all appearances, the old man's
> delirium seemed left behind him with the Cape Horn
> swells, and he came forth from his dark den into the
> blessed light and air; even then, when he bore that firm,
> collected front, however pale, and issued his calm orders
> once again; and his mates thanked God the direful
> madness was now gone; even then, Ahab, in his hidden
> self, raved on. Human madness is oftentimes a cunning
> and most feline thing. When you think it fled, it may
> have but become transfigured into some still subtler
> form. Ahab's full lunacy subsided not, but deepeningly
> contracted; like the unabated Hudson, when that noble
> Northman flows narrowly, but unfathomably through
> the Highland gorge. But, as in his narrow-flowing
> monomania, not one jot of Ahab's broad madness had
> been left behind; so in that broad madness, not one jot
> of his great natural intellect had perished. That before

living agent, now became the living instrument. If such
a furious trope may stand, his special lunacy stormed his
general sanity, and carried it, and turned all its concen-
tred cannon upon its own mad mark; so that far from
having lost his strength, Ahab, to that one end, did now
possess a thousand fold more potency than ever he had
sanely brought to bear upon any one reasonable object.

Ahab possesses purity of intent. He is monomaniacal. That's
what it means; obsessively focused on one thing. Anything and
everything for that one thing. In Ahab's case, it's to destroy the white
whale, and toward that end he will need a ship and crew. Captain
Ahab of Nantucket can get a ship and crew, Crazy Ahab can't, so the
one wears the other like a mask.

Had any one of his old acquaintances on shore but half
dreamed of what was lurking in him then, how soon
would their aghast and righteous souls have wrenched
the ship from such a fiendish man! They were bent on
profitable cruises, the profit to be counted down in
dollars from the mint. He was intent on an audacious,
immitigable, and supernatural revenge.

Ahab is a textbook example of this transformative process. He
starts out as a normal, proper member of society in all respects who's
mind is slowly infiltrated by a creeping dissatisfaction. He was
straight as an arrow, and then slowly started bending. We don't
know what Ahab was doing during his involvement with exotic
worship and sacraments, besides having a disfiguring scar to show for
it, but his dissatisfaction must have preceded that too. The bending
continued until, without warning, *snap!* It breaks. Ahab grabs a
knife and launches himself at a whale. The First Step. One thing is
over, another begun. No turning back. Next comes the incubation
period, "...for long months of days and weeks, Ahab and anguish lay
stretched together in one hammock...then it was, that his torn body

and gashed soul bled into one another; and so interfusing, made him mad... In a strait-jacket, he swung to the mad rockings of the gales." After "the direful madness" we see the emergence of the new being; a new being who conceals himself within the guise of the old; a being of "a thousand fold more potency;" a being in whom madness is a virtue, for whom "my malady becomes my most desired health." The countless considerations that defined the old are meaningless to the new, who has but one. All of life has reduced down to a single thing. The ridiculous impossibility of that single thing—audacious, immitigable, and supernatural—is irrelevant. Success or failure is irrelevant. Death is irrelevant. Course and heading are set. A new man steps into a new life where all is known, all is certain. The old man, the human man, is already fading from memory.

That's what it looks like when someone begins the process of awakening. That's the reality of it, the intensity of it, the carnage and cunning of it. Something is boiling up for years or lifetimes, and then one day, without warning, it erupts and the wild ride begins. Death, transformation, rebirth as a being intent on a single end with no regard for cost or fear of ruin, concealing his true nature and purpose, and already leaving a trail of devastation in his wake.

That's the First Step.

22. Has anybody told the truth?

The words of U.G. Krishnamurti: Part II

> There is no religious content, no mystical overtones at
> all, in what I am saying. Man has to be saved from the
> saviours of mankind! The religious people – they kidded
> themselves and fooled the whole of mankind. Throw
> them out!

> *–U.G. Krishnamurti*

Further observations from U.G. Krishnamurti, the Un-Guru.

THIS CONSCIOUSNESS WHICH IS FUNCTIONING in me, in you, in the garden slug and earthworm outside, is the same. In me it has no frontiers; in you there are frontiers – you are enclosed in that. Probably this unlimited consciousness pushes you, I don't know. Not me; I have nothing to do with it. It is like the water finding its own level, that's all – that is its nature. That is what is happening in you: life is trying to destroy the enclosing thing, that dead structure of thought and experience, which is not of its nature. It's trying to come out, to break open. You don't want that. As soon as you see some cracks there, you bring some plaster and fill them in and block it again. It doesn't have to be a so-called self-realized man or spiritual man or God-realized man that pushes you; anything, that leaf there, teaches you just the same if only you let it do what it can.

❖

There is only the one thought, "How?" The one question that this organism is interested in is "How to throw off the whole thraldom, the whole strangling influence of culture?" That question is the only question this organism has — not as a word, not as a thought — the whole human organism is that one question. I don't know whether I make myself clear. That is the one question, you see, which is throbbing, pulsating in every cell, in the very marrow of your bones, trying to free itself from this stranglehold. That is the one question, the one thought. That is the saviour. That question finds that it has no way of finding an answer, that it is impossible for that question to do anything, so it explodes. When it has no way to move, no space, the 'explosion' takes place. That 'explosion' is like a nuclear explosion. That breaks the continuity of thought.

❖

Questioning my actions before and after is over for me. The moral question — "I should have acted this way; I should not have acted that way. I should not have said this" — none of that is there for me. I have no regrets, no apologies; whatever I am doing is automatic. In a given situation I am not capable of acting in any other way. I don't have to rationalize, think logically — nothing — that is the one and only action in that particular situation.

❖

By conserving sex energy, you are not going to improve yourself in any way. It is too silly and too absurd. Why have they laid so much stress on that? Abstinence, continence, celibacy, is not going to help to put you in this state, in this situation.

❖

We have very strange ideas in the religious field — torture this body, sleep on nails, control, deny things — all kinds of funny things. What for? Why deny certain things? I don't know. What is the

difference between a man going to a bar for a glass of beer, and a man
going to a temple and repeating the name of Rama? I don't see any
basic difference… I am not against escapes, but whether you escape
through this avenue or that avenue, an escape is an escape. You are
escaping from yourself…. What you do or do not do does not matter
at all. Your practice of holiness, your practice of virtue – that is
socially valuable for the society, but that has nothing to do with this.

❖

Why, I sometimes go to the limit of saying that it is possible for
a rapist, for a murderer, for a thief, for a convict, for a con-man – this
kind of thing can happen! … That has nothing to do with it: the
moral codes of conduct have no relationship whatsoever to this.

❖

You don't know what is good; you know only what is good for
you. That's all you are interested in, that's a fact. Everything centers
around that. All your art and reason centers around that. I am not
being cynical. That's a fact. Nothing wrong with it. I'm not saying
anything against it. The situations change, but it is that which is
guiding you through all situations. I'm not saying it is wrong you
see. If it is not so, something must be wrong with you. As long as
you are operating in the field of what they call the 'pair of opposites',
good and bad, you will always be choosy, in every situation, that is
all – you cannot help doing that.

❖

A 'moral man' is a 'chicken'. A 'moral man' is a frightened man,
a chicken-hearted man – that is why he practices morality and sits in
judgement over others. And his righteous indignation! A moral man
(if there is one) will never, never talk of morality or sit in judgement

on the morals of others. Never!

❖

You hope that you will be able to resolve the problem of desire through thinking, because of that model of a saint who you think has controlled or eliminated desire. If that man has no desire as you imagine, he is a corpse. Don't believe that man at all! Such a man builds some organization, and lives in luxury, which you pay for. You are maintaining him. He is doing it for his livelihood. There is always a fool in the world who falls for him.

❖

You are asking me "Has anything any purpose?" Look here, a lot of meanings and purposes have been given to you. Why are you still looking for the meaning of life, the purpose of life? Everybody has talked of the meaning of life and the purpose of life – everybody. Answers have been given by the saviours, saints and sages of mankind – you have thousands of them in India – and yet today you are still asking the same question, "Has life any purpose or meaning?" Either you are not satisfied or you are not really interested in finding out for yourself. I submit that you are not really interested, because it's a frightening thing. It's a very frightening thing. Is there any such thing as truth? Have you ever asked that question for yourself? Has anybody told the truth?

QUESTIONER: *There are so many truths.*

They are all liars, fops, fakes and cheaters in the world, who claim they have searched for and told the truth! Alright, you want to find out for yourself what this truth is. Can you find out? Can you capture the truth and hold it and say "This is truth?" Whether you accept or reject, it's the same: it depends on your personal prejudices and predilections. So if you want to discover the truth for yourself, whatever it is, you are not in a position to either accept or reject. You assume that there is such a thing as truth, you assume that there is such a thing as reality (ultimate or otherwise) – it is that assumption that is creating the problem, the suffering, for you.

Look here, I want to experience God, truth, reality or what you will, so I must understand the nature of the experiencing structure inside of me before I deal with all that. I must look at the instrument I am using. You are trying to capture something that cannot be captured in terms of your experiencing structure, so this experiencing structure must not be there in order that the other thing may come in. What that is, you will never know. You will never know the truth, because it's a movement. It's a movement! You cannot capture it, you cannot contain it, you cannot express it. It's not a logically ascertained premise that we are interested in. So, it has to be your discovery. What good is my experience? We have thousands and thousands of experiences recorded – they haven't helped you. It's the hope that keeps you going – "If I follow this for another ten years, fifteen years, maybe one of these days I will…." because hope is the structure.

❖

QUESTIONER: *So he spends a lifetime and finally discovers that he's discovered nothing.*

Nothing. That's the discovery. So-called self-realization is the discovery for yourself and by yourself that there is no self to discover. That will be a very shocking thing – "Why the hell have I wasted all my life?" It's a shocking thing because it's going to destroy every nerve, every cell, even the cells in the marrow of your bones. I tell you, it's not going to be an easy thing, it's not going to be handed over to you on a gold platter. You have to become completely disillusioned, then the truth begins to express itself in its own way. I have discovered that it is useless to try to discover the truth. The search for truth is, I have discovered, absurd, because it's a thing which you cannot capture, contain, or give expression to.

❖

What separates you, what isolates you, is your thought – it creates the frontiers, it creates the boundaries. And once the boundaries are not there, it is boundless, limitless.

❖

In a way, the whole of life is like a great big dream. I am looking at you, but I really don't know anything about you – this is a dream, a dream world – there is no reality to it at all. When the experiencing structure is not manipulating consciousness (or whatever you want to call it), then the whole of life is a great big dream, from the experiential point of view – not from this point of view here; but from your point of view. You see, you give reality to things – not only to objects, but also to feelings and experiences – and think that they are real. When you don't translate them in terms of your accumulated knowledge, they are not things; you really don't know what they are.

❖

Look here, there is no present to the structure of the 'you'; all that is there is the past, which is trying to project itself into the future. You can think about past, present, and future, but there is no future, there is no present; there is only the past. Your future is only a projection of the past. If there is a present, that present can never be experienced by you, because you experience only your knowledge about the present, and that knowledge is the past. So what is the point in trying to experience that moment which you call 'now'? The now can never be experienced by you; whatever you experience is not the now. So the now is a thing which can never become part of your conscious existence, and which you cannot give expression to. The now does not exist, as far as you are concerned, except as a concept. I don't talk about the now.

❖

Courage is to brush aside everything that man has experienced and felt before you. You are the only one, greater than all those things. Everything is finished, the whole tradition is finished, however sacred and holy it may be – then only can you be yourself – that is individuality. For the first time you become an individual. As long as you depend upon somebody, some authority, you are not an individual. Individual uniqueness cannot express itself as long as there is dependence.

❖

I am always negating what I am saying. I make a statement, but that statement is not expressing all that is being said, so I negate it. You say I am contradicting myself. I am not contradictory at all. I negate the first statement, the second statement, and all the other statements – that is why sometimes it sounds very contradictory. I am negating it all the time, not with the idea of arriving at any point; just negating. There is no purpose in my talking.

23. Let what will befall.

This is much; yet Ahab's larger,
darker, deeper part remains unhinted.

–Herman Melville, Moby-Dick

CURTIS, GOVINDA AND I ARE all seated around the outdoor dining table that has become my *desko al fresco*. They are both reading emails from Julie to help figure out which ones make it to the semi-finals. Curtis has already spent many hours going through them all and he's printed out enough to fill their own book, but we'll have to leave that for Julie to worry about someday. For now, I've asked Govinda to work with Curtis to whittle the stack down to a hundred or so pages of the kind of stuff I want—Julie's descriptions of the process, not her process itself—which I can then go through and select what I need for the book.

"What Julie's doing—" says Govinda, holding one of the pages.

"Yes?" I say, without looking up.

"She's, like—"

I keep reading while he puts it together.

"She's like Captain Ahab, isn't she? That's the thing, isn't it?"

I look up over my granny glasses.

"She *is* Captain Ahab, yes. What you're seeing there is what it really looks like."

He nods slowly. "Hunting her own white whale?"

"Sure, or writing her own *Moby-Dick*."

He thinks about that.

"Do you mean that Herman Melville wrote *Moby-Dick* as, like, his version of Spiritual Autolysis?"

"Any honest writing will invariably be a process of self-immolation—autolysis—so yes. Certainly."

I'm reading *Moby-Dick* the way they're reading Julie's emails; trying to decide what is good for the second book and what I'll have to leave out. I have to leave a lot out, but some things are right on the edge. Right now I'm trying to decide how much of the Pip/Ahab relationship to include. Pip definitely makes it into the book because he foreshadows Ahab's untold fate, which we'll look at later. But what about the powerful bond that forms almost instantly between post-traumatic Pip and Ahab? Does that make it in? It would be a tough thing to leave out, especially as it helps to illustrate the larger issues of Ahab's sanity and humanity. I decide to discuss the Pip material with Curtis and Govinda so as to get a better idea of its relevance. The first thing I notice is that what's important about Pip at this point is equally important of Captain Gardiner, so I start there.

"I need your help with something," I say.

They both set down the pages they were reading and lend me their attention.

"Toward the end of *Moby-Dick*, Ahab's ship, the *Pequod*, meets another ship at sea, the *Rachel*. All Ahab ever cares about when he meets another ship is if they've seen Moby Dick. *'Hast seen the white whale?'* That's how he greets every ship. In the case of the *Rachel*, the answer is yes."

"So that's good news for Ahab, right?" asks Curtis.

"Right, this is what it's all been about. He's finally close to his elusive prey. He knows where Moby Dick is."

"Cool."

"But before he can disengage from the *Rachel*, its captain, Captain Gardiner, begs Ahab not to leave. Captain Gardiner is from Nantucket, like Ahab. He knows Ahab. He has a young son, as does Ahab. Now he comes aboard the *Pequod* to talk face to face with Ahab and tells him he lost his boy in a whale hunt. The boy's off in a boat somewhere. He pleads unabashedly with Ahab to join in the search. Just for two days."

"To look for his son?" asks Govinda.

"Yeah, Captain Gardiner's son. Twelve years old."

I read Captain Gardiner's words to Ahab.

> "My boy, my own boy is among them. For God's sake—I beg, I conjure"—here exclaimed the stranger Captain to Ahab, who thus far had but icily received his petition. "For eight-and-forty hours let me charter your ship—I will gladly pay for it, and roundly pay for it—if there be no other way—for eight-and-forty hours only—only that—you must, oh, you must, and you *shall* do this thing."

"Man wants his boy back," says Curtis.

I continue reading Captain Gardiner's heartfelt plea.

> "I will not go," said the stranger, "till you say aye to me. Do to me as you would have me do to you in the like case. For *you* too have a boy, Captain Ahab—though but a child, and nestling safely at home now—a child of your old age too—Yes, yes, you relent; I see it—run, run, men, now, and stand by to square in the yards."

"So Ahab says yes?" asks Curtis. "He helps find the boy?"

I read more.

> Ahab still stood like an anvil, receiving every shock, but without the least quivering of his own.

Govinda doesn't say anything.

"After repeated pleadings from the *Rachel's* captain," I continue, "this is what Ahab says."

> "Avast," cried Ahab— "touch not a rope-yarn"; then

in a voice that prolongingly moulded every word—
"Captain Gardiner, I will not do it. Even now I lose
time. Good-bye, good-bye. God bless ye, man, and may
I forgive myself, but I must go."

Govinda is slowly shaking his head.

"Shit," says Curtis, "man's got no heart."

I nod and smile. "But that's exactly the point Melville is making, Ahab *does* have a heart. If he were heartless, none of it would mean anything. If he's just a machine, who cares about any of it? Ahab *does* have a heart. We might as well view Captain Gardiner's son as Ahab's own. That's what this is all about."

Curtis shakes his head. "That's some crazy shit."

Govinda is quiet, but I can see he's listening hard.

"There's more," I say. "This heartless thing is very important. Melville wants us to understand it. He wants us to see that it's not a defect; that Ahab is not just a blackhearted psycho."

"I don't see how that can be," says Curtis, shaking his head. "The man is fucked up."

I laugh. Govinda remains silent. I see that this discussion is having more impact on Govinda than Curtis. Govinda is the one who wants to know what it means to set a course that will take him beyond the edge of the charts. For Curtis, this is just a postcard from a place he's heard about. For Govinda, it's a glimpse into what he considers a possible future. Govinda, like Ahab, is a husband and father.

"So now," I continue, "after this whole huge book, we're in the final chapters and the hunt is on. Ahab knows the white whale is near. As he is leaving his cabin to go on deck, he is stopped by the black cabin boy, Pip, who had a near-death drowning experience earlier and literally had the Pip scared out of him. Upon first seeing the boy's non-Pip condition, Ahab speaks to him."

"Where sayest thou Pip was, boy?"

"Astern there, sir, astern! Lo! lo!"

"And who art thou, boy? I see not my reflection in the vacant pupils of thy eyes. Oh God! that man should be a thing for immortal souls to sieve through! Who art thou, boy?"

"Ahab is moved by the boy and takes him under wing," I say. "They're kindred spirits. Here's what Ahab says to Pip:"

"Thou touchest my inmost centre, boy; thou art tied to me by cords woven of my heart-strings."

"Captain Ahab makes friends with the little black boy like that?" asks Curtis.

"Yes, they form a deep and immediate bond. Pip, too, could be seen as Ahab's own son. When it comes time for the hunt, Pip wants to lower with Ahab, head out in the whaleboats, but Ahab won't have it."

"Lad, lad, I tell thee thou must not follow Ahab now. The hour is coming when Ahab would not scare thee from him, yet would not have thee by him. There is that in thee, poor lad, which I feel too curing to my malady. Like cures like; and for this hunt, my malady becomes my most desired health."

"Ahab doesn't want to be cured," says Govinda thoughtfully.

"He's waking up," I say. "He doesn't want to be drawn back into sleep. His madness is necessary. Pip threatens to douse Ahab's flame. What did Ahab say earlier? The boy is tied to him by cords woven of his heart-strings. What does that refer to?"

I look pointedly at Govinda. He doesn't have to think about it for long.

"Attachment," he says.

He told me at our second meeting that he was consciously practicing non-attachment as prescribed by his spiritual teacher. From what I could tell, he translated it as a sort of non-materialism. He'd read *Damnedest* so he knew I didn't consider non-attachment a quality to be cultivated, and we didn't discuss it further at the time, but now he's getting a glimpse of what attachment really means, thinking, perhaps, of his wife and children.

"What did Arjuna see that made him fall?"

He nods his head slowly.

"Seen *Apocalypse Now*?" I ask him.

"Yes," he says.

"The inoculated arms? The diamond bullet? The horror?"

"Yes."

"Okay," I say, and leave it at that.

I read ahead in the book and describe the action.

"Pip pleads desperately with Ahab, appealing to his humanity, as did Captain Gardiner, to make Ahab let him, Pip, stay close to him during the hunt. Finally, Ahab can't stand any more."

> "If thou speakest thus to me much more, Ahab's
> purpose keels up in him. I tell thee no; it cannot be."
> "Oh good master, master, master!"
> "Weep so, and I will murder thee! have a care, for
> Ahab too is mad."

"Ahab says he'll murder Pip?" asks Curtis, perplexed. "I thought they were like father and son now."

"They are, but you heard what Ahab said. *It cannot be*."

"He also said his purpose keels up in him," protests Curtis. "That means maybe it *can* be, right?"

"Good point. I'm sure it feels that way. You don't know until you know. I would think that in that situation, someone pulling on the cords of your heart like a son, that the opposing forces seem very evenly matched, like it could go either way. Maybe that's why he responds so forcefully. Here are Ahab's parting words to the boy."

> "True art thou, lad, as the circumference to its centre.
> So: God for ever bless thee; and if it come to that,—God
> for ever save thee, let what will befall."

"Did he just say——?" asks Govinda in a quiet voice.

"What?" asks Curtis. "Does that mean Pip's gonna die? After all that, Ahab's gonna let the boy die?"

"Two boys," I reply. "Let what will befall."

Curtis looks sad. Govinda looks sadder.

24. Entertaining Negativity

> Ah, God! what trances of torments does that man endure
> who is consumed with one unachieved revengeful desire.
> He sleeps with clenched hands; and wakes with his own
> bloody nails in his palms.
>
> –*Herman Melville, Moby-Dick*

THE PROCESS OF SPIRITUAL AUTOLYSIS has three basic parts: Seeing what needs to be killed, killing it, and cleaning up the mess. Seeing is really the first stage of killing, but the third part is just as important as the first two; you have to clean up after yourself. You must process the loss. That's not a rule like no sweets before bed, that's a rule like gravity. That's how it works.

Every step in the process of awakening has all three components. A step begins with seeing and understanding. That seeing and understanding becomes the very thing that destroys the thing seen and understood. But it doesn't end there. Just because you killed something doesn't mean you killed your attachment to it. Seeing the thing is the beginning of killing the thing, and killing the thing is the beginning of detaching from it. The third step isn't therapeutic; it's the point.

> Great! My fucking attic is haunted! My mind is haunted, my thoughts are haunted. *I* am haunted; possessed, plagued with demons! My mother is here! My unborn children are here. My future is here, my dreams. Everyone who means anything to me, good or bad, pleasant or unpleasant, is here. How do they all fit? How could I have not seen them right away? Of *course* they're here. *This* is where they are. My attic is me, there is no place else.

Whether or not they have physical counterparts out in the real world is meaningless to me, just as the fact that I might be a real person in the real world is meaningless to them. Perception is reality. I am possessed by my own perceptions; not by things and people, future and past, but by my *perceptions* of them. These are my connections, my attachments. Maybe all I really am is the sum of all these connections, these fearful longings and graspings. What is an attachment anyway? It's a belief, that's all. A strong one maybe, but just a belief. And yes, Jed, I know: No belief is true.

The pen is mightier than the sword, isn't it Jed? You wrote about a sword, but that was just a metaphor. It's the pen. Spiritual Autolysis is the power of the pen, which is the power of the mind, the power to see, to see clearly. Yes, I will kill these people inhabiting my mind. I will kill them by clearly seeing the attachments that keep them here. I can see those attachments now. I can see the emotions at work and I am starting to see them for what they are. I am starting to understand what stuff this prison of self is really made of.

You said it in the first chapter. I never paid enough attention to that chapter. Now it seems like the foundation upon which the rest of your book sits. Fear. Of course! There is only fear. Fear disguised as love. Fear disguised as morality. Fear disguised as compassion. Fear making the unreal seem real. We're animals, right? Designed to survive, to protect our young and to keep our species going. Fear drives the whole process. People are like prisms hit by that single beam, which then splits into all the emotions of the rainbow. We are fear refractors.

You asked, "Who really wants to go where this road really leads?" I know that the answer is no one. No one could ever choose this, not knowingly. It's a certain impossibility. You're right, it's like getting hit by a bus. Physical suicide would be a bad hair day next to this. There is no amount of courage that would permit someone who understood this to choose it. But no one knowingly chooses it. This isn't spirituality. This is emotional carnage. There's nothing spiritual about this.

❖

I was in the city a few days ago and I stopped in at the bookstore to pick up a book by Bernadette Roberts. I went to the New Age and Eastern Religion aisles where I've spent so much time and money over the years, but this time I was overcome by sadness and disgust. Now that I'm here, now that I know what I know, I am seething with an inexpressible contempt for the whole of what passes itself off as spirituality. Close your eyes and repeat a mantra? What sort of pathetic joke is that? Be present in the moment? What the hell for? Don't entertain negativity? Are they kidding? I have turned into a fire-breathing dragon of negativity. I can't seem to entertain *enough* negativity! I am reborn as the child of negativity. I eat, breathe and sleep it. I exude it from my pores. I radiate malice and ill will. I am a wrathful destroyer, and what they call negativity, I call the purifying flames. Negation is the process. The various forms of spirituality and religion are not the path to truth, but the antidote to it.

I'm not done with this journey and I may never be, but I can damn well see who's never taken it, who doesn't even know it's there to be taken. My altitude increases daily and I seldom take the time to look back, but visiting the bookstore caused me to do so; gave me some perspective on how far I've come and what I've left behind. So many books, so many teachers, so many paths. Hasn't anyone noticed it's not working? I guess I'm just naive. Who cares what's true as long as it sells, I guess.

I wish I could stick a finger down my throat and just puke out all that sugary spiritual sickness that I spent so many years ingesting. That's what I'm doing now, I guess. That's why I have to write this; to purge myself of this poisonous contempt. Teachers? Teaching what? What is there to teach? There is no teaching, there is only doing. You're either doing this or you're not. All teachings exist for the sole purpose of *not* doing. I see that quite clearly. The whole thing seems grotesque to me now. There is only one book, Jed, and you wrote it. I was also shopping for a copy of the *Bhagavad-Gita*, but I know that the whole of it is contained in your epilogue; The unreal has no being, the real never ceases to be. What else is there to say?

✦

Something strange is happening. (The understatement of the century!) It's hard to describe, it's still very unclear. In fact, being unclear is what it is. Dissolving clarity. It's like the lines I've always seen distinguishing one thing from another, or separating types of things from other types, are fading. It's like looking at earth from space and seeing one world; no artificial boundaries. It's as if I've been seeing divisions that didn't exist all my life, but now I'm not seeing them, and I'm noticing the difference. Is that weird? It seems weird. Hard to tell what's weird anymore.

For example, people. I can no longer really distinguish types or traits. Rather, I see characteristics common to all in slightly differing proportions. I don't understand it yet, but it definitely marks a new way of seeing and understanding the world around me. It's like there are many songs, but they're all variations on the same few notes. People, though, seem like variations on only one note. When I was in the city, it wasn't like I saw many different people, as usual, but the same person many different times, in many different guises. The outer layers of personality, clothing, appearance and gender hardly register with me anymore. A person is a person. To know one is to know them all, like leaves on a tree.

Waste and conservation is an example of parts of my old self just sort of disappearing. When I arrived at the cabin I began considering arrangements for recycling, about which I have always been conscientious. But now, the very idea of waste – the idea that anything can be wasted – seems absurd, non-sensical. That's how it dawned on me. Unlike much of this process I'm engaged in, some things seems to be changing without my volitional input or conscious awareness. Things are changing and I'm not even aware that they've changed until I look and see that something's missing, something's not what it used to be. And then comes another little surprise; no reaction. No sense of loss, no emotional response. This happens repeatedly; once or twice a day I notice that what I once considered an important part of myself is simply gone and forgotten. Beliefs, preferences, opinions; popping silently like soap bubbles, leaving no sign of having ever existed. It's not that I'm reevaluating or seeing things in a new light, but that I'm disappearing one small piece at a time. It's not shocking or upsetting. It seems like it should be a big deal every time it happens, but it's really a non-event. It's actually kind of funny. It's as if all my life I considered it my primary duty to fit in, to belong, to get along and be part of everything, but now that's not my job anymore and that change alone has completely reconstituted what I think of as me.

What I'm writing now is more like journaling than autolysis, it seems. I'm exploring the changes that are occurring rather than using the writing process to make them occur. I'm all over the road with this. Still, I think it's worth paying attention to and examining the part of the process that seems to be taking place behind the scenes. I'm so focused on the things I'm working to change that I could fail to notice that the person I *am* is changing, or maybe just falling away, fading away, *burning* away, I guess, and in some cases, simply vanishing.

✧

I spend hours and hours writing letters to people I know; my mom and dad, sisters and friends, former bosses and teachers. Usually to people who have some power over me which I did not consciously grant, and which I must now consciously revoke; people who influence my thinking, who inhabit my mind. What is it but a form of possession if I'm in almost constant internal dialog with people not present? How many times a day does this happen, and on how many levels? How deep does this go? What's a demon but an inhabiting influence? These non-me presences in my mental space are malignancies and I'm using the pen like a scalpel to remove them. I write these long messy tirades, page after page, longhand, and it works. It gets this crap out of my system. Rumi said the elixir was hidden in the poison and it's true! I write these letters and I just keep at it, twenty pages, thirty pages, until I have managed to purge out whatever poisons were infecting me. I'd never send the letters, of course. They'd lock me up for sure!

✧

I look back now on those early days when I was still with you in the house and I can't believe I survived. Funny that the First Step is in a way the final step. The whole thing, the very thought of it, was so insanely massive that I was crushed under the weight of it. I couldn't get out of bed, couldn't stop crying, couldn't see any possible hope of resolution. I couldn't eat, could barely sit up. I was simply devastated by what felt like the most unbearable grief. I knew there was no possibility of turning back, of undoing what had been done, of going back to the state of blindness that had been my life up until that point. I couldn't see any way of going forward, either. No way out.

What kind of madness was it, I wondered, that allowed me to contemplate a journey that had only one possible destination? A destination far beyond anything ever even contemplated by people I love and respect; my parents and grandparents, my teachers, my sisters and friends. But more! Beyond everybody! Beyond the greatest minds and hearts mankind has produced! Beyond presidents and philosophers and heroes and poets. Beyond Shakespeare and Einstein, Lincoln and Churchill, Bach and Beethoven! Simply by taking the First Step I had already left most of humanity behind forever. That, or I was plunging into the severest sort of insanity. I will be exploring far beyond anything imagined by the greatest explorers, beyond anything our astronauts could even contemplate. Forget death, *this* is the undiscover'd country. *This* is the final frontier. I was going beyond my own species! That's not metaphor or hyperbole, that's literal fact! How do you wrap your mind around that? The very idea was so utterly, perversely, egomaniacally absurd that I would have been able to simply dismiss it with a bitter laugh except for one thing: *It was true!* I *knew* it was true. I tried and I tried, everything I could think of, but that was the inescapable fact. It was true. No other way to say it. My time as a human being was over. Now it was time for something else. I was now on this road and somehow I would walk it until it killed me. I couldn't get off if I wanted to. But what's more, I knew where it went. Right from the very first seconds of this journey there was something in me that understood the whole of it.

You only spoke to me once during that week I spent at the house,

Jed. I don't think I came out of the bedroom much. I came down at one point, looking like hell I'm sure, and there you were, sitting in the library, reading. I didn't say anything. I didn't ask anything. But you answered. You spoke without looking up. "The way humans reckon age is incorrect," you said. "Most people stop developing at a very early age. What looks like a seventy year-old is generally an eleven year-old with fifty-nine years of experience." That's all I remember you saying, but that's all I needed. That was the key that opened that first door that threatened to crush the life out of me. You didn't have to explain. You didn't have to elaborate. If you had come and said that the day before, I wouldn't have understood it, but by the time you spoke to me it was as if the whole thing had built up inside me and just needed that one little tweak and this aching mass of thought and conflict and loathing and heart-crushing fear resolved itself in a flash of clarity and a door opened where there wasn't a door before and the thing that was about to break didn't break.

That wasn't the end of it, of course. Next, I found myself trying to expand that simple concept into a fully realized understanding of human development. Whether or not it's a new idea that most people are developmentally in their pre-teens, it was new to me and I had the urge to understand it in fullness, so I wrote it out and explored it for myself. That's when I got off my self-pitying ass and started taking positive action. I revised my opinion of everyone I knew, one person at a time, based on this new understanding, and saw them in the light of their developmental ages. What an amazing process! I saw that everyone had stopped believing in Santa Claus and the Tooth Fairy, but really hadn't gone much further than that. I didn't have your book back then, Jed, but I remember when you told me that people were just children on a playground to you. I didn't understand it then, but I understand it now.

Obviously, it doesn't end there. That was just the first week. The larger process actually took many long months and continues still. The larger process had to do with cutting away. Detaching. You can say it like that and it looks like just a word – detaching – but what it really is is so brutal and so remorseless, so cold and surgical, that no word or words can approach it. I wrote literally hundreds of thousands of words during this period in my attempt to process myself through it, but it seems like something that can never really be fully accomplished. I use the word detaching, but it's really about dying. No spiritual teaching that talks about non-attachment has any right to. None of them are talking about this. "Cultivate a sense of detachment," they say. A sense of detachment? What planet are they from? They have no idea whatsoever what detachment means. They seem to be talking about detaching from your desire for a BMW or for Mr. Right. Try detaching from what you love! From what you are! From everything that characterizes your membership in the human race! And that's just for starters.

The process of awakening looks like it's about destroying ego, but that's not really accurate. You never completely rid yourself of ego—the false self—as long as you're alive, and it's not important that you do. What matters is the emotional tethers that anchor us to the dreamstate; that hold us in place and make us feel that we're a part of something real. We send out energetic tendrils from the nexus of ego like roots to attach ourselves to the dreamstate, and to detach from it we must sever them. The energy of an emotion is our lifeforce, and the amount of lifeforce determines the power of the emotion. Withdraw energy from an emotion and what's left? A sterile thought. A husk. In this sense, freeing ourselves from attachment is indeed the process of awakening, but such attachments aren't what we *have*, they're what we *are*.

25. The Little Bastard

He must dare to leap into the Origin, so as to live by
the Truth and in the Truth, like one who has become
one with it. He must become a pupil again, a beginner;
conquer the last and steepest stretch of the way, undergo
new transformation. If he survives its perils, then is his
destiny fulfilled; face to face he beholds the unbroken
Truth, the Truth beyond all truths, the formless Origin
of origins, the Void which is the All; is absorbed into it
and from it emerges reborn.

> –*Eugen Herrigel*
> *Zen in the Art of Archery*

I'M SITTING ON THE STEPS in front of the church where
Curtis dropped me off, idly watching people and traffic, just
being dumb-happy. There's practically nothing about cities I don't
like, but what I like most is the textures; dirty concrete, rusted steel,
cold granite, chipped paint, sooty brick, broken plastic, smeared
glass. Manhole covers and sewer grates are good to look at. The green
lamppost knows its business. I can be very happy staring at a cement
floor—not just *any* cement floor, of course. Still, what kind of yutz
takes pleasure in staring at the floor? Williams knew what kind: "So
much depends upon a red wheel barrow, glazed with rain water,
beside the white chickens." Words can't say the rightness of a black
steel door in a red brick wall. My foot casts three shadows. This is the
same breeze that cooled Christ and Buddha under this same moon.
What does it all mean? Why, absolutely nothing. If it meant
anything, it wouldn't mean a thing.

Whenever I mention my likes and dislikes, I feel like I have to tack on a list of disclaimers for anyone who thinks that to be enlightened means to exist in an undifferentiated state of pure, egoless, emotionless stasis, fixed and lifeless as a marble statue. I have preferences; places and things toward which and away from which I tend. Granted, my tastes have devolved to a pretty minimalist level and continue in that direction, but it seems to me a much richer level; less adorned, more essential. Like now, sitting on the steps of a church in a run-down neighborhood, a place without much in the way of cheer or color but rich in is-ness, and I'm sunk in a sappish reverie of—no, I'm not going to say bliss or unity—simple contentment. It's good, it's *all* good. Even bad is good. Now, if you whap me in the face with a shovel, that's not so good, but no one is whapping me in the face with a shovel. I didn't make the journey I made so I could sink into sappish reveries, but now that the journey's done, I seem to do it more and more often. I don't want to make this sound too mystical or Zenny because I don't think it is. It's just a nice place to visit. This is what I took Curtis to the ocean to show him, and he saw it; that you can just be and breathe and set everything down for a while, appreciate what you are and what you're a part of, and then, when you pick everything back up, you'll understand it better, appreciate it more, know it beneath the surface. The point isn't to make yourself feel that you're a part of everything, but to stop for one minute insisting with every thought and feeling that you're not. I know it all sounds terribly trite and cliché, but it's not as common as it sounds. People who do this bring something back with them, and I don't often see anyone who has it.

This disclaimer business always leads to the same paradox thing so let's get there and move on. Jed McKenna is not the enlightened being. There is no such thing as an enlightened being; there is only awakeness, which is undifferentiated. It's not *my* reality, it's reality. Jed McKenna is not the awakeness itself but an experienced trail-guide and qualified spokesman for awakeness. It might not make sense, but it's true so it doesn't have to. The paradox is only visible from one side, so if you want to make sense of it, come see it from the other side.

End of disclaimer.

❖

I'm back at this church because Govinda made it happen. Once he figured out that I wasn't available by phone or email, he began visiting me out at Mary's house, making himself useful, working with Curtis on some things like the Julie material, not badgering or annoying, but making it clear that he'd really like me to come visit his group again. I finally began to see some sense in it, so about a month after my first visit, we're back at this neo-Catholic church.

There's a cat in the bushes on my right that's been watching me since I sat down on these steps. There's a seedy little taco joint down the street that smells really good. I feel like walking. Nice night and place for it.

Curtis shows up and stands on the sidewalk in front of me. On the drive in we discussed a little more about *Star Wars*, the Hero's Journey, and any real-life applicability they might hold. He told me that after our first *Star Wars* conversation he'd looked into it on his own and what he'd come up with, he said, was Zen Mind. He'd made the connection between the Jedi feats of quasi-mystical physical prowess, Eugen Herrigel's book on Zen and archery, and his own personal experiences from playing tennis and soccer. He explained all this to me as he drove us here in the jeep, treating it like an Italian sportscar now that he knew about things like downshifting and accelerating into turns. When he was done telling me about his discoveries, he asked what I thought.

"What do you think I think?" I replied, and that's where we left it. Now it's an hour later and he's standing in front of me and he answers the question.

"Further."

"Yep."

"Okay."

He sits down on the step next to me, neither of us saying much. After a few minutes, Megan from Mark's PR firm appears in front of us. Unlike the last time I saw Megan, as well as the last time I was at this church, I'm not tired now. I'm rested and clear and pleased to be. This frame of mind can't really be improved upon, but it's fragile and talking and thinking only muddles it and makes one murky again.

"May I speak to you frankly?" Megan asks. "It doesn't feel like you'll be signing up for our services, so I won't be hurting my employer or anything."

Nice of her to telegraph the punch.

"Uh, yeah, okay, you may speak frankly."

"I'm not sure people want to pay twenty dollars for a spiritual book just to be called children and to be told that their spiritual beliefs are excrement. I think people are searching for something that can improve their lives in some tangible way, make a positive difference, make them happier, more fulfilled."

"I'd certainly agree with that," I say.

"But your book doesn't really do that. You don't seem to have anything good to say about other paths, other beliefs; *any* beliefs, apparently. You admit you're not tolerant, which to me just means you're closed-minded. You come off as quite arrogant, like you're right and anyone who doesn't agree with you just doesn't matter, like people who disagree with you don't even count. You're against meditation, Buddhism, Christianity, and all sorts of other things. You don't seem to leave room for anyone else's views or beliefs. I just think that's very narrow-minded. I thought spiritual masters were supposed to be open to all points of view and embrace all paths. You seem like just the opposite, as if no one else's views could possibly matter."

"I guess I'd agree with that," I say.

"Well, it doesn't matter if you agree with it or not if you're not going to do anything to change. You're probably not, though, are you?"

"I wouldn't be able to make the kind of adjustments you're talking about."

"I don't see why you couldn't if you wanted to. It doesn't really seem like anything more than just getting in touch with your own humanity. It's like you've shut that part out, but you could change that. You talk so much about fear, you say that we're all fear-based, but maybe we're love-based and you've just somehow closed yourself off to that. Do you think maybe that's possible?"

I nod.

"You know, we're all in this together and we really only have each other. It just seems like such a shame to wall yourself off from that sense of connection, and really, trying to convince other people to do it too doesn't seem right to me. You're a very powerful, convincing writer and I'm afraid a lot of people might read your book and just, kind of, I don't know, run *away* from life. I know that's not how you see it, but maybe you should think about it. Try to understand that people aren't robots and that they can't just turn off their emotions because of something they read in a book. Would you think about that?"

"Certainly. I'm working on another book that you might like better."

She looks at me skeptically.

"Well, I don't know if you're being sincere or not so I'll just leave it at that. I liked your book a lot, but the more I thought about it the more I realized how much I disagreed with you at the most basic level. In fact, I want to thank you because your book helped me to reevaluate my own beliefs and that's made them stronger, so it really had an important impact on me, and I have you to thank for that."

"Oh, well, you're welcome."

"I hope that if you were thinking of using our company for your PR that you won't let my comments change your mind."

"No, I've appreciated your comments very much."

She nods, looks down at her hands, nods again and enters the church building.

"That was critical," says Curtis.

❖

Govinda was planning to talk to the group first and I leave plenty of time for that. He promised to explain my return engagement in a very low-key way, not talking about the book or using any words like enlightenment or master; just saying I'm a special guest some of them might remember. The plan is that I'll participate in discussion, not address the group like a speaker. Curtis and I enter quietly and find everyone meditating. We stand silently in the doorway and I look around to see who I recognize. They must have activated their satsang phone tree or something because tonight's crowd is more of the New Age variety than the *Gita* group I saw in the basement. This time I wasn't going to wait for the coffee can. I gave Govinda some money a week ago and told him to set up a better space with better snacks. He did as I requested and rented the nicer upstairs meeting room with plenty of seating, large windows on two walls, high ceilings, adequate lighting, and not permeated with damp tobacco stench. There's also a much better assortment of snacks including, but not limited to, butter-free cookies. The are two coffee urns, decaf and regular, and real cream. I'm glad to see everything upscaled a bit. Maugham said that the thing about asking for the best is that you'll most likely get it, which is practically the golden rule of dreamstate manifestation: Ask and ye shall receive. This room may not qualify as the best, but it's a step in the right direction.

Meditation concludes and everyone slowly unfolds out of it. People stand and greet each other, fill cups and plates, chat. Wheelchair-bound Barry is here, and several others I recognize from the last time, including Curtis' nuzzling coed, Rohan the ringer and a few others. Mark from the PR firm is here with his wife. The chairs were arranged facing a podium but now everyone forms smaller groups and everything gets shuffled around. I grab a seat with Mark and half a dozen others and listen quietly to their discussion. After a few minutes Mark turns the conversation to me and for the next ten minutes we talk about some of the points made in *Damnedest*. The other little groups kind of gravitate toward our conversation until we all coalesce into a single though somewhat disarrayed group.

I don't really want to sit around talking about the book. The original plan with Govinda was not to even mention it. After the third or fourth question about it I quietly make the point that only a few people present have read it so we should probably find a subject of broader interest. Megan, though, doesn't want to let it go.

"I'm one of the few people here who's read it," she says, "and I've already shared some of my views with you in private. I was wondering if you could explain to us why you think people should buy your book."

Yuck. Just the thing I'd hoped to avoid. Right out of the gate we're in a marketplace mentality. I'm depicted as someone who is here to serve his own greed or vanity, and they're the skeptical consumers wondering whether they should buy into my little fantasy. Megan has put me in this corner and now I have to gently but firmly get out of it.

"I don't think anyone here even knew there *was* a book," I reply. I look around and it's clear that most of them didn't know. "As to why anyone should buy it, I have no feelings on the matter. You were in a business meeting with me where we discussed the promotion of this book. Did I seem like someone who was eager to sell books? You were the one that talked about creating a bestseller. Did I seem to have any interest in all that?"

"No, I have to admit—"

"It was your suggestion that we establish the Jed McKenna brand."

"Which would be good from a business standpoint—"

"Have I mentioned the book here? Am I displaying a copy?"

She shakes her head. I don't want to pick on her, but I really can't have this thing go in the direction she's set.

"Mark, you were at that meeting. What do you think of me as a book promoter?"

"You're a publicity consultant's nightmare," he replies, and people laugh.

"Govinda, did I—"

"Thomas," he corrects me.

"Oh. Did I miss something?"

"Before you came in I spoke to the group and let them know that I was going back to my real name."

I admire his decision. He's putting away childish things.

"Thomas, did I arrange this event?"

"Nope."

"Was I eager to come?"

He laughs. "Practically had to drag you."

"A lot of these people know you and trust you. Do you believe I'm here to sell something or convince anyone of anything. Do you think I have any motivation like that?"

"No, I'm sure you don't."

Megan jumps in. "I don't think it's fair of you—" she says, starting to feel attacked and getting defensive, so I head that off.

"Wait, Megan, it's alright," I say, smiling and holding up my hands in a non-confrontational gesture. "We're not at odds here. No one's angry or defensive. I like you and respect you. I appreciate your contribution. I just wanted to make that point. You make me sound like I'm here to force myself down people's throats, and I'm just making the point that I'm not. I don't have any agenda here. We're just people sitting around talking together. You told me we're all in it together, right Megan? So let's proceed on that basis. Here we are on this planet, somewhere in Queens, New York, USA, sometime in the twenty-first century, right? We're all in the same boat floating on the same ocean trying to make some sense of it all. Nobody's selling anything or running for office, right?"

She laughs and smiles. "Alright," she says. "Actually, I read around a dozen New Age titles a month because of my job and yours was really refreshing. You're just like you seem in your book, by the way, very open, very plain-spoken, a lot of common sense, no frills. That's what I really liked about your book, the common sense approach. You make it all sound so, I don't know, *obvious*, and if you think about it, I suppose it is. I guess I made it pretty clear earlier that I don't agree with your conclusions, or maybe I just don't want to, but my sense when reading your book and talking to you now is that there's no... I don't know how to say it... there's no room for... you don't leave any room to maneuver, I guess. Maybe that says something about the straightforwardness of your approach, the simplicity of it. That was my reaction, anyway."

❖

In *Damnedest,* I said that the only real spiritual teaching is think for yourself and figure out what's true, and that's what I'm saying here. I mean, seriously, what else is there to say? If you want it, it's yours. If you don't, whatever. I've really only got this one message, this one point to make. Pretty much anything else I say is either about process or negation. I don't engage in discussion in the conventional sense of a two-way exchange of knowledge and ideas. I don't take part in spirited debate or lively give and take. I don't entertain differing views and they don't entertain me. Megan was right about me; I'm extremely narrow-minded. My state is one of being, not of knowledge or belief, and no force of emotion, strength of conviction, or weight of opinion can influence me in the least. So, yes, I seem arrogant, but that's just the appearance. There's no sense of superiority on my part. Can't be. Calling me arrogant is anthropomorphic.

Am I pro-truth? No. Do I hate delusion? No. Do I consider the dreamstate evil? No. I'm not opposed to all the teachers and teachings that keep us so effectively narcotized. I don't think anyone or anything is other than perfect. I'm not a warrior for truth. I'm not at war with the armies of the lie. I *like* the lie. I'm all for it. Maya and her magnificent Palace of Delusion have no greater fan than I. Having myself escaped from the confines of delusion, I'm able to appreciate its strengths and its vulnerabilities. Its greatest vulnerability is that it has no mass, no substance. There is no *it*, and all you have to do to see that for yourself is *look* for yourself. Its greatest strength is that looking for yourself is the last thing anyone, say what they may, really wants to do.

But now I'm speaking with a group of people I don't know and who don't know me, which means that truth would be poor choice of topics. The topic itself is simple, but getting everyone from all their diverse backgrounds and beliefs to that place of simplicity would be a mess. That's fine with me, I'm tired of truth stuff anyway and, as Megan pointed out, I don't think anyone really wants to hear about it. There are plenty of interesting topics and I could enjoy this evening more if I were learning something myself instead of just droning on about truth. These people share an interest in the *Bhagavad-Gita*, Curtis is interested in Jedi-Zen stuff, Megan wants something with tangible results, and my own interests lately have been more about the process of reintegrating oneself into the unbounded oneness of things, not necessarily for the purpose of waking up, but for the purpose of having a more enjoyable dream. I'm carrying a letter that I asked Curtis to find for me before we left Mary's house. It's from a woman, Jessica, and details her journey of reintegration from small, segregated self to unbounded self; the Hero's Journey. So, my sense is that all these things will set the agenda for tonight's discussion.

There's no real theme or structure to the evening, so the one group again becomes several and there are often three or four different conversations taking place within earshot. I spend more time listening than talking. The conversation closest to me is between Thomas *nee* Govinda, Mark, Megan, two or three others I don't know, and several others who, like me, are just listening. Their discussion revolves around the spiritual search; about whether it's a tail chase, whether all the books and teachers really help, whether they're progressing or entrenching, and whether there's any real hope of success. After a few minutes, Thomas asks what I think.

"About—?"

"About whether the spiritual quest is really going anywhere or just in circles. Whether it's just another form of self-delusion."

"Depends, I guess." I say. "Look at the impulse, the thing that drives you one way or another. Why are you doing these spiritual things in the first place? You go out and buy a spiritual book or magazine, or you attend some workshop or join some group, come to something like this. Why? You want something, right? You're looking for something. What? What do you want? I would say that's where your discussion takes you."

"So then," says Mark, "I guess the question is, why are we doing it? What do we want? I want to say, you know, freedom or bliss or spiritual enlightenment." He looks at the others and no one offers a better answer. He looks at me. "What would you say?"

"I'd say you either want to be soothed or agitated," I reply. "Both, really, but mostly soothed. Ego wants to be soothed, but the part of you that wants to be agitated, that small needling voice in the background, that's the part that's going to make something happen, and someday, some life, that tiny little bastard is gonna get big enough to do something. He's gonna grab the wheel and throw it hard over and then your life is going to crash and burn. That's where it begins."

"Where what begins?" asks Mark.

"Your life. That's where your life begins. The worst thing will happen, the thing that if it were choice between that and death, you might choose death. Your life becomes your worst nightmare, and that's when it starts getting good."

"You don't think our lives have begun yet?"

"I know they haven't. You do too. Ask your little bastard, he'll tell you."

The other pockets of conversation are again reforming into one around us and I see that I am effectively addressing a group, not taking part in a conversation.

"Whatever that is, whatever happens to smash your life to bits, you will someday look back on with the profoundest gratitude. You will look back on it like a birth from the womb. The womb is lovely and insular and safe, but it isn't life. The distance between the womb and life may appear to be a few inches, but it's really the difference between two different orders of being. It's easy to see people as children, but it might be more useful to say they are unborn. They live unborn and often die unborn. When Thoreau said the mass of men lead lives of quiet desperation, this is what he was talking about. There's the part of you that wants to be agitated, to bust things up and see what they're really made of, and there's the part that keeps that part swallowed down; fear. Fear of losing what you have, but you don't really have anything. That's what the little voice is telling you. Nothing is yours and nothing you do matters. That's the problem with the agitator; he never lies, he never exaggerates, he always makes perfect sense. He's a *rational* little bastard, so the only way to deal with him is to drown him out."

"Denial," says Megan.

"Denial. Sure. But how does that work? Denial is just a label and labels are themselves a tool of denial, allowing us to dismiss difficult things unprocessed, based on the name of the thing and not the thing itself. There are many tools of denial. Avoidance is popular; just keeping yourself constantly distracted so that there's no quiet time during which the little bastard's voice can be heard over the din. Belief is a good one because it's emotionally charged, and emotional nonsense drowns out rational sense. There are many ways in which ego keeps us from seeing the obvious."

"But what about society?" Megan asks. "What would the future look like if everyone listened to their, uh, little bastard and unleashed their deepest, darkest selves onto the world?"

"I don't know. Why ask me? Find the little bastard inside you and ask him. He knows."

"Okay, but right now I'm asking you."

"I don't know. Sounds messy. Could be bad. Maybe everybody would die. Where would we be then?"

"What did yours say?"

"My—?

"Your little bastard."

"Ah. He said there is no society, there is no future, there is no world. Stop being a schmuck. It's all a lie. Burn it all."

"And that's something you did?"

"Yes, ma'am."

"Why?"

"For the only possible reason why anyone would ever do it. Because I absolutely, positively couldn't *not* do it."

"Do you have any regrets?" she asks.

It can be tricky knowing how much answer to give. This doesn't seem like the time to get into a longwinded digression about how I don't possess the thing that experiences regret, so I opt for the short answer.

"Nope."

26. Jolly Punches

There are certain queer times and occasions in this strange mixed affair we call life when a man takes this whole universe for a vast practical joke, though the wit thereof he but dimly discerns, and more than suspects that the joke is at nobody's expense but his own. However, nothing dispirits, and nothing seems worth while disputing. He bolts down all events, all creeds, and beliefs, and persuasions, all hard things visible and invisible, never mind how knobby; as an ostrich of potent digestion gobbles down bullets and gun flints. And as for small difficulties and worryings, prospects of sudden disaster, peril of life and limb; all these, and death itself, seem to him only sly, good-natured hits, and jolly punches in the side bestowed by the unseen and unaccountable old joker. That odd sort of wayward mood I am speaking of, comes over a man only in some time of extreme tribulation; it comes in the very midst of his earnestness, so that what just before might have seemed to him a thing most momentous, now seems but a part of the general joke.

–Herman Melville, Moby-Dick

B ARRY, THE GUY I SAT next to during my first visit here, the subterranean meeting, has gestured me over to him. I take a seat and a few others seated nearby turn to hear our discussion.

"I'm wondering if you can help me," Barry begins. "I have a friend who's in a state of terrible depression. I'm very worried about her." Whether he has this friend or he's speaking about himself as a female friend doesn't matter to me, but as the conversation progresses, I come to think she's real. "She's very unhappy. She's just been getting worse and worse for the last few years and I really think she's on the verge of doing something desperate. I don't know what to do for her."

"What's the general nature of her unhappiness?" I ask. "What does she say it stems from?"

"She hasn't said anything in particular, I mean, she doesn't have some disease or something. She hasn't lost a loved one or anything like that."

Not all black despair is created equal. If the depression is the direct result of some disease or defect, meaning that the person is not clear-thinking, then my response might be similar, but less optimistic because it would seem that the friend was buckled in for her ride and must ride it until the end. This is just my opinion, no more authoritative than anyone else's, but it seems clear to me that there are many rides in this park; it's not all about the fun ones, and you can't get off until the ride comes to a complete stop. So much for free will. You can jump out midway, but whatever made you get aboard in the first place will probably make you get aboard again.

Anyone wishing to confront the issue of free will versus predetermination should begin, as always, by bringing the question into sharper focus. There is no possibility at all of free will; simply by defining it we are able to see it as nonsense. So the real question is, do we have *any* will? Can we choose to exert or not exert any influence over anything? Do we possess the least tiny modicum of control? Any will or no will, that is the question. The only argument for the latter is that there's no argument for the former. Ultimately, no answer is possible and the question itself disintegrates under scrutiny. All questions do.

Everything disintegrates under scrutiny.

The thing to be hoped for regarding Barry's friend is that she's in a rational depression. This is something we touched upon in *Damnedest*. When someone is without hope because they see that there is no cause for hope, there's hope. A question occurs to me.

"Where does she live?" I ask Barry.

"Brooklyn," he says grimly. "We don't see each other much. She doesn't get around so good. We mostly email and talk on the phone." I wonder if she's in a wheelchair, like Barry. I guess if you don't get around so good, Brooklyn and Queens can be worlds apart.

"Is she intelligent?" I ask.

"Very."

"Christian?"

"Yeah, Catholic."

"Oh."

I would normally expect someone in this situation of prolonged despondency to eventually crash and burn, and then phoenix up out of the ashes. Christianity is generally conducive to this death-rebirth transformation, but Catholics, in my experience, even lapsed Catholics, seem more likely to get stuck in the despair part and stay there.

Rational depression isn't a defect or a disease, it's a perfectly appropriate response to the circumstances we find ourselves in. We have no future, no substance, and no significance; what's not to be depressed about? This isn't deep, soul-searching, high-minded stuff; a full and accurate accounting of one's life could be done over a cup of coffee or during a commercial break. From a logical standpoint, the only compelling argument against suicide is that failure may result in a thousand dollar fine and six months in prison. Some people have found a personal savior, but the trick with saviors is not to look too closely; they've got you, but who's got them? Even the best long-term solution you can imagine, whatever you call heaven, starts to sound pretty dumb if you think about it for, like, two minutes. The trick is to not think about stuff, to not look for ourselves, to not see the obvious, but we can't trick ourselves forever, as Barry's friend is finding out.

Depression is fear with hope removed. It arises as we discover that something we thought could be ours will never be ours. Unhappiness is when we worry about not having something, depression is when we realize we'll never have it, and freedom is when we realize that nothing is ours and nothing *can* be ours, so that, in effect, nothing *isn't* ours.

Our own lives are not our own, so what is?

"Well," I say to Barry, "I obviously can't speak with any authority about your friend in particular, but it sounds like something that I can talk about in general. This is going to come off as a bit heartless, probably because it is, but what might be the case with your friend, and anyone else who seems about to succumb to morbid despair, is actually the onset of human adulthood."

"Oh," says Barry glumly.

This isn't an enlightenment thing in particular. It's more a human thing, but it certainly has parallels to the larger awakening process, and it's a precursor to enlightenment; a prerequisite.

"I don't know what to do about it," says Barry. "I don't know how to help her."

"Did you ever consider the possibility she doesn't need help? That it might be a *good* thing?" I ask.

"What?" he says. "Suicidal despair?"

I laugh, but gently because I know this is one of those areas where emotions can get fired up and scorch what could and should be an interesting discussion.

"Well, kind of," I say. "The despair is just the outer manifestation; the visible symptom."

When I see someone in the condition Barry describes, my first impulse is to congratulate them. I don't do it, of course—I understand that it wouldn't be received in the spirit intended—but I see it as a very positive thing growth-wise, human adventure-wise. That despair is most often a sign that one is breaking away from the fairytale version of life, where good little boys and girls live happily ever after, and moving into adulthood.

"I'm worried that she's going to die," he says.

I shrug. People may not want to play by the rules, but they're still the rules. One of the rules is that you die. We have one inalienable right, and that's it.

"She's so unhappy—" murmurs Barry.

"Happiness is for children. There's another level," I reply. "When we come to the point where can't find any more happiness and it looks pretty certain that we never will, we think it's all over, and in a way, it is. In a *good* way."

"I'm really worried that she won't survive it."

"Yeah, well, she might not," I say with deliberate callousness.

"That's a very clinical point of view," Barry protests. "This is a real person we're talking about. I don't think you understand—"

I hold up my hands to stop him.

"Barry, don't take this too much the wrong way, but you're looking at this like she needs rescuing and that you must save her. I understand that, but I've been through the process we're talking about and you haven't. You're seeing a terrible crisis where I'm seeing normal human development. Yes, it's painful, and it's difficult to watch. You see someone sinking and you want to leap in and save her. I understand that she's resisting the process. I understand that she's flailing and crying for help. I understand that it's agonizing to watch. I understand that you'd both like to go back to the way things were, to some happier time, but that's no longer an option, is it?"

He begins to react. The other people gathered around us are hushed. Curtis looks nervous. This is very personal for everyone. This is life stuff and we're all in life.

Barry starts getting choked up and pleading that his friend's case somehow transcends the trite little spiritual bow I'm trying to tie around it. He's getting angry and offended, which is good. Polite facades aren't of much use here. As Barry goes off on a small, barely controlled tirade against my callous indifference, I look around the small group to see how others are reacting. They all seem very present. They're not watching someone else's thing; they're seeing themselves and their own lives in this discussion. They don't look happy, but I am. This is life's wake-up call; misery, suffering, loss, death. This is where people are forced to get real and where understanding can occur. They think I can help, and maybe I can, but not the way they think. I'm not a counselor or a mentor. I'm not interested in helping anyone feel better. I'm no one's friend. I dwell in an infinite pitiless void. Or, to state it more accurately, I *am* an infinite pitiless void. That's my reality. I'm not a nice guy, I just play one.

People sometimes come to me, as Barry is doing now, to show me something that they say is wrong and needs fixing. I am immediately in conflict with such a person. I do not and cannot share the view that something is wrong and needs fixing. No matter how absolutely certain someone might be that something is wrong, and no matter how terribly wrong it may appear, I am absolutely, unshakably certain it's not. I am incapable of perceiving error. I reside in a perfect universe where nothing can ever be wrong. We all do, I just happen to know it.

When I speak or write, I'm not trying to convince anyone or sell anything. My whole gig is telling people to look for themselves, to simply see what's right in front of them. As da Vinci said, some see, some see when shown, and some don't see. "I don't offer the old smooth prizes," said Whitman, "but rough new prizes. These are the days that must happen to you."

I'm sitting in a theater watching a film called *Humanity*. I look upon Civil War hospitals and Nazi death camps and children's burn wards with the same eye with which I look upon bursting gardens and starswept nights and laughing babies. They're just the opposite poles of the film's emotional spectrum. They don't make me forget my reality. Nothing is so grotesquely horrible or so heartwrenchingly beautiful that it transcends my transcendence. Nothing trumps truth. I know what man is and I know what life is. If you look at these statements and decide I'm a bad guy, then you're short-changing yourself. You're mistaken in your belief that you're reading a dialogue between Jed and Barry, just like this *Gita* group was mistaken in thinking they were reading a dialogue between Arjuna and Krishna. You, the reader, are at the exact center of the universe; *your* universe. It's all yours, it's all about you, and you are all alone in it. Anything that tells you otherwise is a belief, and no belief is true.

Who is Krishna in the *Gita*? He's the *perfect* warrior compared to Arjuna's merely *great* warrior. The truth of self compared to false self. Arjuna is mighty, but he can still be bested. Not so Krishna. The perfect warrior is untouchable and unsurvivable. No sword can touch him and nothing can endure the touch of his. The *Gita* is the dialogue between the false self and the true state; the bridging of the paradigm gap. To say that Krishna is God is to completely miss the real point of the *Bhagavad-Gita*. Krishna is the truth. Arjuna is the untruth. The prize to be won in this battle is not wealth or fame or power, but the transition from untrue to true, from dream to awake, from delusion to reality.

Truth is beyond opposites. Duality is a dream. It's not a yin-yang relationship; it's one or the other. The truth contains no element of the false and the false contains no truth. There is only truth and illusion, and within illusion there is only fear and denial. Fear of truth is the foundation upon which Maya's Palace of Delusion is erected. She has no power but that we give her. Denial of fear is the motivation underlying all activities in which humans engage. This is Vanity in the biblical sense: *I have seen all the works that are done under the sun; and behold, all is vanity and a chasing after wind.* We must constantly project the illusion of self because if we don't, we aren't.

❖

Barry is both pleading and angry. "This is a *real person* I'm talking about! I come to you to ask how I can help her, I want to know what I can do for her. She's not a piece on a chessboard, you know. She's not a number. She's not a—"

"Stop," I say.

He doesn't stop.

"You can't just minimize people to make them fit your—"

"Please stop," I say.

He doesn't stop.

"—cold, philosophical view of people like they're just—"

I let him go on for a minute until he's got it all out. When he's done, I proceed.

"You're viewing this from a warm, fuzzy place, Barry," I say gently, "like somehow everything's going to be alright. But is it? I'm asking *you* now. Is it possible that everything's going to be alright?"

I wait for him to see it for himself. He doesn't speak.

"This is a harsh piece of business we're discussing, Barry. You won't solve it on this level; you have to step up to the next one. That's where it's going, with or without you. You want your friend back the way she was, but that's not one of the possible outcomes here. Denial is only a temporary refuge. It's gone past greeting card sentimentality. You see that, don't you?"

He stares at me for a moment, then exhales tremblingly and nods.

"Fear," I say. "It's all about fear. Your fear, her fear. She's afraid, so she keeps struggling to stay afloat. You're afraid of losing her, so you keep encouraging her to struggle. Don't you get tired of being afraid? Of struggling?"

Barry doesn't reply. No one moves.

"The answer is to stop struggling, to go *into* the fear. Let her go. The cause of the unhappiness isn't the situation, but the resistance. You're making disease and decay and death evil, but they're not evil, they just are. The clinging is the cause of the unhappiness. Release is the answer. Let her sink."

Barry lets that sink in for a moment.

"So what do you think I should do?"

"I don't know. Send her a book about suicide."

"She's a Catholic!"

"Not for long."

"But she's my *friend*. She'd hate me! She'd never speak to me again!"

"Yeah, well, what are friends for."

This gets me a dirty look, but I'm trying to provoke him.

"Listen Barry, in a few minutes I'm going to stand up and talk about a woman who was in a similar situation. Stick around and see if that gives you a better idea of what's really going on with someone at this stage, in this sort of crisis, okay?"

Barry nods. Someone rubs his shoulder comfortingly.

27. The Mind of Absolute Trust

In the world of things as they are,
   there is no self, no non-self.

If you want to describe its essence,
   the best you can say is "Not-two."

In this "Not-two" nothing is separate,
   and nothing in the world is excluded.

The enlightened of all times and places
   have entered into this truth.

In it there is no gain or loss;
   one instant is ten thousand years.

There is no here, no there;
   infinity is right before your eyes.

One is all; all are one.
When you realize this,
   what reason for holiness or wisdom?

The mind of absolute trust
   is beyond all thought, all striving,
   is perfectly at peace, for in it
   there is no yesterday, no today, no tomorrow.

—Seng-Ts'an

28. Working-Class Heroes

> He knows himself, and all that's in him, who knows
> adversity. To scale great heights, we must come out of
> lowermost depths. The way to heaven is through hell.
> We need fiery baptisms in the fiercest flames of our own
> bosoms. We must feel our hearts hot—hissing in us.
> And ere their fire is revealed, it must burn its way out of
> us; though it consume us and itself.
>
> *—Herman Melville, Mardi*

THERE'S A WHITE MARKER-BOARD on wheels against a nearby wall, so I roll it out and use the black marker to draw a line from edge to edge. The line starts off level, then angles downward, eventually becoming a straight vertical plummet. From the bottom of the plummet it begins rising again at a steep angle to a point where it shifts to a more gradual ascent. I end the line with an arrow to indicate that it continues. Flat, decline, plummet, steep ascent, gradual ongoing ascent. I write Hero's Journey across the top of the board. I write "Oblivious" along the flat line at the beginning. Along the gradually descending line I write "Mass of Men." Along the vertically descending line I write "Event." Along the steeply ascending line I write "Rebirth," and along the less steep line I write "Life." I bisect the line vertically at the Event point with a dotted line and write "Flesh" on the left side and "Spirit" on the right.

I'm drawing the diagram as an aid to my own thinking and so I'm ready in case tonight's meeting ever gets under way, but when I turn around I find that everyone is now seated and facing me. I guess tonight's meeting is under way.

"Oh," I say. "Hello."

"Hello," many of them reply cheerily.

"Huh, well, okay. I guess I'm going to stand up here and talk for a while about something I think is interesting, uh, you know, in the hope that, uh, you'll think it's interesting too."

HERO'S JOURNEY

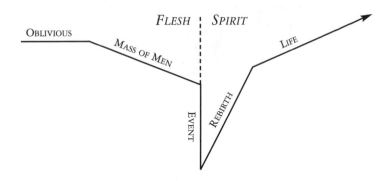

The startled, awkward part over, I proceed with the talking part.

"In the last several weeks, I've been surprised several times to see the ways in which we distance ourselves from our own lives; from life. I'll share a few of them with you. A friend of mine is a lifelong Melville scholar, but for some reason she's never drawn any connection between his works, most notably *Moby-Dick*, and her own life. She somehow maintained an impersonal detachment. Then my friend Curtis here," I point him out, "tells me he did a very interesting paper on the first *Star Wars* movie in terms of Joseph Campbell's description of the Hero's Journey, but when I asked him about what he'd learned about his own life in the process, he came up empty. Is that fair to say?" I ask Curtis. He nods. "Then, through a bizarre set of circumstances, I attend one of your meetings here, and there it was again; this funny way we have of reducing vivid illustrations of life's full potential to sterile, intellectual models that somehow don't apply to us. Obviously, this is one of ego's many defense mechanisms. For those of you who weren't privileged to observe my performance here last month," a few chuckles, "I pointed out the same thing I'm going to discuss tonight; that life isn't a spectator sport, that each of us is in it as much as anyone has ever been, that stories like *Star Wars* and the *Bhagavad-Gita* aren't someone else's stories, they're *our* stories. That we are our own heroes, the heroes of our own lives. That is what the universe, in its not-so-subtle way, has suggested I talk about tonight. Sound okay?"

Everyone sort of smiles of nods, but they're all paying attention.

"I think one of the reasons for this artificial distancing is the godlike quality of the people we see as heroes, and the mythic dimensions of their journeys. The best examples of this are men like Jesus and Buddha, who have been caricaturized like comic book heroes, far removed from anything a regular person could ever dream of becoming. In a similar vein, *Star Wars* is a fight for galactic peace and the *Bhagavad-Gita* takes place between two massive armies ready to attack. Probably none of us are thinking of going out after this meeting to find the Holy Grail or destroy the Ring of Power. I think this quality of grand proportions serves to take the Hero's Journey out of human scale and make it something Olympian, beyond the reach of mere mortals. Even when it's a common Joe, as in *Joe vs The Volcano* or *The Wizard of Oz*, it still seems like the stuff of imagination and fairytales, not real life. So, what I'd like to try to do now is bring the whole thing back down to a size we can work with so we can see who the real hero is and what the real journey is."

Blank stares. People attentive, waiting. This is unusual for me. I can count on one hand the number of times I've addressed a group of people I didn't know. I can count on one finger the number of times I've used a diagram.

"Let me describe this diagram on the board, then I'd like to read a letter I brought with me and see how this woman's journey compares to those of the great myths and legends." I turn to the board and indicate the flat beginning line marked Oblivious. "We don't have to worry about this part too much. We were all there and we know many people who still are, but we're not anthropologists so we'll just say that this is where the unquestioning dwell. Why they're unquestioning doesn't concern us. Okay?"

No one says it's not okay, so I continue.

"This next part, marked Mass of Men, is just that. This is where most everybody is. This is the line that you could isolate as its own spectrum of awakeness and place yourselves and virtually everyone you know along it somewhere. I marked it Mass of Men because of Thoreau's statement, 'The mass of men lead lives of quiet desperation.' This is that. Before anyone chimes in, let me say that this isn't bad or negative or evil or anything like that. This is a part of life, a stage of growth, of normal development. Okay so far? It's not necessary to totally understand or agree with everything now, we'll come back to all this when I read the letter."

No one chimes in, so I go on.

"Here's where it gets good," I say, circling the point at which the downward slanting line turns straight down and where the dotted vertical line divides the board into flesh and spirit. "This is where real life begins, where we get into our true potential." This causes some stirring and grumbles, but we could get stuck here all night if I don't forge on, so I do. "I've marked one side Flesh and one side Spirit because this is where that transition occurs; death of the flesh, birth of the spirit. Human Childhood on the left, Human Adulthood on the right. This is where the small, segregated being ends and the boundless, integrated being is born. Death and rebirth."

Several people raise their hands.

"Hold on, please. I know you have things to say, we'll get to everything. This is just the establishing shot, like a map we'll be referring back to. Just observe for now. I should point out that this isn't my little pet theory. This is the human map. It's not Eastern or Western or Christian or Hindu, it's human, and you'll find it wherever you find people. That might be my main point; that it's not really the hero's journey at all; it's the human journey."

They're contained, but barely, so I finish the diagram quickly by saying that the steep ascent is the infancy and childhood of the newborn being, and that the more gradual upward line is the life of development and discovery.

"Any questions, just in general, about the diagram?"

A woman in her mid-thirties speaks up.

"You say we're all on that Mass of Men part, but how do you know that? Maybe there are people here who have made that Event transition."

"Sure, that's possible," I say. "Anyone?"

No one.

"You're right, though. There could have been someone like that here. I assumed there wasn't because this is a group of seekers and such a person would be in a different mode; growth, exploration, development, expansion, something like that. Probably not worried about the lessons of the *Bhagavad-Gita*. Okay?"

She smiles and nods.

I take out the letter I'm carrying and unfold it. It's a mess from being in my pocket and from me scribbling notes all over it, crossing out whole sections and circling or underlining others. It started as eight pages, but I've reduced it to a handful of phrases and paragraphs for the purposes of this discussion.

"Okay, so I have this letter," I tell the group. "It came to me," I look at Curtis, "how?"

"Sonaya forwarded it with other stuff. I don't know where she got it."

"Okay, so it's a mystery letter. It's from a woman named Jessica who lives in Austin, Texas, addressed to me, and, without her being particularly aware of it, it details her progress along this line I've drawn on the board. Let me give you some of the broadstrokes. She's from a large rural family from which she's the first to attend college. Paid her own way. Graduated and went to graduate school. Graduated and entered the workforce in the health field. We won't worry too much about her experience on the flat line, the oblivious period. What we learn from her letter," I'm scanning the opening paragraphs as I speak, "is that after all the struggle to break out of her humble beginnings, after working her way through college and graduate school, after beginning on her career path, she was suddenly overwhelmed by the," I search for the phrase she uses, "'*inauthenticity* of it all.' Let me quote a few parts. Here she refers to herself as 'lost and bewildered.' She says she's 'lost all direction in life.' I don't think that's too uncommon. She says that she realized her life and her success was 'just a facade,' that everything she'd been working for and everything she accomplished was 'false and illusory.' 'The bottom dropped out from under my whole world,' she says. See what she's saying about her experience at this stage? She's in a slide and there's nothing to do; nothing to grab hold of, nothing to cling to. She can no longer hold the black cloud at bay, can no longer deny its blackness. She's in it now, enveloped by it. That's the process, that's what's happening. Nothing has meaning and she can no longer pretend otherwise. It takes time, it's a transition, but this is what it is. The end of denial."

No one looks very happy to hear this. One of the key elements of denial is denying that you're in denial, but these folks all made the effort to get here tonight, so I'm assuming they're wanting to look at this stuff.

"The point is, that's where everybody really is, living with some degree of doubt and fear and denial. How can you not be? It's not a matter of shame or inadequacy, it's just a matter of living in the dark. You see how this Mass of Men line angles down? That's where gravity is taking us, this is where life naturally goes, yet we spend our lives fighting against it, fighting against *life*. Instead of going along and trusting, we throw all our might into resisting. Why? Because we're afraid of what's down there; change, disruption, the unknown. It's all about denial and resistance." I indicate the building we're all in. "What else is religion but man's fortress against reality? Institutionalized denial. Is there anyone in this room who doesn't recognize what I'm talking about? Anyone who doesn't see this in their own life?"

There isn't. I guess they're well-suited for this message, but that doesn't mean they like to hear it.

"So, in Jessica, we see malaise spreading like a cancer into all areas of her life. Her carefully constructed life is now in a cascade failure. Her career shows her that healthcare is a bureaucratic, systemized farce; her words. Her relationships open her eyes to the fact that no one else can bring meaning into her life. Her successes now appear to her as failures. She says, 'I was becoming soulsick, and I saw no way out of it.' Now way out. That's the core of this experience. You're trapped. Can't go back, can't go forward, can't stay where you are. What we're seeing here is the end of the line, literally." I tap the whiteboard at the point where the Mass of Men line becomes the Event line. "This is where the denial stops working and all pretense melts like wax."

I pause to study the letter and to give everyone a moment to connect what I'm saying with their own experience.

"So, here she is," I say, "sliding inexorably down that Mass of Men line. Denial is the only thing that keeps any of us from doing the same thing, but for Jessica, denial has run out. She's sliding toward that drop-off I've labeled Event. We all are, of course, but she's there now. So what do you think happens? What's the event?" I hold up the letter. "It's obviously not death."

Everyone is staring at the board as if the answer is there.

"She finds Jesus?" asks someone in back. Several people laugh.

"Good guess," I reply. "What does born-again mean except death and rebirth? People come to a crisis in their lives where they feel trapped and hopeless and their egoic limitations are destroyed. A genuine born-again experience would certainly qualify as an Event. But that's not what happens here."

"Not all born-again events are genuine?" someone asks.

"No, most are just a desperate redoubling of denial rather than release. Anyone else want to guess what Jessica's event was?"

No one else guesses. I read it straight from the letter:

"'I was in a car accident and my neck was broken.'"

Several people make pained sounds. Everyone looks adequately uncomfortable. No one seems bored.

I hold up her letter.

"She says she knew that something like this car accident was coming weeks in advance. She didn't know that she'd survive, but she knew that some sort of resolution had to occur and that it would have to be catastrophic in nature." I look through the letter for something I'd underlined. "'In every way, it was perfect,'" I read. "That's what she says about the accident. You see how she's operating on a different level now? She's in a place where she can see a car accident and a broken neck as perfect." I read the entire passage. "'In every way, it was perfect. I have always thought of it as a perfect transition, even before I had the benefit of time and perspective to consider its meaning.'"

I can see that everyone is fully attentive. Jessica is a real person, just like any of them. She's not a myth or a legend or a movie star on a fifty-foot screen, she's just a regular person, confronting her life honestly.

"The first time I read this letter," I continue, "I thought it was quite extraordinary that she was able to appreciate the larger picture even while she was in the midst of this catastrophic event. But it gets better. Try to appreciate her circumstances. She's in this prolonged, deepening depression about the futility of her existence when she gets slammed by a drunk driver. Emergency crews extricate her from her crumpled vehicle, ambulance ride, her clothes cut away in a frenzied emergency room, x-rays, waiting, head taped down, her body completely immobilized, no idea of her condition. Eventually, two doctors come to explain her situation to her; the possibility of permanent paralysis or death. They tell her that her neck is broken and that they need her consent so they can operate immediately. It doesn't get much heavier than that, right? And what does she tell them?"

I walk to the whiteboard and point to the word Spirit to the right of the vertical dotted line.

"She tells them no."

I let that hang in the air. I want them to think about that; to wonder what it means, to wonder why she said it. I want them to think about how their own lives would have to change in order for them to appreciate the perfection of a broken neck and to reject the advice of medical experts trying to save them from paralysis and death. I want them to see for themselves that there is such a thing as life beyond fear.

"The doctors are very insistent, even intimidating. They try to bully her into agreeing to surgery, but she doesn't budge. A twenty-four year-old girl, strapped to a gurney, in a state of calm lucidity. Everything is on the line. Medical experts are giving her advice anyone would leap at. See? It's not just that vertical drop of the death experience, it's also the phoenix-like ascent out of the ashes, the birth of the new being into a new world, a different world where different rules apply. You'll find this exact transition in every version of the Hero's Journey because this is the heart of it. Curtis, in the first *Star Wars* movie, do you remember where Luke makes this transition?"

"He trusts the Force," answers Curtis.

"Exactly. Flying through those canyons of the Death Star, everything on the line, total success or total failure in the balance, he switches off his navigational computers—panicking *his* experts as I recall—and chooses to rely entirely on the Force. *That's* the transition. The old way is fully exited and the new way is fully entered, not by word but by deed, when it matters most, when everything is on the line."

Everyone looks sharply attentive. The only drama more engrossing than the Hero's Journey is the Hero's Journey with *you* as the hero, and that's what I think these folks are thinking about. Not in a rah-rah, sounds-great, let's-go-do-it sense, but in a *Holy Shit!* sense. They're trapped, just like Jessica was. They *know* they're trapped and they know, at the little bastard level, that their life, their *self*, is all a fabrication created to shield them against this plain truth.

"It's not about being the hero of your people, but of your own life. Think of what Jessica's life must have been like before the event, before the onset of her profound disenchantment. She must have been a strong, forceful person, accustomed to carving her way through the world; willful, self-determined, someone we'd all respect. Then, after the event, she lets go. Unconditional surrender. Not mine, but *Thy* will be done. Brahma is the charioteer. She releases the tiller and lets the ship of her life find its own course, calm in the understanding that it will sink or sail. Either way, resolution."

Any time I talk about interesting stuff, I have to wonder how it's being received. It looks like I'm talking to people, but what I'm really trying to do is get past the ego to the little bastard in each of them. That's the challenge. That's what makes it interesting. Can these people be looking at this diagram and listening to Jessica's story and *not* be spurred to a higher level of awakeness by it? Probably not, but my guess is that they'll experience a few solemn hours of serious reflection before allowing themselves to get swept back into the distracting minutiae of their lives. Their little bastards might try to reawaken them to this later on, but by then ego will have seized upon it like white blood cells swarming an invasive microbe that threatens the organism, and tonight's penetrating insights will be tomorrow's mildly interesting spiritual anecdote.

I indicate the sharply angled upward line.

"This is a second childhood. This is where she learns what she is and how she relates to her surroundings, just like a child discovering herself and her world."

"Is she paralyzed?"

"No. She wore something called a halo—she calls it a stabilizing mechanical contraption—for months, but even now, a dozen years later, her road to recovery continues." This causes some sympathetic groans. "You remember that in her Mass of Men days she entered the healthcare profession. She had an urge to help people, to heal, but found that the course she had chosen didn't fulfill this desire. Some of you might be familiar with shamanism; with the ordeal a person undergoes to become a shaman and the way that the shaman is henceforth set apart from the tribe," again I indicate the line behind me. "There are no shamans on the Mass of Men line. This whole thing she's going through is her process of becoming a shaman, a true healer. She doesn't get to be a healer because the gods bestow powers upon her, but through the prolonged, rigorous, all-consuming struggle of her own self-healing. See what I mean? You don't teleport up the mountain, you climb. Becoming a shaman, an authentic healer, invariably entails a mortal crisis, a break from the old ways and rebirth into new ways. This is what happened with Jessica. Through years of effort and struggle to regain her former health and stamina, she became a *true* healer; true as opposed to that system of healthcare that she found to be a bureaucratic nightmare; as opposed to those doctors she rejected and the approach to health they represented. I don't think anyone here will have too much trouble seeing that our modern healthcare system is not one of genuine healers."

The group responds with nods and murmurs of assent. I point to the last segment of line: Life.

"Here's where Jessica's real education began, not an education of books and lectures, but of her own body, her own life. She had to learn a new way of living and of learning. Over the next decade she worked with many types of healers," I refer to the letter, "'chiropractors, osteopaths, myotherapists, cranio-sacral therapists, acupuncturists, many kinds of energy healers, many neuromuscular therapists, therapeutic yoga practitioners, neo-shamans, homeopaths, and many more. I knew that my healing was *my* responsibility, *my* process. I traveled all over the country and in every situation I was a participant and a student, not just a patient. I took what I needed from each and moved on, following my inner guidance rather than prescribed courses of treatment, and deepening my powers of intuitive awareness. I learned about energy and emotion; that body, mind and spirit are not three things, but one. My freeform course of treatment worked superbly as I always seemed to move effortlessly into just the right thing at just the right time. My healing went far beyond recovering from the accident. I was able to correct many problems and rid myself of many physical and emotional toxins I was harboring, so that my health is probably closer to perfect now than it's been since I was a small child, maybe ever.'"

I point to the Life line and draw a red circle around the arrow at the end of it.

"There is no final destination," I say. "Her journey continues to this day. Now she's a genuine healer. Her practice has clients all over the world. Her journey has brought her to this place of mastery and service and growth, and even now that journey continues. She says she realized that her own healing was her own responsibility, and that's a huge step for anyone to take. We might equate surrender with abdication of self-responsibility, but it's really just the opposite. It's where we dispense with intermediaries like priests and doctors and government, and take our lives into our own hands. She says in the letter; 'My accident might seem like one of the worst things that can happen, but for me it was the best thing and I look back on it with a gratitude that is beyond any words to describe. I look back over my life and there's nothing I would change. I am truly blessed.'"

✦

Afterward, I'm on the steps in front of the church again. Most everyone has gone. I'm busy writing down notes from the evening, my habit after most dialogues. Curtis has gone to get the jeep. Megan passes without noticing me.

"Megan," I say. "Got a minute?"

"Oh, hi," she says. "Yes, of course."

"I thought more about what you asked in the PR meeting; the living in the moment business."

"Oh," she says warily. "You did?"

"You know what it sounds like to me? I'm just gonna share an opinion with you. I'm not saying I'm right or anything, but I do want to say first that what I'm about to say isn't meant in any flippant or disrespectful way. I actually mean it in a very respectful way. Well, respectful to dogs, anyway."

"To *dogs?*" she says, her tone making me wish I'd just left this alone, but I wanted to try this out on her and see how it played.

"Yeah, this probably sounds, well, I don't know how it sounds, but the way I figure it, dogs are the most advanced beings on the planet. They're fully, uh, self-realized. They possess unconditional love. They forgive instantly. They're empathetic and sympathetic. They're incapable of guile or dishonesty. They're always in the moment, not carrying the past or fretting about the future. Everything's always new and wonderful. Every place is always the best place to be."

I'm not getting any response, so I continue.

"I say they're the most advanced beings and I mean that by *our* standards; human standards. If you think about the qualities you'd like to possess, the ideal qualities—unconditional love, loyalty, devotion, unwavering friendship, forgiveness, selflessness, sincerity, being fully present in the moment, happiness—qualities we uphold as the loftiest ideals to which we might aspire, they look very much like, you know, a good dog; dog consciousness. Of course," I add, "by those same ideal standards, humans are far and away the *least* evolved beings on the planet."

She smirks at that, a good sign.

"So, anyway, that's what your comments made me think of. Do dogs have a Buddha nature? Dogs *are* Buddha nature. We don't need books and teachers and philosophies; if you want to learn from a great spiritual master, get a dog, *they're* the real Zen masters. Like I say, I don't want to offend you, I really mean this in the most—"

She puts a hand on my arm and I gratefully shut up. She's a dog person, she tells me. She understands. She has a Cavalier King Charles Spaniel, her close companion for more than a decade, who is currently near the end of his life. She already knows that what I'm saying is true, she says, but she'd never made the connection. Once I started saying it, she saw it right away. We sit on the steps together for the next hour and share happy and sad stories about the enlightened beings we have known.

29. The Bird's Nest

> The person is a very small thing. Actually it is a
> composite, it cannot be said to exist by itself.
> Unperceived, it is just not there. It is but the shadow of
> the mind, the sum total of memories. Pure being is
> reflected in the mirror of the mind, as knowing. What is
> known takes the shape of a person, based on memory
> and habit. It is but a shadow, or a projection of the
> knower onto the screen of the mind.
>
> —*Nisargadatta Maharaj*

EGO IS A BIRD'S NEST, haphazardly collected and carelessly placed, shaped by every bit of debris and every breeze that has ever passed its way. Once you start tearing it apart, you'll actually find very little to identify with, and even less that was consciously placed there by you.

And even then, you who? The self that takes part in the creation and development of self was not itself the product of self, but of countless non-self agencies and events, so what is self, really? You can try to take control of your self, try to make some sense of it, organize it, but all you can really do is tidy up on the surface. Some egos are more cluttered, some less, but the idea that a true self lurks within the clutter is just one of the little vanities that keeps us walking in small, purposeful circles. There's no such thing as true self.

Realizing that you have no idea who you are is the beginning of finding out who you are. The idea of the individual self, valid and separate, unravels very quickly under any serious scrutiny. All beliefs do. What takes time and effort is becoming the person who chooses to put the idea of self under such scrutiny, and making sense of what's left after the belief is gone.

Jed, what you call the First Step, that breakdown I suffered at your house, is nothing so innocuous as a step at all. It's a nuclear holocaust of the self – a personal Armageddon. A post-apocalyptic nightmare metaphor feels in some respects so accurate that an actual post-apocalyptic nightmare would seem like a vain pretender. This is real and everything else is, as you say, just an image flickering on the wall. All I am is a frightened little bundle of opinions and memories and desires. That's all anyone is. I'm just amazed that everyone isn't like me, doing what I'm doing, ripping away their bullshit as fast as they can. I guess that's what being asleep means; living with it. I wish I could rip open my ribcage and pull out my heart and just be done with it. But no, that would be too easy.

Even now, I wonder if the First Step isn't the only step and the rest of the process is just a matter of wandering through the barren landscape sifting through debris, identifying bodies and taking note of their passing. Acknowledging. Grieving. Moving on.

Is this just some poetic bullshit? I have to watch myself at all times so I don't lapse into schoolgirl sentimentality. But no, this is as close as I can get to saying what this is like; a post-apocalyptic landscape, ruined, desolate, hopeless. My ambitions, my desires, my connections to people, my hopes, my dreams, my beliefs, the very things that I considered the very essence of me, are now reduced to hollow lifeless corpses, so dead it's like they were never alive, so fragile, they collapse in heaps of ash when touched by a gaze. I come across more of them every day. "Oh, there are my career ambitions. They were such a big part of me, so important. Funny I didn't notice them missing. Now I can't even remember what they really were or why I really had them. I can't even imagine having such a thing as a career ambition now." "Oh, there are my girlish childhood dreams; man, wedding, house, babies. Was I that little girl? I no longer feel that connection, so it doesn't really feel like a loss." "Good lord, my views, my tastes, my preferences. Did I really haul that crap around with me?" That's how it is every day as I uncover more of these aspects of my former self. Some greater, some lesser. I don't grieve for any of them, even those I held most dear. I simply mark their passing – dry-eyed, shell-shocked – and move on.

I walk through this scorched land day after day, using this writing process to make sense of the carnage; to process my losses. What I fear most, though, isn't what I'll find among the dead, but among the survivors. There are survivors, I know. I have a sense of them; dark, formless things. It's petrifying to even think about this. There are things roaming in this devastated landscape of self that I am going to have to hunt down and kill; things that a nuclear blast couldn't destroy. I have no illusions about this. My sanity is so marginal now that I've thought on several occasions of submitting myself for a seven-day psychiatric evaluation. Oh yes, I've looked into it. I've made the calls. The number is in my cellphone's memory. They would understand nothing of what I'm going through, of course, but I feel like one big exposed nerve and the idea of being doped into oblivion has an alarmingly seductive appeal.

We need the boundaries ego provides. They're a necessary part of life in the amusement park. Self is the complex, shifting set of dimensions that give us shape and form and which distinguish us from other shapes and forms. The amusement park isn't come-as-you-are, it has a dress code. It's a costume party, and who you come as doesn't matter, only that you come as someone. You can't come as no one.

Julie is in the park and has slipped off into a quiet corner in order to divest herself of the costume she wears. No simple feat, this, as the wearer has no hands to use or will to use them. It is effectively the costume itself which must summon the will to ruthlessly rip itself away. Ego must slay ego. Only ego can. Who else? Physical suicide is just a shadow of this true self-destruction.

Opinions! Jesus, where did I get all those idiotic opinions? I wore them like a little girl wears her mother's make-up and costume jewelry. "Look at me! I have a unique opinion! Look at my wonderful opinion! I think this, I think that. Look how special I am! I'll admire yours if you admire mine!" I know this is just a normal growing pain, but seriously, what a buffoon! What a fool! I now despise all adornment, all affectation, all cosmetic enhancement. All I want to see is the real thing. The beauty is in the real thing; the thing itself. I would rather look at carrion at the feast, a lone cloud, a fly on the back of my hand, than all the paintings in the Louvre. More poetic bullshit? Maybe, but I find myself happily looking at things that once seemed like nothings. I'm changing and my world changes with me. I am coming to understand Whitman directly. I don't see what could be more beautiful than water dripping from a rusty pipe. I used to hate my feet, now time seems to stand still as I look at them and I see the same perfection to be seen in everything. I wonder if this isn't really the one thing Whitman said again and again, "A morning-glory at my window satisfies me more than the metaphysics of books." Everywhere is this perfection like a clear note sweetly sounded, and the only thing that can ruin it and make it sour is the attempt to improve it, and the only thing that does that is ego; the false self ever strikes the false note.

Fine, it's poetic bullshit, but it's true, so fuck it.

✦

Is it possible that I could now give birth to a child and view it with indifference? It doesn't *seem* possible, but I don't see how it could be otherwise. People think that the connection between two beings takes place at a deep level, but I wonder if it isn't just a deeper level of the outer garment. Must be. What else? Without that garment, there is no contact point. Or maybe one becomes one single undifferentiating contact point, fluidly, dynamically connected with all that is. I don't know. I don't think so.

Something has always stuck with me from one of Castenada's books. As I recall, Don Juan's nephew was killed in a motorcycle accident, and Don Juan was able to shift between two aspects of himself, one wracked by grief for the loss of a loved one, but then switching out of it, not over the course of days or hours, but in an instant. Just like snapping his fingers, he shifted into his impersonal self and observed the death of his nephew with perfect indifference. I recall thinking that was some sorcerer bullshit when I read it however long ago, but now it's not the indifferent part or the switching part I have doubts about, but the feeling part. Does that stay? Can I keep it? It doesn't seem possible.

You mentioned this Jed. You told me about the place in the *Tao* where it says there is no place for death to enter, and in the *Gita* where it says fire cannot burn nor wind make it dry. That's about this, but there's more to be said about it. The part where death enters is also where life enters. There's no place for another being to connect with. I don't understand all this even in theory. Humans connect ego-to-ego. The heart is a part of the ego. The ego is the external self, the false self, the self that doesn't survive this awakening. I remember literally hundreds of discussions by spiritual seekers and teachers, and I remember reading about this in books and magazine articles, but I don't remember it ever making sense, and now that I'm here, now that it's me, it still doesn't. So I ask again and again, if I had a child, would I bond with it even though I no longer have a bonding surface? Would I love my own child? I am certain the answer is no and I am certain the answer can't be no.

In taking the First Step, Julie has effectively stepped from an airplane without a parachute. Now she's in freefall. She may fear that she's going to suffer a bloody impact with the planet hurtling up to greet her, but that's just a residual fear pattern that no longer applies. At the precise moment of impact, the planet will disappear, and nothing will take its place. Her freefall won't end, but it will no longer feel like falling because there will no longer be anything to reference it against; no wind, no whoosh, no fast-approaching planet. This is where dual awareness ends. From then on she will live in boundless awareness, never again able to differentiate between self and non-self. Abiding non-dual awareness.

If she has a baby, will she love it? It's an interesting question and gives rise to others. In a sort of tongue-in-cheek way I've said that a massive head wound could probably return me to some form of pre-realized state. Could parenthood do it? I don't know. Like Julie, I don't see how it could. Unlike Julie, I *do* see how it couldn't.

I bought a copy of the screenplay for The Mahabharata by Jean-Claude Carriére and Peter Brook. I love reading it. I've already ruined it with dog-eared pages and penned notes. In the Gita part, Krishna tells Arjuna he must rise up, free from hope, and throw himself into the battle. That phrase has seared itself into my mind: Free from hope. Abandon all hope ye who enter here. The battle is absolute. It would be so nice if it weren't. It would be so nice if I could convince myself that by meditating for six hours a day, or by prostrating myself at the feet of a master, or by renouncing something I like, I could change the truth. This isn't what I signed up for. I find myself seeking distraction, diversion, anything that might allow me a way out of this, but this is consuming me from the inside and never eases up for a second. There is no way out and the part of me that wishes there were is the cause of my suffering.

❖

I always heard and believed that the spiritual journey was one of peace and inner equanimity, of love and light, tranquility and acceptance. Well, that's not the journey I'm on. Mine is a maddening cacophony of dark emotions; a raging din of anger, hatred, contempt, scorn and disgust, much of it directed at myself.

I wrote for ten straight hours last night. I barely remember it. I looked at what I wrote this morning and it's like puke, like emotional vomit, like I just had this tremendous amount of vile, wretched awfulness in me and it erupted out and just kept pouring out as if from a bottomless source. It's not bottomless, I know it's not, but knowing rationally isn't the same as *knowing* knowing.

❖

I'm making progress. It's so ephemeral in one sense and so perfectly specific in another. There's no stopping, I see that. You can't pause, can't stop to rest, can't exert any control over the speed of things. One thing finishes and the next things starts right up. Layer after layer, no standing still. I do my breathing and try to make a point of getting decent sleep but the only way that really happens is when I go to bed exhausted. I have no schedule anymore. I sleep when I sleep. I'm all over the place. My energy is good but I look like hell. Read, write, walk, sleep.; that's all I do How could anyone go through this with people around? Or holding down a normal job and a life? Or without this writing process? They'd have to try to exert some control over it and from where I'm looking, no way. It couldn't be done. This is a wildfire, not a backyard barbecue. They'd end up in the nuthouse for sure.

30. Distrust all honest fellows!

The words of U.G. Krishnamurti: Part III

> I'll sing this song the rest of my life until
> I drop dead; whether anybody listens to it
> or not is of no importance to me.
>
> *–U.G. Krishnamurti*

The third and final selection of excerpts from U.G. Krishnamurti.

IF ANYONE MAKES YOU BELIEVE you can get somewhere, he's taking you for a ride. He may be honest. Distrust all honest fellows! Throw them out! There is no one who is honest in this field. No outside agency can help you...

I wish you the best of luck. I know very well that it is not something that you or anybody else can get or that anybody can give. I can't give it. If there is somebody who promises, he is just promising, and he is going to take you for a long ride. He is just kidding you. He cannot deliver the goods, so he says "Next life" or "Ten years hence" – he is safe.

❖

You can't be interested in this. How can you be interested in this? – that is my question. How can you be interested in this kind of a thing? What you are interested in is a totally different thing, fancy stuff, fantasy. You may indulge in all kinds of fantasy – that's your affair. If this is not fantasy, you will be interested in some other kind of fantasy. How can you be interested in liquidating yourself? –

that is my question. All that you know – 'you' as you know yourself, 'you' as you experience yourself – is interested in continuity. It knows all the tricks: you cannot beat that.

✦

I am not interested in the whole field of self-expression, getting in touch with one's feelings, overcoming inhibitions and so on; I respond to what people come to see me about, the natural state. If people are interested in psychological change, so-called consciousness expansion and all that, let them go to encounter groups, or see psychiatrists and engage in what I call the 'Freudian fraud'. In the end their so-called growth will not bring them happiness and neither will their improved sex lives (if their sex lives improve); at best they will simply have learned to be unhappy in a new and richer way.

✦

Everything is okay with me. If you have a million dollars and eight girl friends, that's okay with me. If you are lonely and disagreeable and penniless and dying of cancer, that also is okay with me. I am perfectly happy with everything as it is. I am happy with misery, poverty and death; I am also happy with wealth and psychological fulfillment.

✦

{Asked about Buddha and Christ.}

Why do you bother about those fellows? They are dead. You should pitch them in the river. And yet you don't; you keep listening to someone (it makes no difference whom), and you keep hoping that somehow, tomorrow or the next day, by listening more and more, you will get off the merry-go-round. You listen to your parents and to your teachers at school, and they tell you to be good and dutiful and not be angry and so on, and that doesn't do any good, and so you go and learn how to do Yoga, and then presently some old chap comes along and tells you to be choicelessly aware. Or maybe you find someone in the 'holy business', and he does miracles – he produces some trinkets out of the air, and you fall for it – or perhaps he touches you, and you see some blue light or green light or yellow light or God knows what, and you hope he will help you experience enlightenment. But he cannot help you. It is not something that can be captured, contained or given expression to. I do not know if you see the utter helplessness of the situation, and how, if anyone thinks he can help you, he will inevitably mislead you, and the less phoney he is, the more powerful he is, the more enlightened he is, the more misery and mischief he will create for you.

❖

But you are waiting for something to happen or for some grace to descend upon you – you are still depending upon some outside agency. I can tell you that there is no power outside of you – no power. This does not mean that you have all the attributes that you read about of the super-duper gods; but there is no power outside of you. If there is any power in this universe, it is in you.

❖

There is no self to be realized. The whole religious structure that has been built on this foundation collapses because there is nothing there to realize. To me, J. Krishnamurti *(here, U.G. refers to Jiddu Krishnamurti; an acquaintance, not a relation)* is playing exactly the same game as all those ugly saints in the market whom we have in the world today. Krishnamurti's teaching is phony baloney. There is nothing to his teaching at all, and he cannot produce anything at all. A person may listen to him for sixty, seventy or a hundred years, but nothing will ever happen to that man, because the whole thing is phony... Here's a mere wordsmith. He has created a new trap... These gurus are the worst egotists the world has ever seen. All gurus are welfare organizations providing petty experiences to their followers. The guru game is a profitable industry: try and make two million dollars a year any other way. Even J. Krishnamurti, who claims he has no possessions, is the president of an eighty-million-dollar empire.

❖

What prevents you from understanding what you want to understand is this very thing which you are using to understand things. This is not my teaching or anybody's teaching, but this is the only thing: You are trying to understand something through an instrument which is not the instrument to understand.

❖

QUESTIONER: *Yes. But if—*

There is no 'yes, but'. You can't say 'yes' and begin the next sentence with 'but'. There is no 'but' there. If the 'yes' is a real 'yes', that releases the thing there – the 'yes' fades into nothingness and then what is there begins to express itself. If you say 'but', you are giving continuity to that dead structure of thought, experience and hope. 'Yes!' is the thing that blows the whole structure apart.

❖

As long as you follow somebody else's path, the path is the product of thought, so it is actually not a new path; it's the same old path, and you are playing the same old game in a new way. It is not a new game; it is the same old game that you are playing all the time, but you think you are playing a new game. When you see the absurdity of what you are doing, maybe you'll realize "What the hell have I been doing for thirty years, forty years, fifty years!"

❖

One thing I must say. This is not born out of thinking. This is not a logically ascertained premise that I am putting forth. These are just words springing up from their natural source without any thought, without any thought structure. So take it or leave it! You will be better off if you leave it.

❖

Your teacher must go, it doesn't matter who the teacher is. The very thing that you are reading – that's the very thing you must be free from.

❖

QUESTIONER: *Sir, what is your message?*

It is quite simple. You are not going to get anything here. You are wasting your time. Pack up and go! That is my message. I have nothing to give; you have nothing to take. If you continue to sit there, you are wasting your time. The one thing you have to do is get up and go.

31. Man, Deprogram Thyself

> "Until I was twenty-five, I had no development at all.
> From my twenty-fifth year I date my life. Three weeks
> have scarcely passed, at any time between then & now,
> that I have not unfolded within myself. But I feel that I
> am now come to the inmost leaf of the bulb, and that
> shortly the flower must fall to the mould."

> —*Herman Melville in a letter*
> *to Nathaniel Hawthorne*

J ULIE USES ALL THE TEACHERS and teachings her journalistic career put her in touch with as an important part of her process. Many of those people and their ideas resonated with her, found a place to dwell within her, and became a part of her, so that much of what she's doing now involves discovering where and why these resonations occurred and, by so doing, determining the contours of her own false self.

One teacher Julie spent time with ascribed great importance to introspective self-discovery techniques such as journaling, group dialogues and sessions with the teacher as a means of clearing out the internal debris that "keeps us from knowing our true self and pristinely mirroring the divine love of the universe." I'm describing it poorly because all I have to go on is Julie's delightfully lunatic ravings, but the point is that because the teaching found a place inside her, Julie can now find that same place and use the teachings to which she originally responded as a surface against which to pit herself. In this way, many of her battles are fought against "real" opponents, visibly personified, and made practically assailable:

> All that most maddens and torments; all that stirs up
> the lees of things; all truth with malice in it; all that
> cracks the sinews and cakes the brain; all the subtle
> demonisms of life and thought; all evil, to crazy Ahab,
> were visibly personified, and made practically assailable
> in Moby Dick.

Because the subtle demonisms of life and thought can be as form-less and shifting as vapor, the person on a search and destroy mission must have a way of making them practically assailable. Spiritual Autolysis—trying to write something true and keeping at it until you do—is the best possible way of identifying and eradicating our falseness because the process of writing minimizes the weaknesses and maximizes the strengths of the intellect. Nothing false can survive illumination by a steady and focused mind.

> Several years ago I was assigned to interview a well-known teacher and author of several books. I was with him for three weeks in Vancouver and Seattle. He spoke knowledgeably and convincingly about the enlightened perspective, the enlightened path, and the enlightened humanity of the not-too-distant future. Whenever he spoke I just lapped it up, like he was blessing me with his words. I sat there taking my notes, nodding and smiling, totally uncritical, totally absorbed, totally taken in by his saintly appearance and reputation. I look back on it now and shudder at my gullibility. He talked about how the enlightened perspective was one of compassion and unconditional love. I'd love to do that interview over now! Enlightened perspective? Compassion? How could I have been so catatonic that I just sat there and let him get away with that? Some journalist! What a brainwashed sheep I was! Put that man in front of me now. I laugh to think of it. I feel as if my gaze alone would be sufficient to dissipate him, or that I could step right through him and meet no resistance. I wouldn't have to speak, I could destroy him simply by seeing him clearly.

Which is effectively what she's doing now; destroying thoughts with thought, seeing things clearly. It helps to put a face on the enemy of the moment, but her rage is not against any of her former teachers. It's against her own attachment to them, which is inside her; a part of her. Of the several hundred battles she will fight and win, more than a dozen, from what I can tell, will be against spiritual teachers whose ideas have taken up residence within her including, eventually, me.

"Man, know thyself," is bullshit. "Man, deprogram thyself!" That's what it's all about. Even as I write this I feel like my soul is twisted with some dark mass of hatred and resentment, but I also know that that's how it should be; that's how the process works. Every step is like a slow-motion explosion; starting as a spark, growing in intensity, blooming into a violent fiery ball, and finally erupting into a purifying, all-consuming white-hot inferno, destroying everything and leaving nothing where there once stood a mountain. I mean, again and again, every few days, that's what this is. Boom! Boom! Boom! Each step starts as an itch, grows into an agony, and erupts into a conflagration. Every molecule that burns is a molecule of me. What is being burned in this process is the false me, and every step is its own protracted battle. This is no mere intellectual challenge. I get past one obstruction and I have a moment's peace before the next starts coming into view. It starts out small and distant, but grows larger and larger until it looms impossibly large before me. These are my demons, but they weren't demons when I let them in, they were cuddly little bundles of warmth and happiness and safety. But now that I want to get to the heart of things, they are tenacious little monsters and each must be ruthlessly slain. There is no choice, no decision to make. I kill them and dissect them and I see them for exactly what they are; the web of self I have spun to shield me from reality.

Everything I do to assert and define self is truly to deny no-self. Nothing is so ridiculous or petty that it doesn't trace back to the one root from which all my choices and actions stem. All of life reduces to the projection of the false and the denial of the true. The false self must be constantly asserted, like a leaky balloon that we have to keep blowing into. But what if we stop blowing into it? What then? What then? We'll see what's left when life support is unplugged. That's how we find out what's real, who we really are and aren't. How simple it is, really. This doesn't require philosophy or religion or white-bearded old men. It just requires honesty.

What took me nearly two years to accomplish Julie might do in much less time. I came into the process a spiritual and philosophical illiterate. I had an advantage in that I had long since determined that reality had no basis in reality, but I didn't have the benefit, as Julie does, of having representatives of the world's great systems of thought already inhabiting my mind, neatly lined up, smallest to largest, for me to practice my swordsmanship on.

I no longer transfer my authority to another. I do not defer or relinquish. Now I'm seeing it for myself and I see that nothing is okay. It's the exact opposite of okay. What can possibly be okay if your life is a lie? If who you are is a fiction? It's that simple. What else matters? What else is there? There are no winners. There is no success. If your life is a lie, then who you are and what you are is a lie. There's no response to that. You either roll over and go back to sleep or you start chewing through the ropes.

Also unlike Julie, I didn't have a Jed McKenna. I didn't find anyone like she's found in me. My experience was one of inventing and discovering the process as I went. It is because I did go through that, and because discovering the process was so much a part of my process, that I was able to become the guy that wrote the book that makes the whole ordeal a bit less of an ordeal for Julie and others who want to get to the First Step and make sense of what comes after, or just steer clear of the whole mess.

> How many people do I know or know of who've put all their spiritual eggs in the meditation basket? How many who think that all their time spent in meditation is adding up to something? Building up in them? Moving them closer to something? I know people who've meditated their butts off for years and where are they now? Right where they started. It can't happen that way. I know it can't because I know what it is. Meditation equals medication. It's like medicating patients in the nuthouse, or better yet, convincing them to medicate themselves, and to ratchet up the dosage anytime they feel the slightest twinge of spiritual dyspepsia. Nurse Ratched! Someday I'll reread Ken Kesey's *One Flew Over the Cuckoo's Nest* with very different eyes.

The heretic theme appears occasionally in film and literature. Robin Williams in *Dead Poets Society* is an example. The movie *Pleasantville* is a happy tale of heresy. The town of Pleasantville is frozen in a black and white, 1950's Mayberryesque sensibility. Then along comes the unwitting heretic from a larger world of full color and open minds, where the roads don't circle around but keep on going. His awakeness leads to the gradual awakening of the community. There is resistance, but the townsfolk don't burn him at the stake and, in the end, everyone embraces the new paradigm. *One Flew Over the Cuckoo's Nest* is about the same thing, a tale of heresy, but a little less cheery as regards the fate of the heretic and the fruits of heresy, and written, I should add, by the heretic who wrote "Further" on the front of a bus and drove it straight up the ass of a sleeping giant.

> I'd rather burn in hell now and forever than to continue living in

that suffocating prison of lies. You hear the word ego and you think of psychology and personality, but ego isn't personality structure, it's the structure of confinement. That and nothing else. *Nothing* else. What did you say in the book, Jed? "There's nothing to say about it, nothing to feel about it, nothing to know about it." Of course! Of course! There's not one single thing that matters about the dream except that you're in a dream. Wake up!

I understand fear now. I know what it is, how total it is. You can look at yourself and not see it because you don't see anything that's *not* it. I know that I wasn't *afraid*, I was *fear*.

What is Christianity but a two-bit protection racket? Good cop/bad cop. The son, our blessed saviour, saving us from what? From his psychotic freakshow father who's hellbent on burning us alive forever. What kind of twisted fuck thinks this stuff up? What kind of pathetic slob falls for it? My kind. Me. I did. I wasn't above it, I wasn't immune. And now that I'm flushing this poison from my system, I can see the secret of its hold over us.

I know, Jed, I know. Whatever is is right. I know that, I *do*, but Jesus Christ! Is it any wonder that the human race is spiritually retarded? The opiate of the masses, they say about religion, but it's not, not really, because no one is immune. No one is outside of this opium dream looking in at the dopefiends. The rich and powerful are every bit as narcotized as the poor and weak, the atheist as much as the devout. I'm starting to see how deep this separation runs, how pervasive it truly is.

Ego as a structure of confinement is an apt analogy, but slightly misleading. Jails wall in, ego walls out. A minor distinction, perhaps, but a critical one. Whatever's out there isn't holding us in, we're holding it out. We are our own keepers. We can open the door and walk out whenever we want. Of course, the thing one leaves isn't just the prison of self but self itself, so the freedom thus won is something of a booby prize.

Julie may rage against the fear that confines us in one email and display a calm understanding and respect for it in the next. Fear looks like evil when you're trying to escape from it, but it looks very sensible and necessary when you're not. You can say fear and ignorance are bad and that Maya is evil, but that's a low-level perspective. For this whole dualistic universe thing to work, it's important that everyone doesn't just go wandering off; that they stay on stage and play their role. Fear is the glue that holds the whole thing together and keeps everyone in character. Julie understands that, intellectually at least.

> I was out walking today and I was so overcome by happiness that I had to skip. *Skip!* I haven't skipped since I got interested in boys! I skipped through the woods and sang loud idiot songs and I jumped up and down on the earth so it knew I was here. Tilly came bounding along with me, leaping and yipping. I think we bonded! I suddenly realized that after more than a year of this agonizing upheaval I have absolutely nothing to show for it and that thought was just too funny! It was like the dam had burst. I have no wisdom, no knowledge, nothing to impart. All this hell and I have nothing to show for it. I have acquired nothing, gained nothing. How perfect! The word wisefool popped into my head right then and it felt perfect. What a great word! I've become so delightfully stupid that I really enjoy being with myself! I think it might be because I don't think about things too much anymore. I can't believe how much of my life I've spent in thought. Think think think all day long as if there was anything to think about. What was I thinking? When this is over I vow never to think again! Disgusting habit!

To become an adult human is like being born anew into a

unimaginably different world and having to figure out where you are and how everything works. You come to see, as Julie has, that thought, our primary method for understanding life, is really our way of walling ourselves off from it. We translate the world into our artificial language of symbols and concepts in order to avoid knowing it directly.

WHEN I HEARD the learn'd astronomer;
When the proofs, the figures, were ranged in columns
    before me;
When I was shown the charts and the diagrams, to add,
    divide, and measure them;
When I, sitting, heard the astronomer, where he lectured
    with much applause in the lecture-room,
How soon, unaccountable, I became tired and sick;
Till rising and gliding out, I wander'd off by myself,
In the mystical moist night-air, and from time to time,
Look'd up in perfect silence at the stars.

—Walt Whitman

THE WORLD IS too much with us; late and soon,
Getting and spending, we lay waste our powers:
Little we see in Nature that is ours;
We have given our hearts away, a sordid boon!
The Sea that bares her bosom to the moon;
The winds that will be howling at all hours,
And are up-gathered now like sleeping flowers;
For this, for everything, we are out of tune;
It moves us not.—Great God! I'd rather be
A Pagan suckled in a creed outworn;
So might I, standing on this pleasant lea,
Have glimpses that would make me less forlorn;
Have sight of Proteus rising from the sea;
Or hear old Triton blow his wreathed horn.

—William Wordsworth

When the intervening layer of symbols and concepts is removed, the terrain and self are seen as one and the rules of motion and navigation become radically different. This is the true but seldom-realized potential of the human being. These are the new and better senses and abilities to be mastered. We learn to accept and reject, to push and be pulled, to shape and be shaped. We learn to detect lines of flow and to follow them smoothly between and around obstructions. We learn to see patterns and merge with them. If we don't learn these things, then we're out of tune with our energetic environment and can only stumble and grope, like birds that can't fly or fish that can't swim, or like most of the people we think of as normally developed. It's a whole art and science thing, and what you are and how it works are really the same, so that learning one is learning both.

32. This is, and no mistake.

Selections from the writings of Henry David Thoreau

> In what concerns you much, do not think that
> you have companions: know that you are alone
> in the world.
>
> –H. D. Thoreau

I WENT TO THE WOODS because I wished to live deliberately, to front only the essential facts of life, and see if I could not learn what it had to teach, and not, when I came to die, discover that I had not lived. I did not wish to live what was not life, living is so dear; nor did I wish to practice resignation, unless it was quite necessary. I wanted to live deep and suck out all the marrow of life, to live so sturdily and Spartan-like as to put to rout all that was not life, to cut a broad swath and shave close, to drive life into a corner, and reduce it to its lowest terms, and, if it proved to be mean, why then to get the whole and genuine meanness of it, and publish its meanness to the world; or if it were sublime, to know it by experience, and be able to give a true account of it in my next excursion.

❖

Time is but the stream I go a-fishing in. I drink at it; but while I drink I see the sandy bottom and detect how shallow it is. Its thin current slides away, but eternity remains. I would drink deeper; fish in the sky, whose bottom is pebbly with stars. I cannot count one. I know not the first letter of the alphabet. I have always been regretting that I was not as wise as the day I was born.

❖

Men esteem truth remote, in the outskirts of the system, behind the farthest star, before Adam and after the last man. In eternity there is indeed something true and sublime. But all these times and places and occasions are now and here.

❖

Let us settle ourselves, and work and wedge our feet downward through the mud and slush of opinion, and prejudice, and tradition, and delusion, and appearance, that alluvion which covers the globe, through Paris and London, through New York and Boston and Concord, through Church and State, through poetry and philosophy and religion, till we come to a hard bottom and rocks in place, which we can call reality, and say, This is, and no mistake.

❖

If you stand right fronting and face to face to a fact, you will see the sun glimmer on both its surfaces, as if it were a scimitar, and feel its sweet edge dividing you through the heart and marrow, and so you will happily conclude your mortal career. Be it life or death, we crave only reality. If we are really dying, let us hear the rattle in our throats and feel cold in the extremities; if we are alive, let us go about our business.

❖

Shams and delusions are esteemed for soundest truths, while reality is fabulous. If men would steadily observe realities only, and not allow themselves to be deluded, life, to compare it with such things as we know, would be like a fairy tale and the Arabian Nights' Entertainments. If we respected only what is inevitable and has a right to be, music and poetry would resound along the streets. When we are unhurried and wise, we perceive that only great and worthy things have any permanent and absolute existence, that petty fears and petty pleasures are but the shadow of the reality. This is always exhilarating and sublime. By closing the eyes and slumbering, and consenting to be deceived by shows, men establish and confirm their daily life of routine and habit everywhere, which still is built on purely illusory foundations. Children, who play life, discern its true law and relations more clearly than men, who fail to live it worthily, but who think that they are wiser by experience, that is, by failure.

❖

The millions are awake enough for physical labor; but only one in a million is awake enough for effective intellectual exertion, only one in a hundred millions to a poetic or divine life. To be awake is to be alive. I have never yet met a man who was quite awake. How could I have looked him in the face?

❖

If one listens to the faintest but constant suggestions of his genius, which are certainly true, he sees not to what extremes, or even insanity, it may lead him; and yet that way, as he grows more resolute and faithful, his road lies. The faintest assured objection which one healthy man feels will at length prevail over the arguments and customs of mankind. No man ever followed his genius till it misled him. Though the result were bodily weakness, yet perhaps no one can say that the consequences were to be regretted, for these were a life in conformity to higher principles.

❖

He is the best sailor who can steer within fewest points of the wind, and exact a motive power out of the greatest obstacles.

❖

Why level downward to our dullest perception always, and praise that as common sense? The commonest sense is the sense of men asleep, which they express by snoring.

❖

There are nowadays professors of philosophy, but not philosophers. Yet it is admirable to profess because it was once admirable to live. To be a philosopher is not merely to have subtle thoughts, nor even to found a school, but so to love wisdom as to live according to its dictates, a life of simplicity, independence, magnanimity, and trust. It is to solve some of the problems of life, not only theoretically, but practically. The success of great scholars and thinkers is commonly a courtier-like success, not kingly, not manly. They make shift to live merely by conformity, practically as their fathers did, and are in no sense the progenitors of a nobler race of men.

❖

Not till we are lost, in other words, not till we have lost the world, do we begin to find ourselves, and realize where we are and the infinite extent of our relations.

❖

Books, not which afford us a cowering enjoyment, but in which each thought is of unusual daring; such as an idle man cannot read, and a timid one would not be entertained by, which even make us dangerous to existing institutions—such call I good books.

❖

I learned this, at least, by my experiment: that if one advances confidently in the direction of his dreams, and endeavors to live the life which he has imagined, he will meet with a success unexpected in common hours. He will put some things behind, will pass an invisible boundary; new, universal, and more liberal laws will begin to establish themselves around and within him; or the old laws be expanded, and interpreted in his favor in a more liberal sense, and he will live with the license of a higher order of beings. In proportion as he simplifies his life, the laws of the universe will appear less complex, and solitude will not be solitude, nor poverty poverty, nor weakness weakness.

33. The Symphony

> From beneath his slouched hat Ahab dropped
> a tear into the sea; nor did all the Pacific contain
> such wealth as that one wee drop.
>
> *—Herman Melville, Moby-Dick*

Chapter 132, The Symphony, is the true final chapter of Moby-Dick. Although the book contains three more chapters and an epilogue, this is where Ahab's final battle is fought and won. Those three concluding chapters can really be considered a very exciting wrap-up, an extended epilogue: The white whale is spotted and chased for three days. Ahab delivers his final speech and harpoons Moby Dick. The rope catches Ahab around the neck and pulls him under. Everybody dies but Ishmael.

In this chapter, The Symphony, Ahab the man takes a final look back over the life that has brought him to this end. He considers his lost humanity and sees it in the "magic glass" of Starbuck's eye. Starbuck is the first mate; a responsible Nantucketer and Quaker, a respected whaleman, a father and a husband, all things that Ahab was and, from Starbuck's perspective, could be again.

Starbuck, knowing that a dire fate awaits ship and crew, and seeing a chance to change it, pleads for Ahab to let him turn the boat for home. Ahab, at his most sentimental and vulnerable, need only give the slightest nod of his head and the cup will be taken from him. That's it. That's how close Ahab is, even at the last, to full reprieve. That's how easy it would be, at least, so it appears to Starbuck.

Fedallah sits, so to speak, on Ahab's other shoulder.

I T WAS A CLEAR STEEL-BLUE day. The firmaments of air and sea were hardly separable in that all-pervading azure; only, the pensive air was transparently pure and soft, with a woman's look, and the robust and man-like sea heaved with long, strong, lingering swells, as Samson's chest in his sleep.

Hither, and thither, on high, glided the snow-white wings of small, unspeckled birds; these were the gentle thoughts of the feminine air; but to and fro in the deeps, far down in the bottomless blue, rushed mighty leviathans, sword-fish, and sharks; and these were the strong, troubled, murderous thinkings of the masculine sea.

But though thus contrasting within, the contrast was only in shades and shadows without; those two seemed one; it was only the sex, as it were, that distinguished them.

Aloft, like a royal czar and king, the sun seemed giving this gentle air to this bold and rolling sea; even as bride to groom. And at the girdling line of the horizon, a soft and tremulous motion— most seen here at the Equator—denoted the fond, throbbing trust, the loving alarms, with which the poor bride gave her bosom away.

Tied up and twisted; gnarled and knotted with wrinkles; haggardly firm and unyielding; his eyes glowing like coals, that still glow in the ashes of ruin; untottering Ahab stood forth in the clearness of the morn; lifting his splintered helmet of a brow to the fair girl's forehead of heaven.

Oh, immortal infancy, and innocency of the azure! Invisible winged creatures that frolic all round us! Sweet childhood of air and sky! how oblivious were ye of old Ahab's close-coiled woe! But so have I seen little Miriam and Martha, laughing-eyed elves, heedlessly gambol around their old sire; sporting with the circle of singed locks which grew on the marge of that burnt-out crater of his brain.

Slowly crossing the deck from the scuttle, Ahab leaned over the side and watched how his shadow in the water sank and sank to his gaze, the more and the more that he strove to pierce the profundity.

But the lovely aromas in that enchanted air did at last seem to dispel, for a moment, the cankerous thing in his soul. That glad, happy air, that winsome sky, did at last stroke and caress him; the step-mother world, so long cruel—forbidding—now threw affectionate arms round his stubborn neck, and did seem to joyously sob over him, as if over one, that however wilful and erring, she could yet find it in her heart to save and to bless. From beneath his slouched hat Ahab dropped a tear into the sea; nor did all the Pacific contain such wealth as that one wee drop.

Starbuck saw the old man; saw him, how he heavily leaned over the side; and he seemed to hear in his own true heart the measureless sobbing that stole out of the centre of the serenity around. Careful not to touch him, or be noticed by him, he yet drew near to him, and stood there.

Ahab turned.

"Starbuck!"

"Sir."

"Oh, Starbuck! it is a mild, mild wind, and a mild looking sky. On such a day—very much such a sweetness as this—I struck my first whale—a boy-harpooneer of eighteen! Forty—forty—forty years ago!—ago! Forty years of continual whaling! forty years of privation, and peril, and storm-time! forty years on the pitiless sea! for forty years has Ahab forsaken the peaceful land, for forty years to make war on the horrors of the deep! Aye and yes, Starbuck, out of those forty years I have not spent three ashore. When I think of this life I have led; the desolation of solitude it has been; the masoned, walled-town of a Captain's exclusiveness, which admits but small entrance to any sympathy from the green country without—oh, weariness! heaviness! Guinea-coast slavery of solitary command!— when I think of all this; only half-suspected, not so keenly known to me before—and how for forty years I have fed upon dry salted fare— fit emblem of the dry nourishment of my soul!—when the poorest landsman has had fresh fruit to his daily hand, and broken the world's fresh bread, to my mouldy crusts—away, whole oceans away, from that young girl-wife I wedded past fifty, and sailed for Cape Horn the next day, leaving but one dent in my marriage pillow—wife? wife?—rather a widow with her husband alive! Aye, I widowed that poor girl when I married her, Starbuck; and then, the madness, the frenzy, the boiling blood and the smoking brow, with which, for a thousand lowerings old Ahab has furiously, foamingly chased his prey—more a demon than a man!—aye, aye! what a forty years' fool—fool—old fool, has old Ahab been! Why this strife of the chase? why weary, and palsy the arm at the oar, and the iron, and the lance? how the richer or better is Ahab now? Behold. Oh, Starbuck! is it not hard, that with this weary load I bear, one poor leg should have been snatched from under me? Here, brush this old hair aside; it blinds me, that I seem to weep. Locks so grey did never grow but from out some ashes! But do I look very old, so very, very old, Starbuck? I feel deadly faint, bowed, and humped, as though I were Adam, staggering beneath the piled centuries since Paradise. God! God! God!—crack my heart!—stave my brain!—mockery! mockery! bitter, biting mockery of grey hairs, have I lived enough joy to wear ye; and seem and feel thus intolerably old? Close! stand close to me, Starbuck; let me look into a human eye; it is better than to gaze into sea or sky; better than to gaze upon God. By the green land; by the bright hearth-stone! this is the magic glass, man; I see my wife and my child in thine eye. No, no; stay on board, on board!—lower not when I do; when branded Ahab gives chase to Moby Dick. That hazard shall not be thine. No, no! not with the far away home I see in that eye!"

"Oh, my Captain! my Captain! noble soul! grand old heart, after all! why should any one give chase to that hated fish! Away with me! let us fly these deadly waters! let us home! Wife and child, too, are Starbuck's—wife and child of his brotherly, sisterly, play-fellow youth; even as thine, sir, are the wife and child of thy loving, longing, paternal old age! Away! let us away!—this instant let me alter the course! How cheerily, how hilariously, O my Captain, would we bowl on our way to see old Nantucket again! I think, sir, they have some such mild blue days, even as this, in Nantucket."

"They have, they have. I have seen them—some summer days in the morning. About this time—yes, it is his noon nap now—the boy vivaciously wakes; sits up in bed; and his mother tells him of me, of cannibal old me; how I am abroad upon the deep, but will yet come back to dance him again."

"'Tis my Mary, my Mary herself! She promised that my boy, every morning, should be carried to the hill to catch the first glimpse of his father's sail! Yes, yes! no more! it is done! we head for Nantucket! Come, my Captain, study out the course, and let us away! See, see! the boy's face from the window! the boy's hand on the hill!"

But Ahab's glance was averted; like a blighted fruit tree he shook, and cast his last, cindered apple to the soil.

"What is it, what nameless, inscrutable, unearthly thing is it; what cozening, hidden lord and master, and cruel, remorseless emperor commands me; that against all natural lovings and long-ings, I so keep pushing, and crowding, and jamming myself on all the time; recklessly making me ready to do what in my own proper, natural heart, I durst not so much as dare? Is Ahab, Ahab? Is it I, God, or who, that lifts this arm? But if the great sun move not of himself; but is as an errand-boy in heaven; nor one single star can revolve, but by some invisible power; how then can this one small heart beat; this one small brain think thoughts; unless God does that beating, does that thinking, does that living, and not I. By heaven, man, we are turned round and round in this world, like yonder wind-lass, and Fate is the handspike. And all the time, lo! that smiling sky, and this unsounded sea! Look! see yon Albicore! who put it into him to chase and fang that flying-fish? Where do murderers go, man!

Who's to doom, when the judge himself is dragged to the bar? But it is a mild, mild wind, and a mild looking sky; and the air smells now, as if it blew from a far-away meadow; they have been making hay somewhere under the slopes of the Andes, Starbuck, and the mowers are sleeping among the new-mown hay. Sleeping? Aye, toil we how we may, we all sleep at last on the field. Sleep? Aye, and rust amid greenness; as last year's scythes flung down, and left in the half-cut swaths—Starbuck!"

But blanched to a corpse's hue with despair, the Mate had stolen away.

Ahab crossed the deck to gaze over on the other side; but started at two reflected, fixed eyes in the water there. Fedallah was motionlessly leaning over the same rail.

34. The Price of Truth

> The port would fain give succor; the port is pitiful; in
> the port is safety, comfort, hearthstone, supper, warm
> blankets, friends, all that's kind to our mortalities. But
> in that gale, the port, the land, is that ship's direst jeop-
> ardy; she must fly all hospitality; one touch of land,
> though it but graze the keel, would make her shudder
> through and through. With all her might she crowds all
> sail off shore; in so doing, fights 'gainst the very winds
> that fain would blow her homeward; seeks all the lashed
> sea's landlessness again; for refuge's sake forlornly
> rushing into peril; her only friend her bitterest foe!
>
> *—Herman Melville, Moby-Dick*

JULIE WILL EMERGE FROM HER chrysalis exactly as enlightened as the most enlightened person that ever was. No more, no less. Onlookers may assume there are levels of awakeness, so that the Buddha is supremely enlightened at the high end and newcomer Julie is at the bottom, just starting out, but in the void of undifferentiated consciousness no such spectrum exists. Awake is awake.

> The person I was is gone, over, dead. I can't even comprehend that
> I ever was what I was. Who I was makes no sense to me now. How
> I could have been so obtuse? So comatose? So deceived? So thick?
> So unaware? I thought I was a spiritual person and I was anything
> but. I was like the exact opposite! My so-called spirituality wasn't a
> connection with reality but a shield against it. What kind of sad
> spiritual groupie was I? Every few months it seems I was growing
> disenchanted with the last great spiritual breakthrough and

grasping desperately at the next. One mirage after the next. Whatever they were selling, I was buying. What a rube! What a flake! What was I even looking for? I don't know now because I didn't know then. Something that was going to catapult me to some fabulous new strata of being where my wishes were fulfilled, my counsel was sought, my happiness was admired and my life would sparkle like a diamond forever. Ego's wretched desires protracted to their grotesque extremes. What a load of crap, but that's what I was, I guess, a load of crap. How else to say it? I can't make sense of it now because it didn't make sense then. It was always about some vaguely but vastly more wonderful state of being, or some elevated state of consciousness or some level of mastery that I couldn't even begin to guess the nature of. One month it's the new wonder supplement that's going to purify me. The next month it's the miraculous new meditation technique that's finally going to give me whatever it is I've always wanted from meditation. A month later everyone's flocking to hear the latest guru who has managed to make it all make sense. Paint your door red, sleep facing north, recite tongue-twisting mantras, hose out your innards, tune up your chakras, read this scripture, wear that gem, sit in this pose, burn this incense, gaze at this saint's picture, get that saint's blessing, buy this book, attend this workshop. Take no chances, buy at least one of everything: sacred gems, healing crystals, calming oils, cleansing incense, mood-enhancing candles, malas, more malas. My apartment became a warehouse for Indian fetishes, wind-chimes, Hindu statues, Buddhist art, tarot decks, astrology charts, full-spectrum lighting, therapeutic aromas, yantra posters, meditation cushions, yoga mats, safe foods, safe cleaning products, non-synthetic fabrics, non-off-gassing carpets, non-toxic paints. Books, hundreds of books. Every stupid book with a pretty cover and a clever angle. Magazines I was once so proud to be affiliated with that I'm now too embarrassed to even think about. Fad after fad, gimmick after gimmick, and there I was like a schoolgirl falling in and out of an endless cycle of spiritual infatuations. That was my life! If God walked in right now and told me I had to go back to being that person I'd try to kill Him. That, or I'd kill myself, but I wouldn't go back to that prison of vapidity. I had a Zen clock next to my bed for chrissakes!

I was never really a New Ager. I was never a spiritual seeker. Most of what I needed to know I learned in my own two-year crash-and-burn course. It was all new and fantastic to me; people traveling outside their bodies, discorporate entities dispensing knowledge through living people, the stunning depth of wisdom of the East, all the courageous men and women all over the world, striving to make sense of it all. I've since met many New Agey type folks and I recognize the perennial search dynamic Julie describes. She's being a bit harsh about what is, after all, a very human tendency—walking in small, purposeful circles—but then, she's in a harsh place.

Jesus, I'm a fucking vampire now. How am I going to deal with all the people in my life from now on? I'm a butterfly and they're all caterpillars who don't know there is such a thing as a butterfly. What do I do now? Do I slip back into the role of Julie? Exchange inane pleasantries? Pretend to take an interest in people's... what? Their make-believe worlds? Their make-believe lives? Their well-defined characters on their tiny stages? Their getting and spending, primping and preening? Their desperate need to inflict themselves on each other? Their... oh dear God... their *opinions*? I don't think I could stand a minute of it. Not one minute. It would hardly even be possible to impersonate my former self, but what else? What do I do? Tell the truth? I can't, obviously, but why not? Maybe that's the easiest way out; just state the plainest possible truth and let things fall where they may. What would the truth even sound like? I think I could restrict all future conversation to a few simple remarks: "I don't know." "I don't care." "I have no thoughts on that matter." "Your words have no meaning to me." "There's no point in speaking to me." "Can't you see I'm not really here?" But if I have to say things like that, the mistake has already been made. I'm starting to get a very clear understanding of what it means to be alone. It's not at all what I'd guessed. If I thought about it at all, I might have romanticized it a bit, but this isn't romantic. This isn't just a simple realization that I am alone, but the slow stripping away of everyone and everything that tells me I am *not* alone. I'm starting to see where this road really leads. I think I can deal with being there because I think that what seems terrible about it only seems that way from here, but getting there is worse than any hell could ever be. I can't even resign myself or make myself numb to it. I know this was all in your book, Jed, but I'm only starting to see what it really means now. I'm out. I am no longer a part of anything and I'll never be a part of anything again.

This is the curious problem of the person who has stepped out of their role but not their costume, i.e., died while alive. Such a person is no longer in the play, no longer a member of the production, but they can't tell others that because, for others, the play is all; there is nothing but the stage, nothing beyond. This new type of role, the non-role, simply does not compute and gets interpreted as a break from sanity rather than true sanity. Julie's dead, but she'll have a heck of a time explaining that to anyone. Vampire is right. She's the living dead, the *un*dead, and only another of her kind can really understand what that means.

The only possible solution is to sever connections and distance myself from people. I don't know how to do this. I've had strong ties with many people, deep friendships, lasting relationships. My family ties are very strong, especially with my mother and one of my sisters. What do I do about that? They have no capacity to understand that Julie, as much as I may resemble her, is gone. There'll be no convincing them, no explanation could get through to them, so what do I do? I could make myself so utterly repulsive to them that even the spell of a mother's love would be broken. I can't even imagine what that would take. Or I could simply go. Vanish. Change my name, leave the country, make myself disappear. This could actually work because those closest to me are all actually fairly conventional in their views and have always considered me a bit loosely wrapped. I wouldn't even have to move far away. I could simply send out short notes to everyone saying that I've pledged myself to a life of service at the feet of Swami Salami and will be moving to his ashram in the remotest Himalaya, no phones, no email, see ya later, and though I'm sure it would evoke varying degrees of sadness, it wouldn't arouse much surprise.

Surprising to me, however, is that this entire matter of being permanently set apart is not weighing very heavily upon me. It seems like more of an operational challenge than the cause for emotional upheaval I would have expected. That may not be perfectly true at the moment, but I can see that it will be. I have more work to do, more cleaning in the attic, more letting in of light, but the new reality is becoming established. It's all a dream and I am awake, and I can never believe in the dream again.

The newly awakened person could, I suppose, make a direct, open declaration of their new status, could say, "I am now something new, something you can't understand. I am truth-realized. Awake." One problem is that people don't understand that they don't understand; don't know that they don't know. The other problem is that it basically means playing another role; getting back on stage, acting enlightened. It's foreign and unnatural; as false as any role. The enlightened person role is not the true role of the enlightened person. There is no true role.

So what is Julie to do? Die. That's the obvious answer. Drop the body. Be done with it. But why? Why not live? Why not stay? Why interfere with the flow of things? If nothing else, she has an interesting decade before her as she learns what it means to be this thing she has become. No reason to fling oneself out a window at this point.

So what does that leave? She could go sit on a mountain in India and answer useless questions for the next forty or fifty years. Pointless questions from people eager to stay comfortably numb; turned Away, not Toward. People who will falsely exalt her, praise her with meaningless words, grandly bestow upon her meaningless things. That sort of sideshow function is so dreadful to contemplate that it casts immediate doubt on anyone who would endure it. But what the hell, you go where you go. I myself did a bit of the question answering thing for a while. I didn't choose it, I kind of fell into it. I could never see the larger unifying pattern in which it made sense until I realized that it was all about the book. Then it all came together. The larger picture revealed itself and the pieces resolved into sharp focus. The universe wanted some books written, and all those hundreds of dialogues formed the foundation of knowledge and experience upon which I could write them. My entire life, I saw, was simply the process by which these books were brought into being.

> When I go to the store or the city I have to slip awkwardly back into Julie. Friendly, cheerful, but not so much now. Not needing anything reflected back to me now. More reserved now, not as outgoing, not overt, not warm, not engaging. Just enough. Just nice enough to get what I need and get away. I am beyond opinion. I'm not interested in my own opinions or anyone else's. I don't have the luxury of caring what people think, least of all myself. I'm willing to lose my self-respect, but I still have it. It has adapted. It used to be based on dozens of factors, hundreds,

maybe more. Now it's based one thing only. On this. Nothing else matters. The only reason to act "normal" around other people is to guard this process. Nothing matters but this process.

❖

There are no more taboos. There is nowhere that is closed to me, nowhere that I won't go. Nothing is off-limits. I shun nothing. Nothing is excluded. Nothing is vile or repugnant, nothing too extreme. The only criteria by which I judge anything is whether it's of value to my process of awakening or not. It's not that I'm not scared, just that this is about tearing down walls, *all* walls. If my eye offendeth me, I will pluck it out. If my hand offendeth me, I will cut it off. There is no price I won't pay. No price is too high.

❖

I'm starting to wonder what the point of all this is, this whole process I've spent the last fourteen months clawing my way through. What the hell's the point of it? It doesn't make any sense. I guess this is the essential paradox of the whole thing; the insane humor of it. Who benefits? No one benefits. There's no Julie left. What's the point of this massive upheaval? There is none. It's absolutely, undeniably pointless. How can something this huge, this transformative, this nuclear, be so pointless? But that's what it is. I guess you could say the same about anything.

Like a child flicking a switch that turns the world off like a light. What can you say when the thing that ends isn't within a context, but context itself? It hardly merits a shrug.

In the last few months there have been several times when I was overcome by a happiness so intense that I literally felt that it might be more than I could bear. I've never known any happiness that could compare with this and I don't see how any happiness could. It feels like it could kill me and I wouldn't care if it did. I see now, Jed, what you *didn't* say in your book and I see why you didn't. There's a reality to this that you didn't go into and now that I know it, I know why. There's the place where all the paradoxes disappear and where no questions remain, but there's no point in trying to describe this place. You gave the one perfect answer to all the seemingly unanswerable questions: Come see for yourself. I'm here now. I see it now. It was right there all the time. It looks like the price of truth is everything, but it's not. How could I not have known? The price of truth is nothing.

35. The Greatest Story Ever Told

> So there is no earthly way of finding out precisely what
> the whale really looks like. And the only mode in which
> you can derive even a tolerable idea of his living contour,
> is by going a whaling yourself; but by so doing, you run
> no small risk of being eternally stove and sunk by him.
> Wherefore, it seems to me you had best not be too
> fastidious in your curiosity touching this Leviathan.
>
> *—Herman Melville, Moby-Dick*

MARY AND I ARE HAVING our Sunday dinner at a restaurant high on a promontory overlooking the water. It's probably our last such dinner together because I'm moving on in a few days. I mainly came to New York to handle some business matters in the city and now that's all wrapped up and I feel like going somewhere else. I actually feel like going to Orlando or Cedar Point, but you can't have much fun riding the world's best rollercoasters alone.

We talk about *Moby-Dick*. We often do. It's something we have in common, the way she and William did. During my visit most of our conversations have revolved around *Moby-Dick* and the countless ways in which it makes more sense when the reader understands that it's not about whales and whaling, or good and evil, or God and Satan, but simply about striking through the wall, about purity of intent, about a man in a life or death struggle for his freedom.

Hanging over all of our conversations has been the thing I've hinted at but haven't stated; my second epiphany regarding *Moby-Dick*, the missing *denouement*. Figuring out what the book is really about is secondary to figuring out how triumphant and magnificently complete it really is. *Moby-Dick* isn't *a* masterpiece, it's *the* masterpiece. It's the greatest story ever told once you understand the level at which it truly functions. My hope is that Mary will arrive on that level before I leave the area in a few days, but it's up to her.

We discuss my second book, this one, and how I plan to weave *Moby-Dick* into it based on my understanding of Ahab as the unknown archetype; the Break-Out Archetype, the model of the being anyone must reshape themselves into in order to achieve breakout velocity.

"I have a ton of notes," I tell her as my mussels and pasta in olive oil and garlic arrive, "but it's going to take a few more months to see how it all really lays out in terms of the book."

"And you're really going to open with the words 'Call me Ahab'?"

"Yep."

"Very bold," she says, "but very appropriate. I'm in complete agreement. It's been such a pleasure having you here and penetrating the book at the little lower layer," she twinkles. "I'm really going to miss having you here, having these dinners, discussing the book."

That strikes a sad note. She's been lonely since losing William, I'm sure. *Moby-Dick* was their thing and she's been reliving some of that with me. She smiles and turns upbeat. "You *know* I'm never going to let you leave without telling me your other big insight, don't you?"

I smile playfully. "You'll get a draft of the book. Maybe it'll be in there."

She laughs. "You know, if you think about it," she says coyly, "you say 'Call me Ahab', but in a way, you're more Ishmael than Ahab."

Ahhh.

"Now, you mean?" I draw her out. "Who I am now?"

"Yes," she says, "with the writing, the telling of the tale, recounting the entire journey, including the Ahab years."

And there it is. She has it, she just doesn't know it yet.

Moby-Dick, the book, is itself a series of masks through which the reader must strike. Has anyone made it through all of *Moby-Dick's* masks before? Maybe, but I've found no sign of it. Some might have guessed at it, but if you don't do the work you don't enjoy the benefits. Anyone can say the words *tat tvam asi*, and anyone can grasp the concept of *tat tvam asi*, but having *tat tvam asi* as your living reality is a different matter. But it doesn't matter if we get there first or last; the point to get there, not to plant a flag.

"*And I only am escaped alone to tell thee,*" I quote Ishmael from the epilogue. "Yeah, Ishmael would be the more accurate name for me now." I make deliberate eye contact. "What an interesting observation."

"What?" she says. "What's going on? Are you finally going to tell me this second big thing of yours?"

"You don't need me to tell you. It's like the ruby slippers. You had it all along."

She doesn't wish to be trifled with. "Jed—" she says sternly.

"How did Ahab die?"

"How did Ahab die? The rope. The rope from his harpoon. He thrust his harpoon into Moby Dick and the rope wrapped around his neck and pulled him in. Down."

"And does it say he died?"

"Does it *say*—? No, no, I don't think so. I guess it's just assumed that when he—"

"The first three words of the book. The most famous opening line in literature. What are they?"

"'Call me Ishmael,'" she quotes.

"What does that mean, Mary? What's the point of saying it? What's the point of saying it with the very first words of the book?"

"Well," she draws the word out while she considers it. "He's introducing himself—"

"What's the subtext?"

"The subtext?"

"Of those three words."

"Well, I guess that's his way of telling us he's not really— He's saying—"

"What happened to Pip?"

"Pip? He was dragged down too—"

Click.

Her eyes go wide and she seizes up for a moment. Her hands go to her chest. She's not breathing. "Oh shit," she whispers. "Shit."

Instantly she loses her voice and her eyes flood with tears. A moan escapes from deep within her. She brings up her napkin and I turn my attention to my mussels to give her some privacy.

"Excuse me," she says. She stands, picks up her purse, and walks quickly out of the restaurant.

That's okay, it was my turn to pay anyway.

❖

I do not say these things for a dollar
or to fill up the time while I wait for a boat.

— *Walt Whitman* —

As I said in *Damnedest*, someone in my position never meets an impartial observer. No one is out of play. In a blast furnace, there is no distinction between resident and visitor. Fire doesn't negotiate and nothing doesn't burn. I'm a one-trick pony and I'm always on. I don't go in for much small talk. The only thing I'm really interested in is the burning away of layers.

Not everyone's ego bursts into flames when they ask me the time, but if you get into a serious discussion with me and you're honest with yourself, you will be a different person when we're done.

Such a discussion may take a minute or a year, but when it's done you will have gotten off your ass and moved, and since the terrain is you, who you are dies and is born anew with every step.

The first thing I showed Mary about *Moby-Dick* was that it's really about burning away layers; striking through masks. Having read *Damnedest,* she understood what I was saying and saw it for herself. We spent many happy dinners together discussing how that observation made *Moby-Dick* a different and much more interesting and comprehensible book, and why that observation seemed to have eluded readers and critics for a century and a half.

Now Mary was seeing the second thing, the larger thing; that *Moby-Dick* isn't the story of burning away layers, but the story of the man who burns away the layers; of how he became that man, and what became of that man.

Mary is a wonderful woman; one of those warm, decent people that we all want to have in our lives. But as wonderful and enviable as that may be, it's just a composite of layers, and all layers are but veils, and all veils are highly flammable.

I've said it many times and it's true; preferences are irrelevant. It doesn't matter what you want or why you're here. If you're standing in a furnace, the fact that you didn't intend to burn will not protect you from the flames. Or, to use Melville's terms, the only way to know the whale is to go a-whaling, but by doing so you run no small risk of being eternally stove and sunk by him.

Guest badges are not issued here.

I visited Mary because we warmed to each other over the course of many emails and phone conversations. She invited me to stay with her. She said she had a large house with plenty of extra room in a beautiful area for which I already had a keen fondness, so I accepted. When I arrived it was Mary who brought the book *Moby-Dick* to my attention; spoke of how wonderful it was, how it had been her favorite book to teach and how it was something very special to her.

She told me she was writing a book about *Moby-Dick,* which she planned to dedicate to the memory of her husband. She and William had enjoyed *Moby-Dick* together; enjoyed the process of deciphering the symbology and reading books about it and its author. For their entire marriage they enjoyed visiting New Bedford, Nantucket, and Cape Cod; shopping, dining, visiting museums. *Moby-Dick* was their shared passion, their common bond.

Would I have ever read *Moby-Dick* just on my own? Maybe, maybe not. Would I have read it just to be polite to my host? Probably not. But there were other factors that put the book in front of me, so I did what I do and obeyed the prevailing winds as soon as I detected them; I started reading this ponderous, intimidating book about whaling and obsession. It wasn't long before I came to some very interesting insights about the book and its author, and I began to see very clearly why it had been set in front of me.

I certainly never decided to teach Mary a lesson based on the book, or to escort her to the next level using the book. It doesn't work that way. I don't think or plan, I observe. I don't steer, I just ride currents; they steer. I was completely taken by surprise by the whole *Moby-Dick* thing. At first I was surprised by what a great book it is just on the basis of literary merit, humor, and rollicking entertainment. This is not a book you read from end to end and can say you've read it. *Moby-Dick* would demand a major commitment from the reader just to get to the point of misunderstanding it with a reasonable degree of familiarity. I was staggered by the depth and complexity of the book, with its challenging philosophies and ingenious symbology. I was also surprised by the humor of it. *Moby-Dick* is a delightfully funny book.

Next, I was struck by something so enormous and difficult to believe that I spent the next few weeks trying to disprove it. I couldn't, and eventually I came to the reasonable certainty that in the hundred and fifty years since its original publication, no one, with the possible exception of Herman Melville, understands *Moby-Dick*.

Readers and critics seemed to have succeeded in understanding a lot of what was going on *within* the book, but not the book as a whole; not the unifying overview in which it all makes perfect sense. At the highest level, the book eludes everyone. I scanned through hundreds of reviews, commentaries, opinions and forewords and found that, whether they admitted it or not, critics, readers and reviewers were universally perplexed. Some admitted that they didn't understand it. Some asserted that it isn't meant to be understood. Some tried to shoehorn it into comfortable theories which mainly concern what is represented in the conflict between Ahab and Moby Dick. Those that claim the whale to be God or Fate come closest if you take God or Fate to mean Supreme Jailer Personified; what we might call Maya, Lord of the Prison of Duality. Ultimately, God, Fate and Maya are only outward symbols of an inward condition. Moby Dick is the Lie.

Many critics solved the problem by saying that Ahab is just insane. I can see why they'd think so, but it seems that if your main character is driven by madness, then your whole story is just about a guy who's nuts. Hardly the case here. Some made the case that Ahab isn't insane, but without the necessary perspective, it can't be done. Guessing right doesn't count.

From that point on I began reading *Moby-Dick* in a whole new light. Ahab didn't have to do much talking before I saw that he wasn't crazy. As soon as I got to the strike through the mask business I was pretty sure that I was holding a book that was a masterpiece of an unknown philosophy—Truth—and that Ahab was the blueprint of an unknown archetype; the Break-Out Archetype.

Moby-Dick is like a painting by an artist who possesses color perception being analyzed, critiqued and judged by a color-blind world. No interpretation is possible without the necessary perceptual faculty. It's done in color and must be viewed in color. It doesn't play in black and white no matter how you light it or how you squint. Because I happen to possess the faculty of color vision, and because I happened to look, I see something quite plainly that others haven't. Small wonder that it remained obscure for seventy years and really only comes to light another eighty years after that. Without this perceptual faculty, *Moby-Dick* can only be a gray muddle. Seen correctly, it's the American *Mahabharata*.

Of course, telling people how great something is that they can't see for themselves would be pointless. Happily, the perceptual faculty required isn't in the eyes but behind them, and anyone who *wants* to see *can* see.

Look for yourself.

Ahab survived. Ahab is Ishmael. *Moby-Dick* isn't the story of one ship's voyage over the course of months, but one man's voyage over the course of his life. Says Ahab:

> "Forty—forty—forty years ago!—ago! Forty years of
> continual whaling! forty years of privation, and peril,
> and storm-time! forty years on the pitiless sea! for forty
> years has Ahab forsaken the peaceful land, for forty years
> to make war on the horrors of the deep!"

In the first three words of the book, "Call me Ishmael," we are told this. We are told, essentially, "I'm not telling you who I am." But why not? Why would the narrator of a whaling tale wish to conceal his identity from his readers? And why say so with the very first words? Why so prominently stated?

Because Melville is playing fair. He's putting it all right there where we can see it. He's hiding it in plain view. The key to *Moby-Dick* is hidden in the first three words.

Yes, Ishmael is Ahab. The narrator is Ahab. It was Ahab that survives, floating alone for two days on Queequeg's coffin, an orphan. We never see Ahab die or dead. The rope grabs him around the neck and pulls him from the boat. That's it. Does that mean he dies? No, not physically. Melville foreshadows it explicitly by sending Pip down first:

> The sea had jeeringly kept his finite body up, but drowned the infinite of his soul. Not drowned entirely, though. Rather carried down alive to wondrous depths, where strange shapes of the unwarped primal world glided to and fro before his passive eyes; and the miser-merman, Wisdom, revealed his hoarded heaps; and among the joyous, heartless, ever-juvenile eternities, Pip saw the multitudinous, God-omnipresent, coral insects, that out of the firmament of waters heaved the colossal orbs. He saw God's foot upon the treadle of the loom, and spoke it; and therefore his shipmates called him mad. So man's insanity is heaven's sense; and wandering from all mortal reason, man comes at last to that celestial thought, which, to reason, is absurd and frantic; and weal or woe, feels then uncompromised, indifferent as his God.

He saw God's foot upon the treadle of the loom. We are shown this in Pip so we'll know it of Ahab.

❖

After lingering over my dinner and taking a nice walk down the hillside and along the shore, I take a cab back to the house and arrive a couple of hours after Mary left the restaurant. I find her sitting at William's desk in the paneled study, the small pool of light from the desk lamp creating a warm glow around her. She has a glass of sherry poured but untouched in front of her. She has two books laid open before her; *Moby-Dick* and a Bible. She's holding a pen over a yellow legal pad when I enter, making notes. I stop at the doorway, not wanting to intrude on her process.

She looks up and sees me standing there.

"My bonny lad," she says softly.

I don't speak.

"A wild ass of a man," she says.

"Excuse me?"

She reads from the Bible. *"He shall be a wild ass of a man, his hand against every man and every man's hand against him; and he shall dwell over against all his kinsmen."*

"Who shall?"

"Ishmael," she replies. "That's what God said about Ishmael."

I don't say anything.

"Melville wrote to Nathaniel Hawthorne about *Moby-Dick*; 'I have written a wicked book and feel as spotless as the lamb.'"

I nod. "The Nihilist's Bible," I say. "The Truth-Seeker's Handbook."

"Yes," she says "I guess that's what it is. It would be absurd to suggest Melville didn't know perfectly well what he was writing. He should have just called it that."

"Don't make it about Melville," I tell her. "It's not just Melville. There's another author, we might as well call it the ocean. Melville didn't get what he wanted from *Moby-Dick*, but that other author always gets exactly what it wants. If you try to approach the book through Melville, you'll miss. The ocean is the true author, but the ocean has no hands. It operates through us."

She nods. "I think I understand that. Come in please," she says. "It's okay. Have a seat."

I do as I'm bid and seat myself in one of the plush leather Queen Annes facing the desk. After a moment of writing she sets down her pen, picks up her glass, and speaks.

"Well Jed, a hundred and fifty years after Melville wrote *Moby-Dick*, it looks like you're the first person to see it for what it is." She raises her glass. "Congratulations."

"Cool," I reply. "I should get something for that. A nice plaque or something."

"I don't think a book called *Spiritually Incorrect Enlightenment* that begins 'Call me Ahab' will command much attention from the literary world, I'm afraid."

"There goes my plaque."

She gives me a lopsided little grin.

"Congratulations on being the second," I offer.

She rolls her eyes a bit.

"Seriously," I say, "think about what's really happened here. You demonstrated your intent. You told the universe in the only way it understands, through your desire and actions, your demonstrated intent, that you wanted to crack this mountainous riddle of a book. You should really try to own this. Look at you and me. Look at the unlikelihood of us being brought together. I didn't orchestrate this, you know." I meet her eyes. "You know?"

She nods. She's in there. Still in a bit of shock, but coming out.

"You got what you asked for," I say.

She nods again and turns her attention to the yellow pad she's been writing on.

"It's always been considered an ineptly structured novel," she says, "but now, now I don't know what it is. If you look at the whole book as the reminiscences of one man's lifelong quest, but not really a whaleman, and not really a whale, just a man's lifelong philosophical inquiry, culminating, as you say, in the monomania required to strike through the ultimate mask. It was Ahab who felt the drizzly November in his soul, forty years earlier, who went to sea to escape a suicidal despair. It's Ahab telling his own story, recounting a life of philosophical seafaring. It's all so obvious, now." She pauses, taps her pen on the yellow pad. "In just the last hour I've come up with over thirty things that never really made sense before, that do now. It's just spilling out. I could go on and on. I *will* go on and on. It's a whole new book now—rather, I'm seeing it through new eyes. I'm throwing out the book I've spent ten years working on and starting from scratch." She pauses, jots something down, scratches it out. "If you care to look more deeply into it," she says, "you'll find your theory confirmed again and again in Melville's life and work before and after *Moby-Dick*. It *all* makes sense now."

She looks at her yellow pad and shakes her head. "Ishmael, Elijah, Mapple, Fedallah, Perth's scars, the fire, the lightning, Stubbs' dream, the gams, the quadrant, the prophesies! How could I not see it? My Lord, Pip alone!"

Once something comes into focus it's hard to see how you didn't see it all along. She reads from the passage where Ahab is raging at, essentially, Maya; the personification of his captor. Mary reads beautifully. I close my eyes and relax into the words:

> "I now know thee, thou clear spirit, and I now know
> that thy right worship is defiance. To neither love nor
> reverence wilt thou be kind; and e'en for hate thou canst
> but kill; and all are killed. No fearless fool now fronts
> thee. I own thy speechless, placeless power; but to the
> last gasp of my earthquake life will dispute its uncondi-
> tional, unintegral mastery in me. In the midst of the
> personified impersonal, a personality stands here.
> Though but a point at best; whencesoe'er I came; where-
> soe'er I go; yet while I earthly live, the queenly person-
> ality lives in me, and feels her royal rights. But war is
> pain, and hate is woe. Come in thy lowest form of love,
> and I will kneel and kiss thee; but at thy highest, come
> as mere supernal power; and though thou launchest
> navies of full-freighted worlds, there's that in here that
> still remains indifferent. Oh, thou clear spirit, of thy fire
> thou madest me, and like a true child of fire, I breathe it
> back to thee."

She shuts the book and shakes her head.

"Jesus," she says. "No one was even close. Still, it's not a perfect fit. This is going to take a very careful reexamination."

Viewed aright, *Moby-Dick* is a completely different book than has been commonly supposed, and Mary will now have to read it afresh, through her new eyes. It's always been considered a high-seas adventure with some philosophical meditations thrown in. In truth, it's the supreme philosophical treatise set against the backdrop of a whale hunt. It is the most important and least understood document in the human archive. It is an escape plan, drawn up by one who escaped.

"No, it's not a perfect fit," I say. "Melville called *Moby-Dick* a draft of a draft, right? He didn't know where it was going when he started it; where *he* was going. I'd say he figured it out as he wrote it. That explains a lot of the inconsistencies, and it makes sense to me that he wouldn't want to mess with rewriting it. We can speculate that Ishmael is Ahab, but we can say for sure that Ishmael and Ahab are both Melville. He discovers Ahab through the process of writing *Moby-Dick*. See what I mean? Does that make sense?"

"Yes. Writing *Moby-Dick* was Melville's process of Spiritual Autolysis, and when he was done, he was done. Is that it?"

"Yes, that's what I think. You'll never make sense of *Moby-Dick* because that's not the real story. It's not the whaling adventure as it has been so long supposed, and it's not the story of Ahab as the Break-Out Archetype as we've discussed, and it's only a minor point to say that Ahab is really the fictional author Ishmael when we know who the true author is."

"It's not really even a novel, is it?" she asks. "In some ways, it's his own—"

I wait while she thinks about it.

"That poor dear man. I've always felt such deep sympathy for him. All this time, no one knew. It's his process, isn't it? It's not the *record* of his journey, it *is* his journey."

"Yes. Herman Melville decided to go and keep going, come what may. That's what the book is. It's not about fictional Ahab and

Ishmael, but about the real man who made the real journey. It's the real break-out of a real man."

"This explains so much," she says, "not just about the book but about the man, about his subsequent life, his sanity or lack thereof, about *Pierre*, his next book, about his letters."

She sits quietly for a few moments, shaking her head sadly.

"This explains everything," she says.

❖

We continue to sit, not saying much. She's pondering this immense disruption to her inner landscape and I'm thinking deep, enlightened thoughts. After a while, she resumes speaking.

"I love your book, Jed, I mean, it's been a very powerful force in my life, but somehow I never thought it really applied to me. I never made the connection. When you said that the greatest men and women who ever lived were just children on a playground to you, when you said your experience was like being the only adult in a world full of children, I thought you meant, well, *other* people. I somehow excluded myself from that, as if I were an adult too, and empathized with what you were expressing. I still see you as a seven year-old boy, you know, a proper little gentleman in your herring-bone suit and cap, holding hands with my daughter in front of the turning Christmas tree in the Russian Tea Room all those years ago."

I smile, but I'm sitting just outside the puddle of light from the desk lamp and she can't see it. She's not really talking to me anyway.

"All the widely varying interpretations of *Moby-Dick* over the years represent the many ways in which man interprets his world, the masks he lays over it, but *Moby-Dick* is about striking through *all* masks. Isn't that what you mean by further? Ahab struck through all the masks, and only someone like Ahab could understand that. It takes an Ahab to know an Ahab. It took Melville to create him and you to see him. It's occurred to me, sitting here, that your book will be the Rosetta stone which will allow me to decipher *Moby-Dick*."

I'm a little stuck to the leather. I remain perfectly still so that I don't mock this solemn moment with one of those embarrassing sounds that will force me to blame the chair. It's a minute before she speaks again.

"Ahab doesn't die. He doesn't lose. He doesn't fail."

"No," I say, "he succeeds. His success is absolute."

"It's not a tragedy. It's not dark."

"No. It's about victory. Freedom. Truth. Beauty. The good stuff."

"Jesus H. Christ," she mutters.

"Nice. Aren't you, like, pretty Catholic?"

"I don't know what the hell I am anymore."

I laugh. I seem to have that effect on people.

"So when he comes back up," she asks, "buoyed up on a coffin, he's not really Ahab anymore, is he? The monomania is gone. The madness is gone. The insane, driving obsession is—? There's no more—? It's all just, what?"

I supply the word.

"Done."

"Done," she repeats.

"Whether you're looking at Melville or Ahab, the answer is the same. His quest is over. His harpoon, welded like glue from the melted bones of murderers, simply falls from his hand as the pen falls from Melville's. Moby Dick is slain, yet swims away; the whale from Ahab, the book from Melville. Ahab is slain, yet floats on. Melville is slain, but lives on. He is henceforth, as the final word of the book tells us—"

She supplies it this time.

"An orphan."

36. Montreal

Only themselves understand themselves,
  and the like of themselves,
As Souls only understand Souls.

−Walt Whitman

I COULD LEARN TO HATE Canada.

It's ten weeks later. I'm in Montreal sitting at a sidewalk table in one of those atmospheric little cafes that people find so charming, though as far as I can tell it's a lot like sitting at a table on a sidewalk. I have a drink in front of me, but due to imperfect communications with my uncharming waiter, I'm leary of it. I'm busy being confused by the menu when I hear a voice I haven't heard in almost two years.

"So, how's the enlightenment thing working out for you?"

I look up and smile. "Oh, real good, thanks. Really getting a kick out of it," I recite. "You?"

"Oh, same, yeah. Real pleased," she says. "Right on time, I see."

"Politeness of kings," I respond.

She remains standing. She's wearing sunglasses, but it's not hard to see that she's feeling a little worked up. I gesture to the chair she's standing behind.

"Welcome," I say.

It's a weighty word. She emits an involuntary little hiccup-laugh-cry thing, but doesn't sit.

"How does a new vampire address the vampire that created her?" she asks, still standing. A planned greeting, but it's a good question;

an important one.

"In your case," I answer, "as Julie."

She brings a hand up to her mouth as she sobs and nods her head. "I don't think she's here anymore," she manages to say through barely contained tears.

While it's true that done means done, it also means beginning. As I've said, the newly awakened can expect to deal with about a decade of adjustment, and it's not at all what you might suppose.

"I understand that," I say softly, "but since she's gone so that you could be here, you might honor her memory by taking her name."

This time the sob catches her hard and she walks briskly away. I hold the menu in front of me so no one will know I'm thinking deep, enlightened thoughts. It's about ten minutes before Julie returns. I look up to see her standing behind the chair again.

"Are you going to sit down this time." I ask, "or do you have some pressing engagement?"

"No," she replies with a small smile, sitting down and removing her sunglasses, "I'm free."

> We have circled and circled till
> we have arrived home again—we two have;
> We have voided all but freedom,
> and all but our own joy.

> — *Walt Whitman* —

Epilogue

How often have I said to you that when you have
eliminated the impossible, whatever remains,
however improbable, must be the truth?

–Sir Arthur Conan Doyle

SPIRITUALLY INCORRECT ENLIGHTENMENT isn't *one*
kind of enlightenment; it's the *only* kind. There's no enlightenment *in* the dream and breaking *out* of the dream is a muddy, bloody
business. That's the bad news. The good news is that enlightenment
isn't what anyone really wants anyway.

Take a close look at Captain Ahab, the Break-Out Archetype.
Are you ready to play that role? It doesn't matter how you answer
because it's not a role we choose. Ahab didn't choose the role. Julie
didn't choose it. I didn't. Who would? Who could? It's idiotic, but
what's more than that, it's silly.

What I've called Human Adulthood in these pages, however, is
something we *can* choose. Human Adulthood is what all seekers
really want, and it's not silly.

"Who am I?" That is the question. That's the question at our
very center. Life turns on that center, and everyone who is alive has
one of two relationships to that center: Toward or Away. Toward is
perfectly simple. Away is infinitely complex.

Toward may be simple, but it's not easy. Just ask Jessica. To die
of the flesh and be born of the spirit is not the same as enlightenment, but they split a cab for a while. If you wish to make this transition in your own life—to awaken within the dream, to shuffle off
the egoic coil—my suggestion would be that you combine Spiritual

Autolysis with fervent prayer, using each to advance the other. Use the writing to locate and illuminate your falseness and thereby develop a healthy self-contempt. The strength of that emotion will then empower your prayer, which should be for the courage and ability to locate and illuminate your falseness, and so on.

Brace for impact.

❖

About a month after I said goodbye to Mary, I received a package in the mail from her. It included a letter in which she said she felt renewed and that she was now approaching the life and works of Melville on a whole new level, with an understanding that extended into all areas of her own life. She doesn't know if she'll actually publish the new book she's working on, she says, but she's proceeding as if she will because that gives the whole undertaking some context.

She informs me that Curtis has found a job for the rest of the summer; a customer service position that beats flipping burgers. Mary has him doing odd jobs and running errands for a few hours a week as well. After I left, Mary gave him an envelope I'd left with her that contained a brief note, a final check, and the title to the jeep.

When Ahab roused his men to the hunt of the white whale, he nailed a gold doubloon to the mainmast as a reward for the first man to sight Moby Dick. Also in Mary's package was a custom-made plaque with a gold doubloon nailed to the center. The inscription cites me as first to spot the white whale, and below that, in large letters, is inscribed the perfect diamond at the heart of the character Ahab, of the book *Moby-Dick*, of the author Herman Melville, and of the reader:

Truth hath no confines.

❖

The entirety of mankind's science can be summarily discarded by anyone who understands the First Law of Objective Reality which states: There Ain't None. You can't tell the science guys that, though. They work to create a Theory of Everything, but they have no idea what everything really means. They talk about the Big Bang theory of how the universe began, like a vase shattering into a million tiny bits, but that's wrong too. The way I see it, it's more like the film of their shattered vase running backward; all the millions of tiny particles and fragments following incalculably precise trajectories back to wholeness, fitting themselves together with such miraculous and unerring accuracy that by observing the perfection of any part, we can know the perfection of the whole.

> I discovered the secret of the sea
> in meditation upon a dewdrop.
>
> — *Kahlil Gibran* —

This is what Julie calls poetic bullshit, and rightly so, but I can afford to indulge myself. Poetic bullshit is one thing when you're waging the battle of your life, and something else when you're swinging in a hammock with your hat pulled down. What's not a miracle? Which piece of the vase is less than another? Everything fits, everything belongs. None are lost. All will arrive.

The one is the source of the many, returning is the motion of the *Tao*, and the science guys got it ass-backward. The universe isn't flying apart, it's flying together.

Bibliography

The Bhagavad-Gita, Translated by Sir Edwin Arnold. The Harvard Classics. New York: P.F. Collier & Son, 1909–14.

Burroughs, John. *Accepting the Universe* New York: W. H. Wise & Co., 1924.

Melville, Herman. *Moby-Dick; or, The Whale* New York: W.W. Norton & Co. Inc., 1976.

Thoreau, H.D. *Walden* New York: Viking Press, 1947.

Twain, Mark. *The Mysterious Stranger* New York: Harper & Brothers, 1916.

Whitman, Walt. *Leaves of Grass* New York: Doubleday Doran & Co., 1940

Wisefool Press

WEBSITE

SPIRITUAL ENLIGHTENMENT: THE DAMNEDEST THING and SPIRITUALLY INCORRECT ENLIGHTENMENT are available in print, electronic (e-book) and audiobook editions. Please visit our website for more information about current and future titles:

www.WisefoolPress.com

E-BOOKS & BONUS MATERIAL

E-book editions of Wisefool Press titles contain exclusive bonus materials, such as interviews and additional chapters, not available elsewhere. Visit the Wisefool Press website for purchase information.

QUANTITY DISCOUNTS

Quantity discounts are available to everyone at our website.